ARCHITECTURAL DRAWINGS OF THE EIGHTEENTH CENTURY

LES DESSINS D'ARCHITECTURE AU XVIIIe SIÈCLE

I DISEGNI DI ARCHITETTURA NEL SETTECENTO

Translation into english:
Ian Monk.

Traduzione in italiano:
Ivana Costa.

Revisione:
Maria Laura Bardinet Broso.

© 2001, Bibliothèque de l'Image
46 bis, passage Jouffroy - 75009 Paris.
Tél. 01 48 24 54 14 - Fax : 01 45 23 08 83

English edition: ISBN 2-914239-24-6
Edition en français : ISBN 2-914239-26-2
Edizione in italiano: ISBN 2-914239-27-0

ARCHITECTURAL DRAWINGS OF THE EIGHTEENTH CENTURY

LES DESSINS D'ARCHITECTURE AU XVIIIe SIÈCLE

I DISEGNI DI ARCHITETTURA NEL SETTECENTO

DANIEL RABREAU

Directeur du Centre Ledoux
(Université de Paris I)

Bibliothèque de l'Image

Contents

Sommaire

Sommario

À la mémoire de
Jean-Pierre Mouilleseaux

INTRODUCTION

Drawing remains one of the best sources for charting the history of civilisations because it has always been an essential tool in both the sciences and the arts, or indeed in any field in which man has wanted to create *figures*. It has commonly been accepted as a language and as a means of expressing thought, from hieroglyphic writing to the most individual artistic creations. Being indispensable to both the savant and the workman, this vital instrument is perfectly adapted to interpreting the changes of taste in whatever artistic field it is used: painting, sculpture, architecture, decorative or applied arts, or on the stage. Since it can be reproduced using different engraving techniques, and is associated with the illustration of texts and collections of *images*, through the ages drawing has become one of the most important vehicles for the expression of knowledge.

In modern times, three centuries of publishing activity were crystallised and magnified by the publication of the plates in Diderot's *Encyclopédie* (1751-1772). Architecture, which philosophers called the "mother of the arts", was included as drawings that illustrate its history, theory and practice. It conditions the physical context of other professions and, sometimes, thanks to the pure pleasure of symbolic association, contrasts figures drawn from another discipline. It is sufficient to cite anatomical plates, in which human skeletons meditate in front of a finely conceived Greek-style sarcophagus. From reconstructions of the Mausoleum at Halicarnassus to the revolutionary architects' grandiose plans for cemeteries, without forgetting the humble tombstone or the ancient pyramids, graves and ruins stimulated the imagination of Enlightenment designers. The paper image then also became an object of meditation. It summoned up nostalgia, and a study of the great yet ephemeral cycles of the natural world. When popularised as prints, drawing runs the risk of being betrayed, simplified, made rigid or bland. However, when they are not used for a downmarket illustration, and are employed by a first-rate artist, etchings and engravings can faithfully communicate drawings to the general public. The evolution of these two graphic techniques (which

INTRODUCTION

Instrument obligé des sciences et des arts, le dessin demeure une des sources privilégiées de l'histoire des civilisations, dans tous les domaines où la main de l'homme s'est plu à créer des *figures*. Moyen d'expression de la pensée il est communément admis comme langage, depuis l'écriture hiéroglyphique jusqu'aux métamorphoses de l'imaginaire artistique le plus individuel. Indispensable au savant comme à l'ouvrier, informateur par essence, il se prête à l'interprétation et aux changements du goût dans tous les domaines de l'art où il intervient : peinture, sculpture, architecture, arts décoratifs ou appliqués, arts du spectacle. Reproductible, par les différents procédés de la gravure, associé à l'illustration de textes ou recueils d'*images*, le dessin est devenu au cours des âges un des agents privilégiés de la connaissance.

Dans les Temps modernes, trois siècles d'activité éditoriale ont été cristallisés et magnifiés par la publication des planches de l'*Encyclopédie* (1751-1772) dirigée par Diderot. L'architecture, « mère des arts » selon le philosophe, y est présentée à l'appui de dessins qui illustrent son histoire, sa théorie, sa pratique ; elle conditionne le cadre même des métiers et, parfois par un pur plaisir d'association symbolique, elle sert de faire-valoir à des figures d'un autre genre. J'en veux pour preuve telle planche d'anatomie où le squelette humain médite devant un sarcophage d'une belle facture « à la grecque »... Des restitutions du mausolée d'Halicarnasse aux projets de nécropole mégalomane des architectes révolutionnaires, sans oublier l'humble stèle ou l'antique pyramide, le tombeau, avec la ruine, stimule l'imagination des dessinateurs du Siècle des lumières. L'image de papier se confond alors avec un objet de méditation ; elle sollicite la nostalgie et symbolise la réflexion sur les grands cycles éphémères du monde soumis à la nature. Vulgarisé par l'estampe, le dessin risque parfois d'être trahi, simplifié, durci ou affadi. Toutefois, lorsqu'ils ne se bornent pas à l'illustration hâtive, lorsqu'un artiste de premier plan les exécute, l'eau forte et le burin deviennent les auxiliaires fidèles du dessin destiné au plus grand nombre. L'évolution de ces deux procédés d'art graphique (il n'est pas question de les confondre) fut

INTRODUZIONE

Strumento obbligato delle scienze e delle arti, il disegno resta una delle fonti privilegiate della storia delle civiltà, in tutti i domini in cui la mano dell'uomo s'è dilettata a creare delle figure. Mezzo d'espressione del pensiero, esso è comunemente accettato come linguaggio, a partire dalla scrittura geroglifica fino alle metamorfosi del più individuale immaginario artistico. Indispensabile all'erudito come all'operaio, informatore per definizione, esso si presta all'interpretazione e ai cambiamenti del gusto in tutti i settori dell'arte in cui interviene: pittura, architettura, scultura, arti decorative o applicate, arti dello spettacolo. Riproducibile, attraverso le diverse procedure di stampa, associato all'illustrazione dei testi o raccolte di immagini, il disegno è divenuto nel corso del tempo uno degli agenti privilegiati della conoscenza.

Nell'età moderna, tre secoli d'attività editoriale sono stati cristallizzati e glorificati con la pubblicazione delle tavole dell'*Enciclopedia* (1751-1772) diretta da Diderot. L'architettura, "madre delle arti" secondo il filosofo, è qui presentata grazie al contributo di disegni che illustrano la sua storia, la sua teoria, la sua pratica; essa condiziona il quadro stesso dei mestieri e, a volte per un piacere di associazione simbolica, serve a valorizzare figure d'altro genere. Si pensi ad esempio alla tavola d'anatomia dove lo scheletro umano medita davanti a un sarcofago dalla bella fattura "alla greca"... Dalle ricostruzioni del Museo d'Alicarnasso ai progetti delle necropoli megalomani degli architetti rivoluzionari, senza dimenticare l'umile stele o l'antica piramide, è la tomba, insieme alla rovina, a stimolare l'immaginazione dei disegnatori del Secolo dei Lumi. L'immagine di carta si confonde allora con un oggetto di meditazione; stimola la nostalgia e diventa il simbolo della riflessione sui grandi cicli effimeri del mondo sottomesso alla natura. Diffuso dalla stampa, il disegno rischia qualche volta d'essere tradito, semplificato, irrigidito o impoverito. Tuttavia, quando non si limita a semplice antecedente dell'illustrazione e quando viene realizzato da un artista di primo piano, l'acquaforte e il bulino diventano i fedeli ausiliari del disegno destinato ad essere riprodotto.

should not be confused) was closely linked to an unprecedented reciprocal development in the eighteenth century. Piranesi, one of the most skilled and influential architectural designers of the age, owes his immortal glory to his prints.

These introductory remarks raise a series of questions which should be examined before we turn to the specific nature of eighteenth-century architectural drawings. The historical question is uncomplicated. The nature of drawing, according to its various disciplines and according to the concept of genres which thus resulted (by analogy with painting), as well as the widespread distribution of specialised collections of engravings, are perfectly well-established historical trends during the sixteenth and seventeenth centuries, based on a figurative tradition and innovation (with the plan, elevation, section, perspective and bird's eye view preceding axonometric projection). However, specialisation and variety increased during the eighteenth century. Philosophical debate relativised the fields of knowledge and how they were to be represented. From *fine art* drawings, which were collected and exhibited in the Louvre, to the techniques of descriptive geometry that were taught by Monge (i.e., from pictures of buildings to analytical blueprints), there was an extraordinary variety in the technical and plastic means used to depict architecture.

Drawing – architecture's starting point

To understand the reasons for such rich inventiveness it will be necessary to examine the purposes of an art (drawing) which conditions both the perception and conception of another art (architecture). Drawing is thus at the heart of architectural theory, which wavers between two definitions that can be seen as either contradictory or complementary.

One states that *the art of building*, as a service to Mankind's physical and social needs, is a science whose functional purpose is enriched by decorative symbolic designs.

The other states that *architectural art* (the art of drawing) is an intellectual activity dependent on the metaphysics of Beauty, and as such is a *cosa mentale*.

In a century that had rediscovered aesthetics, the act of building merely represented the specific final stage of one of the liberal arts. Abbé Batteux[1] (a successful mid-eighteenth-century theorist)

étroitement liée par un essor réciproque, exceptionnel, au XVIIIᵉ siècle. Un des dessinateurs d'architecture, parmi les plus virtuoses et les plus influents du temps, Piranèse, doit sa gloire immortelle à ses estampes.

Ces remarques liminaires posent toute une série de questions qu'il est utile d'examiner avant d'aborder la nature et la spécificité du dessin d'architecture au XVIIIᵉ siècle. La question d'ordre historique est claire : la nature du dessin selon les disciplines envisagées, selon le concept de genres qui en résulte (par analogie au domaine de la peinture) et l'ample diffusion de recueils gravés spécialisés, relève de données parfaitement établies au cours des XVIᵉ et XVIIᵉ siècles, fondées sur une tradition et une innovation figuratives (le plan, l'élévation, la coupe, la vue perspective, la vue à vol d'oiseau, précèdent l'axonométrie). Spécialisation et variété s'intensifient toutefois au XVIIIᵉ siècle. Le débat philosophique relativise alors les champs de la connaissance et leurs moyens d'expression. Du *beau* dessin, collectionné comme une œuvre d'art ou exposé au Louvre, jusqu'aux techniques de la géométrie descriptive enseignées par Monge (c'est-à-dire du tableau d'édifice à l'épure analytique), les représentations de l'architecture connaissent une extrême diversité de moyens techniques et plastiques.

Le dessin, premier élément de l'architecture

On ne saurait comprendre les raisons de cette richesse inventive sans s'interroger sur les finalités d'un art (le dessin) qui conditionne à la fois la perception et la conception de cet autre art qu'est l'architecture. Le dessin est donc au cœur de la théorie de l'architecture qui oscille entre deux définitions comprises comme antithétiques ou complémentaires.

L'une affirme que l'*art de bâtir,* au service des besoins physiques et sociaux de l'homme, est une science dont la finalité fonctionnelle s'enrichit, par le décor, d'intentions symboliques.

L'autre considère l'*art architectural* (art du dessin) comme une activité spirituelle dépendant de la métaphysique du beau et, à ce titre, initialement comme *cosa mentale*.

Pour ce siècle qui découvre l'esthétique, édifier, bâtir, ne représente que la phase finale spécifique d'un des arts libéraux. L'abbé Batteux[1] (théoricien à succès du milieu du XVIIIᵉ siècle), mettant en parallèle les arts et la poésie, exclut toujours

---

L'evoluzione di queste due procedure dell'arte grafica (non è il caso di confonderle) fu strettamente legata, per uno sviluppo reciproco, eccezionale, al XVIII secolo. Uno dei disegnatori d'architettura tra i più abili ed influenti del tempo, Piranesi, deve la sua gloria immortale alle sue stampe.

Queste osservazioni preliminari pongono tutta una serie di interrogativi che è utile esaminare prima di affrontare la natura e la specificità del disegno d'architettura nel XVIII secolo. La questione d'ordine storico è evidente: la natura del disegno secondo le discipline affrontate, secondo la concezione di genere che ne risulta (per analogia al settore della pittura) e l'ampia diffusione di raccolte stampate specializzate rilevano dei dati perfettamente stabilizzati nel corso del XVI e XVII secolo, fondati su una tradizione e un'innovazione figurativa (il piano, l'alzato, lo spaccato, la vista prospettica, la vista in linea d'aria, antecedente dell'assonometria). Specializzazione e varietà s'intensificano tuttavia nel XVIII secolo. Il dibattito filosofico relativizza allora i campi della conoscenza e i loro mezzi di espressione, dal "bel" disegno, collezionato come un'opera d'arte o esposto al Louvre, fino alle tecniche della geometria descrittiva insegnate da Monge (cioè del quadro d'edificio al disegno tridimensionale analitico), le rappresentazioni dell'architettura conoscono un'estrema diversità di mezzi tecnici e plastici.

Il disegno, primo elemento dell'architettura

Non si saprebbero comprendere le ragioni di questa ricchezza inventiva senza interrogarsi sulle finalità di un'arte (il disegno) che condiziona al tempo stesso la percezione e la concezione di quell'altra arte che è l'architettura. Il disegno è dunque al centro della teoria dell'architettura che oscilla tra due definizioni intese come antitetiche o complementari.

L'una afferma che l'*arte del costruire*, al servizio dei bisogni fisici e sociali dell'Uomo, è una scienza la cui finalità funzionale s'arricchisce, attraverso la decorazione, d'intenzioni simboliche.

L'altra considera l'*arte architettonica* (arte del disegno) come un'attività spirituale dipendente dalla metafisica del Bello e, a questo titolo, inizialmente come *cosa mentale*.

Per questo secolo che scopre l'estetica, edificare, costruire, non rappresenta che la fase finale specifica di una delle arti liberali. L'abbé Batteux[1] (teorico di successo della metà del XVIII secolo),

excluded architecture from the fine arts by drawing a parallel between art and poetry. These were *imitative arts*. In Batteux's opinion, architecture does not *imitate* nature because it uses its own materials – stone, wood, and so on. However, it must be admitted that architectural drawing, which by 1750 was considered to be an almost independent artistic speciality, was one of the principal refutations of Vitruvius's utilitarian definition of the art.

From Vitruvius to new archaeological and geographical curiosity

Since the start of the Italian Renaissance, the theory of western architecture had been regenerated by the study of antiquities and in commentaries on Vitruvius's famous architectural treatise, written at the time of Augustus. During the sixteenth and seventeenth centuries, the ten books of the *De Architectura*, which epitomised the Graeco-Roman tradition, inspired many architects, such as Alberti, Serlio, Palladio and Vignole, and introduced above all the notion of *orders*. Until at least the middle of the eighteenth century, official academic studies were limited to discussing the relative merits and characteristics of these orders. So it was that, until the nineteenth century, the repertoire of codified architectonic forms was based on rules, to which academics tried to attach an elusive norm. However, since Vitruvius's text lacks the drawings which may have illustrated it, interpreting it was and remains problematic, in particular because of the huge variations that can be observed in surviving Roman constructions. In the eighteenth century, when the Hellenistic world was at last accessible to architects and academics (in Greece itself, Sicily, and Asia Minor), Vitruvianism declined when faced with fresh symbolic, aesthetic, anthropological and historical values provided by previously unknown archaeological sites. The discovery of Herculaneum and Pompeii and the early digs there (between 1719 and 1748), as well as the study of the Doric temples of Paestum, Aegina, Agrigentum or Athens, resulted in a new prolifically inventive *Antiquarianism* which set all of Europe alight. A stimulating debate about the origins of architecture and, via the arts, about the foundations of civilisation led to a flurry of hypotheses that were fit to fire architects' imaginations. So drawing, as a vital tool in spreading images to aid creation and educate the public, became a fundamental Enlightenment preoccupation. Treatises illustrating the orders were replaced

l'architecture du domaine des beaux-arts. Ceux-ci, en effet, sont des *arts d'imitation*. Or, pour Batteux, l'architecture n'*imite* pas la nature, car elle met en œuvre ses propres matériaux : pierre, bois, etc. Cependant, il faut admettre que le dessin d'architecture, reconnu comme une spécialité artistique quasi autonome autour de 1750, participe au premier rang des réfutations de la théorie utilitariste de l'art de Vitruve.

De Vitruve aux nouvelles curiosités archéologiques et géographiques

Depuis les débuts de la Renaissance italienne, la théorie de l'architecture occidentale, régénérée par l'observation des Antiques, glosait sur le fameux texte de l'architecte du temps d'Auguste, Vitruve. Les *Dix livres d'architecture*, somme de la culture gréco-romaine, qui avait inspiré aux XVIe et XVIIe siècles de nombreux architectes, comme Alberti, Serlio, Palladio, Vignole, introduisait principalement la réflexion sur les *ordres*. Jusqu'au milieu du XVIIIe siècle, au moins, les discours académiques autorisés dissertent sur les caractères et les mérites respectifs de ces ordres. Et le répertoire des formes architectoniques codifiées s'appuie jusqu'au XIXe siècle sur des règles dont on cherchait une norme intangible. Or, privé des dessins qui auraient pu l'accompagner, le texte de Vitruve était et demeure difficile à interpréter, notamment à cause des variations extrêmes qui s'observent dans les édifices conservés des Romains. Au XVIIIe siècle, lorsque le monde hellénique fut enfin à portée des architectes et des érudits (en Grande Grèce, en Sicile, à Athènes, en Asie Mineure), le vitruvianisme déclina au profit d'autres valeurs historiques, anthropologiques, esthétiques et symboliques, portées par des modèles archéologiques jusqu'alors inconnus. La découverte et les premières fouilles d'Herculanum et de Pompéi (entre 1719 et 1748), l'étude des temples doriques de Paestum, d'Egine, d'Agrigente ou d'Athènes, furent à l'origine d'une *Anticomanie* d'un nouveau genre, inventive et prolifique, qui enflamma l'Europe. Une dialectique stimulante sur les origines de l'architecture et, à travers les arts, sur les fondements de la civilisation, entraîna une surenchère d'hypothèses propres à échauffer l'imagination des architectes. Le dessin, agent privilégié d'une pédagogie de l'image mise au service de la création et du public, devint un enjeu fondamental de la culture des Lumières. Aux traités illustrant les ordres se substituèrent des recueils encyclopédiques de techniques

mettendo in parallelo le arti e la poesia, esclude sempre l'architettura dal dominio della Belle Arti. Queste, in effetti, sono delle *arti d'imitazione*. Ora, per Batteux, l'architettura non imita la natura, poiché essa mette in opera i suoi propri materiali: pietre, legna, ecc. Tuttavia si deve ammettere che il disegno d'architettura, riconosciuto come una specialità artistica quasi autonoma intorno al 1750, partecipa in prima fila alle confutazioni della teoria utilitarista dell'arte di Vitruvio.

Da Vitruvio alle nuove curiosità archeologiche e geografiche

A partire dall'inizio del rinascimento italiano, la teoria dell'architettura occidentale, rigenerata dall'osservazione degli antichi, si fondava sul famoso testo dell'architetto dei tempi di Augusto, Vitruvio. *I Dieci Libri di Architettura*, summa della cultura greco-romana, che avevano ispirato nel XVI e nel XVII secolo numerosi architetti, come Alberti, Serlio, Palladio, Vignola, introducevano in modo particolare la riflessione sugli ordini. Almeno fino alla metà del XVIII secolo i discorsi accademici autorevoli dissertano sui caratteri e i meriti rispettivi di questi ordini. E il repertorio delle forme architettoniche codificate si appoggia fino al XIX secolo su delle regole di cui si cercava una norma intangibile. Privato dei disegni che avrebbero potuto accompagnarlo, il testo di Vitruvio era e resta di difficile interpretazione, particolarmente a causa delle variazioni estreme che si osservano negli edifici conservati dei Romani. Nel XVIII secolo, quando il mondo ellenico fu alla fine alla portata degli architetti e degli eruditi (in Magna Grecia, in Sicilia, a Atene, in Asia Minore) il vitruvianesimo declinò a vantaggio di altri valori storici, antropologici, estetici e simbolici, portati dai modelli archeologici fino ad allora sconosciuti. La scoperta e i primi scavi di Ercolano e di Pompei (tra il 1719 e il 1748), lo studio dei templi dorici di Paestum, d'Egina, d'Agrigento o di Atene, furono all'origine di un'*Anticomania* di genere nuovo, inventivo e prolifico, che infiammò l'Europa. Una dialettica stimolante sulle origini dell'architettura e, attraverso le arti, sui fondamenti della civiltà, innesca una spirale di ipotesi atte a stimolare l'immaginazione degli architetti. Il disegno, agente privilegiato di una pedagogia dell'immagine messa al servizio della creazione e del pubblico, divenne una posta in gioco fondamentale della cultura dei Lumi. Ai trattati illustranti gli ordini si sostituirono delle raccolte enciclopediche di tecniche figurative,

by figurative technical or encyclopedic works dealing with archaeology, ornamentation, travel and modern *models*, that had been built, planned or dreamt of.

The sumptuously illustrated French translation of Vitruvius's *De Architectura* with its erudite commentary, which Charles Perrault published in two successive editions (1673-1684), was one of the major events in architectural science before archaeological eclecticism. In the *Académie Royale d'Architecture* (founded by Louis XIV in 1671) it sparked off a great debate, analogous to the famous literary dispute that opposed Ancients and Moderns. It was also much talked of in the press, which was developing quickly in the eighteenth century. In 1682, Antoine Desgodets, who had been officially commissioned by Colbert to check the measurements of Roman buildings, published his *Edifices antiques de Rome dessinés et mesurés exactement*. This work, which became internationally renowned, was widely imitated. For example, a study of modern architecture such as *Vitruvius Britannicus* (1715-1725) by Colen Campbell, or the erudite architectural studies published by Lord Burlington in 1727-1728 on unpublished designs by Inigo Jones and Palladio, introduced the Continent to British *Palladianism*. With a view to illustrating and defending idioms, Blondel published his *Architecture française* (1752-1756) to celebrate the "grand style" inherited from the era of the Sun King. Finally, in Germanic countries, as well as a burgeoning number of monographs dealing with the palaces and churches that had been erected between the Rhine and the Danube, the Austrian architect Fischer von Erlach published several of his Viennese works, projects and picturesque ideas for highly ornamental fountains and vases, preceded by an illustrated history of world architecture. His *Entwurf einer historischen Architektur* (1721), in German and French, used bird's eye view landscapes to illustrate buildings from every civilisation: the monoliths of Stonehenge, Egyptian pyramids, the Temple of Jerusalem, palaces and temples from Babylon, Constantinople, Arabia, China, etc., as well as other Wonders of the World. Figurative extrapolations and drawings of *architectural fiction* had now become an artistic discipline intended to stimulate the sensations and imagination. Exoticism and archaeology continually developed hand-in-hand in the libertarian and encyclopedic investigations of the Enlightenment. Draughtsmen of all backgrounds, painters and architects worked

figuratives, d'archéologie, d'ornements, de voyages et de *modèles* modernes, édifiés, projetés ou idéaux.

La traduction des *Dix livres d'architecture* de Vitruve, somptueusement illustrée et savamment commentée, que publie par deux fois Claude Perrault (1673-1684), fut un des événements majeurs de la science architecturale qui précéda l'éclectisme archéologique. Elle entraîna, dans le sein de l'Académie royale d'architecture (fondée par Louis XIV en 1671), un grand débat parallèle à la fameuse querelle littéraire des Anciens et des Modernes, dont la presse, en plein essor au XVIIIᵉ siècle, se fera l'écho. Auparavant, officiellement chargé par Colbert de vérifier les mesures des monuments romains, Antoine Desgodets avait publié en 1682 les *Édifices antiques de Rome dessinés et mesurés exactement*. Ces travaux, connus à l'étranger, suscitèrent une véritable émulation. Recueil d'architecture moderne, par exemple, le *Vitruvius Britannicus* de Colen Campbell (1715-1725), ainsi que les publications que le célèbre érudit, architecte, Lord Burlington, consacra à la diffusion des dessins inédits d'Inigo Jones et de Palladio (1727-1728), initièrent le Continent au *Palladianisme* d'outre-Manche. Dans un esprit d'illustration et de défense des *Idiomes*, Blondel publia l'*Architecture française* (1752-1756) à la gloire du « grand goût » hérité de l'époque du Roi-Soleil. Dans les Pays germaniques, enfin, tandis que se multiplient les monographies de palais et d'églises récemment édifiés entre Rhin et Danube, l'architecte autrichien Fischer von Erlach édita quelques-unes de ses œuvres viennoises, des projets et de pittoresques inventions de fontaines et de vases extrêmement ornés, précédés d'une histoire de l'architecture mondiale par l'image. Son *Entwurf einer historischen Architektur* (1721) au texte bilingue allemand-français, illustre à partir de superbes dessins de paysages vus à vol d'oiseau, les monuments de tous les peuples : mégalithes de Stonehenge, pyramides d'Égypte, temple de Jérusalem, palais et temples de Babylone, de Constantinople, d'Arabie, de Chine, etc., auxquels se joignent d'autres merveilles du monde... Extrapolations figuratives et dessins de *fiction architecturale* s'imposent désormais comme une discipline de l'art d'émouvoir et de faire rêver. Exotisme et archéologie ne cesseront de se développer, conjointement, dans la quête libertaire et encyclopédique du Siècle des lumières ; dessinateurs de toutes formations, peintres, architectes, collaboreront à merveilleux ouvrages illustrés de *voyages* dont le sérieux scientifique, ethnologique ou

d'archeologia, d'ornamenti, di viaggi e di modelli *moderni*, edificati, progettati o ideali.

La traduzione de *I Dieci Libri d'Architettura* di Vitruvio, riccamente illustrata e sapientemente commentata, pubblicata per due volte da Claude Perrault (1673-1684), fu uno degli avvenimenti maggiori della scienza architettonica che precedette l'eclettismo archeologico. Essa comportò, in seno all' *Academie Royale d'Architecture* (fondata da Luigi XIV nel 1671) un gran dibattito parallelo alla famosa *querelle* letteraria degli Antichi e dei Moderni, di cui la stampa, in pieno sviluppo nel XVIII secolo, si farà portavoce. Precedentemente, ufficialmente incaricato da Colbert di verificare le misure dei monumenti romani, Antoine Desgodets aveva pubblicato nel 1682 gli *Edifices antiques de Rome dessinés et mesurés exactement*. Questi lavori, conosciuti all'estero, suscitarono una vera e propria imitazione. Raccolta d'architettura moderna, per esempio, il *Vitruvius Britannicus* di Colen Campbell (1715-1725), così come le pubblicazioni del celebre erudito e architetto Lord Burlington, hanno consacrato alla diffusione alcuni disegni inediti d'Inigo Jones e di Palladio (1727-1728) e iniziarono il Continente al *Palladianesimo* d'Oltre Manica. In uno spirito di d'illustrazione e di difesa degli idiomi, Blondel pubblicò l'*Architecture Française* (1752-1756) a gloria del "gran gusto" ereditato dall'epoca del Re Sole. Nei paesi germanici, infine, mentre si moltiplicano le monografie di palazzi e di chiese recentemente costruiti tra il Reno e il Danubio, l'architetto austriaco Fischer von Erlach pubblicò alcune delle sue opere viennesi, dei progetti e delle pittoresche invenzioni di fontane e di vasi estremamente ornati, preceduti da una storia dell'architettura mondiale attraverso l'immagine. Il suo *Entwurf einer historischen Architektur* (1721), dal testo bilingue tedesco-francese, illustra a partire da superbi disegni di paesaggi visti in linea d'aria i monumenti di tutti i popoli: megaliti di Stonehenge, le piramidi d'Egitto, il Tempio di Gerusalemme, palazzi e templi di Babilonia, di Costantinopoli, d'Arabia, della Cina, ecc. ai quali si aggiungono altre Meraviglie del mondo... Estrapolazioni figurative e disegni di *finzione architettonica* si impongono ormai come una disciplina dell'arte di commuovere e di far sognare. Esotismo e archeologia non smetteranno di svilupparsi congiuntamente nell'ambito della ricerca libertaria ed enciclopedica del Secolo dei Lumi; disegnatori di tutte le formazioni, pittori, architetti, collaborarono a meravigliose opere illustrate di

together on marvellous illustrated *travel books*, whose scientific, ethnological and archaeological themes were expressed by means of the *veduta* of architecture or ruins, landscapes reduced to human dimensions with a clear fascination for the art of building. Examples are Abbé de Saint Non's *Voyage pittoresque et description du Royaume de Naples et de Sicile* (1781-1787), illustrated by Desprez, Pâris, Châtelet, Renard, but also Fragonard and Hubert Robert; Clérisseau's unfinished *Les Antiquités de la France* (1778) and the *Voyage pittoresque des îles de Sicile, de Malte et Lipari* by the landscape painter Houël (1781-1786).

Techniques and new images

The means used to depict architecture, either by planimetry or perspective, had been perfected and diversified during the seventeenth century from methods that had been devised during the Renaissance. In his introduction to Vitruvius, Perrault explicitly presented the motivations behind his choices which, while limited, would still be in force one century later. The architect of the colonnade in the Louvre wrote: "There are three sorts of figures, there are those which are mere outlines to show the measurements and proportions that are set down in the text; others are shaded to show the effects these proportions can have when put into use, and for this very reason some of the shaded figures have been drawn in perspective, when the intention was not to demonstrate the proportions with a compass, but instead appeal to the judgment of the eye"[2]. Science and art are thus clearly distinguished by the graphic technique. The blueprint, restricted to the geometric and arithmetical description of the orders, took its inspiration from the most scientific form of architectural drawing, *stereotomy*, that is to say the sectioning of blocks of stone practised by master masons.

The shading of the body then transposes on to paper the analysis of how the concrete object is to be perceived. Whether as a plan, elevation or section (the three decomposed views of architectural drawing), the pure line or the shaded mass relay the constructional, plastic and harmonic characteristics of a building. But perspective, which can include landscapes, appeals to a different and more artistic perception, which Perrault calls the "judgement of the eye". Subjectivity, taste and relativity are hence introduced into the *graphic representation* of architecture, just as they

archéologique, s'exprime à travers la *veduta* d'architecture ou de ruines, paysages élaborés à l'échelle humaine, où la curiosité pour l'art de bâtir demeure omniprésente. Tels sont, par exemple, le *Voyage pittoresque et description du Royaume de Naples et de Sicile*, de l'abbé de Saint-Non (1781-1787), illustré par Desprez, Pâris, Châtelet, Renard, mais aussi Fragonard et Hubert Robert, *Les Antiquités de la France* (1778), resté inachevé, de Clérisseau, *Le voyage pittoresque des îles de Sicile, de Malte et Lipari*, du peintre de paysage Houël (1781-1786)...

Techniques et nouvelles images

Les moyens utilisés pour figurer l'architecture, soit en planimétrie, soit en perspective, avaient été perfectionnés et diversifiés au XVIIᵉ siècle à partir de solutions élaborées à la Renaissance. Perrault, dans son introduction à Vitruve, expose explicitement les motivations de ses choix qui, pour être limités, n'en seront pas moins en vigueur un siècle plus tard. L'architecte de la colonnade du Louvre écrit : « Les figures sont de trois espèces, il y en a qui n'ont que le premier trait pour expliquer les mesures et les proportions qui sont prescrites dans le texte ; les autres sont ombrées pour faire voir l'effet que ces proportions peuvent faire étant mises en œuvre, et pour cette même raison quelques-unes de ces figures ombrées ont été faites en perspective, lorsque l'on n'a pas eu l'intention de faire connaître ces proportions au compas, mais seulement au jugement de la vue. »[2] Science et art sont donc bien distingués à partir des techniques du trait ; l'épure, réservée à la nomenclature géométrique et arithmétique des ordres, s'inspire du dessin scientifique par excellence de l'art de bâtir : celui de la coupe des pierres, ou *stéréotomie*, pratiquée par les maîtres maçons.

L'effet d'ombre donnant du corps transpose ensuite sur le papier l'analyse de la perception de l'objet concret. En plan, en élévation et en coupe (les trois instantanés décomposés du dessin de relevé), le trait pur ou la masse ombrée informent sur les caractéristiques constructives, plastiques et harmoniques d'un édifice. Mais la vue perspective, qui n'ignore pas le paysage, sollicite cette autre perception qui tient de l'art et que Perrault nomme le « jugement de la vue ». L'arbitraire, le goût, la relativité s'introduisent dans la *représentation graphique* de l'architecture comme ils interviennent traditionnellement, en peinture, dans « l'imitation des objets visibles de la nature » (j'emprunte

viaggi la cui serietà scientifica, etnologica ed archeologica si esprime attraverso la *veduta* d'architettura e di rovine, paesaggi elaborati su scala umana dove la curiosità per l'arte di costruire è onnipresente. Tali sono, per esempio, il *Voyage pittoresque et description du Royaume de Naples et de la Sicile*, dell'abate di Saint Non (1781-1787), illustrato da Desprez, Pâris, Châtelet, Renard, ma anche Fragonard e Hubert Robert, *Les Antiquités de la France* (1778), rimasto incompiuto di Clérisseau, *Le Voyage pittoresque des îles de Sicile, de Malte et Lipari*, del paesaggista Houël (1781-1786)...

Tecniche e nuove immagini

I mezzi utilizzati per rappresentare l'architettura, o in planimetria, o in prospettiva, erano stati perfezionati e differenziati nel XVII secolo a partire da soluzioni elaborate nel Rinascimento. Perrault, nella sua introduzione a Vitruvio, espone esplicitamente le motivazioni delle sue scelte che, per quanto limitate, saranno ancora in vigore un secolo più tardi. L'architetto del colonnato del Louvre scrive: "Le figure sono di tre specie, ce ne sono alcune che non hanno che il primo tratto per spiegare le misure e le proporzioni che sono prescritte all'interno del testo; altre sono ombreggiate per far vedere l'effetto che queste proporzioni potevano generare una volta messe in opera, e per questa stessa ragione alcune di queste stesse figure ombreggiate sono state messe in prospettiva, quando non c'è stata l'intenzione di far conoscere queste proporzioni con il compasso, ma solamente al giudizio della vista".[2] Scienza e arte sono dunque ben distinte a partire dalle tecniche del tratto; il disegno tridimensionale, riservato alla nomenclatura geometrica aritmetica degli ordini, si ispira al disegno scientifico per eccellenza dell'arte di costruire: quello del taglio delle pietre, o *stereotomia*, praticata dai maestri muratori.

L'effetto d'ombra del corpo traspone in seguito sulla carta l'analisi della percezione dell'oggetto concreto. In piano, in alzato e in spaccato (le tre istantanee decomposte del disegno del rilievo), il tratto puro o la massa ombreggiata forniscono informazioni sulle caratteristiche costruttive, plastiche e armoniche d'un edificio. Ma la vista prospettica, che non ignora il paesaggio, sollecita quest'altra percezione che deriva dall'arte e che Perrault chiama "giudizio della vista". L'arbitrario, il gusto, la relatività s'introducono all'interno della *rappresentazione grafica* dell'architettura come essi intervengono tradizionalmente, in pittura,

traditionally are in painting, or in "the imitation of nature's visible objects" (to quote Roger de Piles's *Cours de peinture par principes*, 1708). The illusion of space, depicted by the draughtsman, captures the spectator's senses and invites him to enter, or project himself, into the image. This is no longer a mere question of knowledge and communication. Feelings and emotions have become involved.

Vision, feeling and the illusion of perspective

Following on from Locke, and his successor Condillac who wrote *Le Traité des sensations* in 1754, eighteenth-century artists meditated on the *sensualist* approach to perception and on the active role of the senses; especially in the character sand impressions revealed by eyesight, which was then generally considered to be the first among the five senses. When a sentimental scene, such as Greuze's, or a poetically meditative imagery, such as Piranesi's, rises before our eyes, then such a figure can be considered as a state of feeling. Changing customs and the broader distribution of arts in society (reinforced by the bourgeois appropriation of culture, and its obligatory passage via the theatre that was so popular in the eighteenth century) pointed architectural drawings towards *narrative forms*, which were no longer simple representations, but associated with movement in space. The influence of stage arts and painting on architecture, through drawings destined for an informed clientele, also manifested itself in a technical manner through scientific extrapolations of perspective. The art of the *quadratura*, or the way to decorate the surface of a building with a *trompe-l'œil*, an imaginary full-size building on walls or vaults, had already developed during the seventeenth-century Baroque period. From a desire to evoke the supernatural, above all in the iconography of the Catholic religion, Italian artists had, by means of a paradoxical realist manner, succeeded in visually remodelling space. By playing with aerial and geometric perspective, and by calculating accelerated or double-speed vanishing points, the painters of the *quadratura* produced intellectual artistic specialities with axonometric compositions. This was based on scenography in the theatre, the church, or the entrances to palaces and public places during festivities, and thus became one of the branches of architecture. By means of drawings, it was also depicted in countless theoretical or practical

l'expression au *Cours de peinture par principes*, de Roger de Piles, 1708). L'illusion d'espace, montrée par le dessinateur, capte l'entendement et invite indubitablement le spectateur à s'inclure, ou à se projeter, dans l'image. Il n'est plus seulement question de connaissance, de communication, mais de sentiment et d'émotion.

Vision, sentiment, illusion scénographique

À la suite du philosophe Locke, et de son successeur Condillac, auteur du *Traité des sensations* (1754), les artistes du XVIIIᵉ siècle méditeront sur la théorie *sensualiste* de la perception et sur le rôle agissant des sens ; surtout sur la découverte des caractères et des impressions que révèle la vue. Celle-ci était alors communément admise comme le premier des cinq sens. Qu'une dramaturgie sentimentale à la Greuze, qu'une iconographie poétiquement méditative à la Piranèse, surgissent dans la vision, et la figure peut s'identifier à un état d'âme. L'évolution des mœurs, le partage communicatif des arts en société (renforcé par l'appropriation bourgeoise de la culture et son passage obligé par le théâtre dont raffole le XVIIIᵉ siècle) ont orienté le dessin d'architecture vers des formes *narratives*, associées au déplacement dans l'espace, et non plus seulement illustratives. L'influence sur l'architecture de l'art de la scène et de la peinture, par le biais du dessin destiné à des amateurs éclairés, s'est également manifestée d'une manière toute technique à partir d'extrapolations de la science de la perspective. L'art de la *quadratura*, ou manière de décorer l'architecture édifiée par le *trompe-l'œil*, l'architecture feinte en grandeur réelle sur les murs ou sur les voûtes, s'était développé durant le XVIIᵉ siècle baroque. Dans un désir d'évocation du surnaturel lié d'abord à l'iconographie du culte catholique, les artistes italiens étaient parvenus, d'une manière réaliste paradoxale, à la reconstruction visuelle de l'espace. Jouant de la perspective aérienne et géométrique, calculant des points de fuite accélérés, parfois dédoublés, à partir de compositions axonométriques, les peintres de la *quadratura* diffusèrent une spécialité artistique savante. Elle s'appuyait sur la scénographie, au théâtre, à l'église, dans les entrées de palais et lieux publics lors des fêtes, et devint une des branches de l'architecture. Par le biais du dessin, elle fut aussi illustrée dans d'innombrables traités théoriques ou pratiques et diffusée à l'échelle réduite sous forme de gravure. L'ouvrage du

nell'"imitazione degli oggetti visibili della natura" (prendo in prestito l'espressione dal *Cours de peinture par principes*, di Roger de Piles, 1708). L'illusione di spazio, mostrata dal disegnatore, conquista l'intelletto e invita indubbiamente lo spettatore a inserirsi, o a proiettarsi, nell'immagine. Non è più soltanto una questione di conoscenza, di comunicazione, ma di sentimento e d'emozione.

Visione, sentimento, illusione scenografica

Sulla scia del filosofo Locke, e del suo successore Condillac, autore del *Traité des sensations* (1754), gli artisti del XVIII secolo meditarono sulla teoria "sensualista" della percezione e sul ruolo attivo dei sensi, soprattutto sulla scoperta dei caratteri e delle impressioni che la vista rivela. Questa era allora comunemente riconosciuta come il primo dei cinque sensi. Allora una drammaturgia sentimentale alla Greuze e un'iconografia poeticamente meditativa alla Piranesi sorgono nell'ambito della visione e la figura può identificarsi a uno stato d'animo. L'evoluzione dei costumi, la condivisione comunicativa delle arti nella società (rinforzata dall'appropriazione borghese della cultura e il suo passaggio obbligato attraverso il teatro per cui impazzisce il XVIII secolo) hanno orientato il disegno d'architettura verso forme narrative, associate allo spostamento nello spazio, e non più solamente illustrative. L'influenza dell'arte della scena e della pittura, per mezzo del disegno destinato a degli amatori colti, si è ugualmente manifestato in una maniera totalmente tecnica a partire dalle estrapolazioni della scienza della prospettiva. L'arte della *quadratura*, o la maniera di decorare l'architettura edificata attraverso *il trompe-l'œil*, l'architettura finta in grandezza reale sulle mura o sulle volte, si erano sviluppate durante il XVII secolo barocco. In un desiderio di evocazione del sovrannaturale legato in un primo momento all'iconografia del culto cattolico, gli artisti italiani erano pervenuti, in una maniera realista paradossale, alla ricostruzione visiva dello spazio. Giovandosi della prospettiva aerea e geometrica, calcolando i punti di fuga accelerata, a volte raddoppiati, a partire da composizioni assonometriche, i pittori della quadratura diffusero una specialità artistica sapiente. Essa si appoggiava sulla scenografia del teatro e della chiesa, nelle entrate dei palazzi e luoghi pubblici nel periodo delle feste e divenne uno dei rami dell'architettura. Per mezzo del disegno anch'essa fu

treatises and published in reduced form as engravings. The work of the Jesuit painter Andrea Pozzo, *Perspectiva pictorum et architectorum* (Rome, 1691) is a manual explaining how to construct an illusion of space from a cunning use of perspective. Collections by Ferdinando Galli Bibiena (*L'Architettura civile*, 1711, *Direzioni della Prospettiva Teorica*, 1753) and by his son Giuseppe Galli Bibiena (*Architettura e Prospettive*, 1740) contain the most varied depictions of theatre decors, gardens, antique-style urban *vedute* and the *Theatra Sacra*. Their influence can be seen in concrete terms in the Rococo architecture of northern Italy, Austria, the Germanic countries and the Iberian peninsula.

The Bibiena, tireless propagators of generous and fantastical spatial forms and combinations, had the privilege of teaching two generations of artists. Originally from Bologna, where their name is synonymous with a prestigious regional school[3], the Bibiena family travelled across all of Europe leaving behind them splendid collections of drawings, as well as permanent or ephemeral architectural works.

Emancipation and prestige of drawing

Artists travelled more in the eighteenth century, and drawings that were signed or from grand masters' studios circulated more widely. The artistic prestige and authority of a designer of a *work on paper* were now independent of any actual construction. A similar development can also be seen in how drawings by painters and sculptors were valued: one such example was the great sculptor Bouchardon, who started to specialise in small red-chalk pictures that were snapped up by collectors. A didactic dimension was added to pleasure. The art of drawing, which was traditionally considered to be a *mechanical* activity (we would now say *manual* as opposed to *intellectual*), became one of the essential branches of the Enlightenment's pedagogical approach. Drawing, wrote Roger de Piles "gives a taste for the knowledge of the Arts and for judging them, at least to a certain point. This leads us to consider that this activity is essential in the education of gentlemen"[4]. There was even more enthusiasm for coloured drawings: pastels, watercolours, red chalk, black chalk and wash tints with grey or brown shades. Then, while in the middle of the century engravers were conceiving print that aped pencil drawings

peintre jésuite Andrea Pozzo, *Perspectiva pictorum et architectorum* (Rome, 1691), est un manuel pour apprendre à construire l'illusion spatiale à base de perspective savante ; les recueils de Ferdinando Galli Bibiena (*L'Architettura civile*, 1711, *Direzioni della Prospettiva Teorica*, 1753) et de son fils Giuseppe Galli Bibiena (*Architettura e Prospettive*, 1740), offrent les aspects les plus variés de décor de théâtre, de jardins, de *vedute* urbaines à l'antique, de *Theatra Sacra*. Leur influence se vérifie concrètement dans l'architecture rococo de l'Italie du Nord, de l'Autriche, des Pays germaniques et de la péninsule Ibérique.

Infatigables pourvoyeurs de formes et de combinaisons spatiales, généreuses et fantasques, les Bibiena eurent le privilège de former deux générations d'artistes. Originaires de Bologne où leur art est synonyme d'une école régionale prestigieuse[3], les Bibiena parcourent l'Europe où ils laissent, en plus d'œuvres architecturales édifiées ou éphémères, de splendides collections de dessins.

Émancipation et prestige du dessin

Le déplacement des artistes et la circulation des dessins autographes ou sortis de l'agence d'un grand maître, s'amplifient au XVIIIᵉ siècle. Le prestige et l'autorité artistiques que confère au dessinateur l'œuvre de papier, sont désormais reconnus indépendamment de toute considération constructive. Une évolution similaire s'observe d'ailleurs dans l'art du dessin de peintre, voire de sculpteur : je pense au grand statuaire Bouchardon qui se fit une spécialité des petits tableaux à la sanguine avidement recherchés par les amateurs. À la délectation s'ajoute une valeur didactique. L'art du dessin, considéré traditionnellement comme une activité *mécanique* (on dirait aujourd'hui « manuelle » par opposition à « intellectuelle »), devint une des branches obligées de l'action pédagogique des Lumières. Le dessin, écrit Roger de Piles, « donne un goût pour la connaissance des arts et pour en faire juger au moins jusqu'à un certain point. Ce qui oblige à regarder cette partie comme nécessaire à l'éducation des jeunes gentilshommes[4] ». L'engouement s'accentue pour le dessin coloré : pastel, aquarelle, sanguine, pierre noire, craie blanche et lavis aux nuances grises ou brunes. Et, tandis que les graveurs inventent au milieu du siècle l'estampe en manière de crayon et l'aquatinte qui imite le lavis, les ouvrages pratiques diffusent méthodes et techniques. Les principaux traités sont : *L'art de laver*, de Gautier (1687), les

illustrata negli innumerevoli trattati teorici o pratici e diffusa su scala ridotta sotto forma di stampa. L'opera del pittore gesuita Andrea Pozzo, *Perspectiva pictorum et architectorum* (Roma, 1691), è un manuale per apprendere a costruire l'illusione spaziale sulla base della prospettiva dotta; le raccolte di Ferdinando Galli Bibiena (*L'Architettura civile*, 1711, *Direzione della Prospettiva Teorica*, 1753) e di suo figlio Giuseppe Galli Bibiena (*Architettura e Prospettive*, 1740) offrono gli aspetti più vari di decorazione di teatro, di giardino, di *vedute* urbane all'antica, di *Theatra Sacra*. La loro influenza si può concretamente verificare nell'architettura rococò dell'Italia del Nord, dell'Austria, dei Paesi Germanici e della penisola Iberica.

Infaticabili procacciatori di forme e combinazioni spaziali, generose e bizzarre, i Bibiena ebbero il privilegio di formare due generazioni di artisti. Originari di Bologna dove la loro arte è sinonimo di una scuola regionale prestigiosa[3], i Bibiena percorrono l'Europa dove lasciano, oltre a opere architettoniche edificate o effimere, delle splendide collezioni di disegni.

Emancipazione e prestigio del disegno

Lo spostamento degli artisti e la circolazione dei disegni autografi o usciti dal laboratorio di un grande maestro si ampliano nel XVIII secolo. Il prestigio e l'autorità artistica conferita al disegnatore dall'opera di carta sono ormai riconosciuti indipendentemente da ogni considerazione costruttiva. Un'evoluzione simile si osserva d'altra parte nell'arte del disegno del pittore o dello scultore: penso al grande scultore di statue Bouchardon, che fece sua la specialità dei piccoli quadri in sanguigna, avidamente ricercati dagli amatori. Al piacere si aggiunge un valore didattico. L'arte del disegno, considerato tradizionalmente come un'attività meccanica (si direbbe al giorno d'oggi "manuale" in opposizione a "intellettuale"), divenne uno dei settori obbligati dell'azione pedagogica degli Illuministi. Il disegno, scrisse Roger de Piles, "dona un gusto per la conoscenza delle Arti e per formularne un giudizio almeno fino a un certo punto. E ciò obbliga a considerare questa parte come necessaria all'educazione dei giovani gentiluomini[4]". L'entusiasmo si accentua per il disegno colorato: pastello, acquerello, sanguigna, pietra nera, gesso bianco e *inchiostro acquarellato* dalle sfumature grigie o brune. E, mentre gli incisori inventano a metà del secolo la stampa alla maniera della matita e l'acquatinta che imita l'*inchiostro*

and aquatints that imitated wash drawings, practical manuals publicised various methods and techniques. The main treaties were: Gautier's *L'Art de laver* (1687), the *Nouvelles règles pour la pratique du dessin et du lavis*, by the architect Delagardette (1803) and Buchotte's *Les règles du dessin et du lavis* (1722, second edition 1743), which particularly concerns architectural drawings. The "architecture of the brush", to use an expression applied to Servandoni, Legeay, De Wailly, Boullée or Robert, had became firmly established.

Though a painter's drawings had previously been reserved for sketches, for centring a composition, as preparatory studies or as reproductions of paintings as engravings, they now became exhibition pieces. Boucher and Greuze, for example, perfectly symbolise the *finished* drawing, with or without the intention of transposing it on to canvas, to be exhibited in the Louvre like a painting and to be judged on its own merits. In studios, among collectors and patrons, in portfolios or framed under glass and hung on the wall, architectural drawings also became fully-fledged works of art, worthy of being inventoried and sold (the collection of the Marquis de Marigny, Mme de Pompadour's brother, has remained famous). The circulation of drawings from the Italian and French schools, the uncontested leaders in the eighteenth century, was thus parallel to the distribution of engravings. But it was the value of a unique object, even a reverse-proof, depicting the physical manifestation of an idea and directly communicated by the artist's hand, that gave a great collection its true prestige.

Enlightened princes or monarchs, who had sometimes established their courts off the beaten geographical track, or who wished to beautify their capitals, rapidly acquired collections of drawings of architecture and the decorative arts. The Tessin-Hârleman estate in Stockholm, the collections of George III in London and of Catherine II in Saint Petersburg, as well as the galleries in Berlin and Vienna still today bear witness to the extraordinary flourishing of architectural drawings far away from the most highly reputed centres (Paris, Venice, Rome or Bologna, for example).

Drawings of decorative models

Drawing clearly played a primordial role in the stylistic development of an art which was deeply and lastingly to mark eighteenth-century minds. The changes in social behaviour, as well as an

Nouvelles règles pour la pratique du dessin et du lavis, de l'architecte Delagardette (1803) et *Les règles du dessin et du lavis*, de Buchotte (1722, 2ᵉ éd. 1743) qui concerne particulièrement le dessin d'architecture. L'« architecture au pinceau », selon l'expression attribuée à l'œuvre des Servandoni, Legeay, De Wailly, Boullée ou Robert, était franchement reconnue.

Autrefois réservé à l'esquisse, au cadrage de la composition, à l'étude préparatoire et à la reproduction des tableaux par la gravure, le dessin de peintre connaît enfin la gloire des cimaises. Boucher et Greuze, par exemple, symbolisent parfaitement la pratique du dessin *fini*, avec ou sans intention de le transposer en peinture, que l'on expose au Salon du Louvre comme une toile et que le critique juge. Dans les cabinets, chez les collectionneurs et les mécènes, en portefeuilles ou encadrés sous verre et accrochés au mur, les dessins d'architecture devinrent eux aussi des objets d'art à part entière, dignes d'inventaires et commercialisés (la collection du marquis de Marigny, frère de Mme de Pompadour et directeur des Bâtiments du roi, est restée célèbre). La circulation des dessins des écoles italienne et française, phares incontestés au XVIIIᵉ siècle, est donc un phénomène parallèle à la diffusion des gravures. Mais la valeur de l'objet unique, voire de la contre-épreuve, qui offre un rendu plastique particulier à l'idée directement transmise par la main de l'artiste, devait assurer un réel prestige aux grandes collections.

Princes et souverains éclairés qui fixaient parfois leur cour hors des grands axes géographiques, ou qui souhaitaient embellir leur capitale, se constituèrent rapidement des cabinets de dessins d'architecture et d'arts décoratifs. Le fonds Tessin-Hârleman à Stockholm, les collections de George III à Londres, celles de Catherine II à Saint-Pétersbourg, les cabinets de Berlin ou de Vienne, témoignent aujourd'hui encore, dans les musées, archives et bibliothèques, de l'extraordinaire rayonnement du dessin d'architecture loin des centres les plus réputés (Paris, Venise, Rome ou Bologne, par exemple).

Dessins de modèles décoratifs

Le rôle du dessin est évidemment primordial dans l'évolution stylistique d'un art qui imprégna profondément et durablement les mentalités au XVIIIᵉ siècle ; des changements de comportement de la société, un double appel à la moralisation et au rôle éducatif des arts accompagnèrent aussi cette

acquarellato, le opere pratiche diffondono metodi e tecniche. I principali trattati sono: *L'art de laver*, di Gautier (1687), le *Nouvelles règles pour la pratique du dessin et du lavis*, dell'architetto Delagardette (1803) e *Les règles du dessin e du lavis*, di Bouchotte (1722, seconda ed. 1743) che tratta particolarmente del disegno d'architettura. L'"architettura al pennello", secondo l'espressione attribuita all'opera di Servandoni, Legeay, De Wailly, Boullée o Robert, era ampiamente conosciuta.

Anticamente riservato allo schizzo, all'inquadratura della composizione, allo studio preparatorio e alla riproduzione dei quadri attraverso l'incisione, il disegno di pittore conosce alla fine la gloria dei capolavori. Boucher e Greuze, per esempio, simboleggiano perfettamente la pratica del disegno finito, con o senza l'intenzione di trasporlo in pittura, che si espone al Salone del Louvre come una tela e che il critico giudica. Negli studi, presso i collezionisti e i mecenati, in cartelle o incorniciati sotto vetro o attaccati ai muri, i disegni d'architettura divennero anch'essi degli oggetti d'arte a sé stanti, degni d'inventari e di essere commercializzati (la collezione del marchese de Martigny, fratello di Mme de Pompadour e direttore degli Edifici del re, è rimasta celebre). La circolazione dei disegni delle scuole italiane e francesi, guide riconosciute nel XVIII secolo, è dunque un fenomeno parallelo alla diffusione delle incisioni. Ma il valore dell'oggetto unico, e addirittura della contro-stampa, che offre una resa plastica particolare all'idea direttamente trasmessa dalla mano dell'artista, doveva assicurare un reale prestigio alle grandi collezioni.

Principi e sovrani illuminati che fissavano qualche volta la loro corte fuori dai grandi assi geografici, o che auspicavano di abbellire la loro capitale, si costruirono rapidamente dei gabinetti di disegni d'architettura e d'arti decorative. I fondi Tessin-Hârleman a Stoccolma, le collezioni di Giorgio III a Londra, quelle di Caterina II a San Pietroburgo, i gabinetti di Berlino o di Vienna, testimoniano ancora oggi, nei musei, negli archivi e nelle biblioteche, la straordinaria diffusione del disegno d'architettura lontano dai centri più prestigiosi (Parigi, Roma o Bologna, per esempio).

Disegni di modelli decorativi

Il ruolo del disegno è evidentemente primordiale nell'evoluzione stilistica di un'arte che impregnò profondamente e in modo durevole le mentalità nel XVIII secolo; dei cambiamenti di comportamento della società, un doppio richiamo alla moralizzazione

appeal both to moralisation and to the educative role of the arts accompanied this development. It can even be said that the partisans of the different architectural styles of the first third of the eighteenth century knowingly confronted one another through the use of drawing. This happened in two ways: firstly in the concrete creation of new forms which the images expressed; secondly by a widespread distribution of *professional models*. The virulently naturalist and anti-Vitruvian movement of Rocaille decoration and the Rococo style based themselves on lines that were free, flexible, light and often asymmetric. The *ornamenters* (who could be painters, architects or sculptors, but who all drew ornaments) became prestigious thanks to an unprecedented production of decorative artwork and astonishing graphic freedom. Formal prototypes often appeared as furnishings, decorations for panels or the applied arts (objects made of gold, bronze, cast iron, ceramics etc.) before being transferred to stone. After 1750, the antiquarian reaction, which was first ironically qualified in Paris as "the Greek taste", became opposed to "Rocaille". Borrowings from ancient ornaments and new iconographies reintroduced stable geometric structures, with pure symmetrical forms, drawn directly from ruins or archaeological finds. All of this led to a new syncretism, in which Egypt and Etruria were united with the original Greek model. The *antiquarians*, including learned historians such as Caylus and Winckelmann, considered drawing to be the most highly communicative form of record.

But it was with Piranesi, the architect and engraver of genius, that a new decorative and figurative system arose in Rome, which art history describes as *Piranesian*. His collection of projected fireplaces (*Diverse Maniere d'adornare i Cammini*, 1769) symbolises an Egypto-Etrusco-Greek eclecticism, treated with quite stunning graphic effects, and establishing the *Egyptomania* which the Neo-Classicism of the end of the century would integrate in its "Louis XVI", "Directoire" and "Empire" *styles*.

Stylistic debates and drawing

While this revolution of images and styles was taking place between 1745 and 1775, the Baroque and Classical schools remained dominant in most countries until the middle of the eighteenth century. The Baroque and Rococo, the

évolution. On peut dire que les agents des différents styles de l'architecture des deux premiers tiers du XVIIIᵉ siècle s'affrontèrent sciemment par le truchement du dessin. Et cela de deux manières : d'abord dans la création bien concrète de formes nouvelles que l'image véhiculait, ensuite par l'ampleur de la diffusion des modèles *professionnels*. Libres, ondulantes, flexibles, légères et souvent asymétriques, telles sont les lignes sur lesquelles s'appuie l'unité fortement naturaliste et anti-vitruvienne de l'ornement rocaille et du style rococo. Le rôle des *ornemanistes* (indifféremment peintres, architectes ou sculpteurs d'objets, tous dessinateurs d'ornements) s'est trouvé valorisé par une production sans précédent des arts décoratifs et une étonnante liberté graphique. Des prototypes formels sont apparus souvent dans le mobilier, le décor des lambris ou les arts appliqués (orfèvrerie, bronze, fer forgé, céramique), avant d'être transcrits dans la pierre. Après 1750, la réaction antiquisante, d'abord qualifiée ironiquement à Paris de « goût à la grecque », s'opposa au « goût chicorée » ou rocaille ; relevés d'ornements antiques et nouvelle iconographie réintroduisent les structures géométriques stables, aux formes pures, symétriques, directement dessinées d'après les ruines ou les objets de fouilles ; tout cela combiné dans un nouveau syncrétisme où l'Égypte et l'Étrurie rejoignaient le modèle grec initial. Les *antiquaires*, érudits et historiens comme Caylus et Winckelmann, assignèrent au rôle témoin du dessin des vertus communicatives et exemplaires.

Mais c'est avec l'architecte graveur Piranèse que surgit à Rome le génie de l'invention d'un nouveau système décoratif et figuratif auquel l'histoire de l'art a décerné les vocables *piranésien* et *piranésisme*. Son recueil de projets de cheminées (*Diverse Maniere d'adornare i Cammini*, 1769), symbole d'un éclectisme égypto-étrusco-grec traité avec une efficacité graphique éblouissante, établit l'*égyptomanie* que le néoclassicisme de la fin du siècle intégrera dans les *styles* « Louis XVI », « Directoire » et « Empire ».

Dessin et débats stylistiques

Tandis qu'entre les années 1745 et 1775 s'opère cette révolution des images et des styles, baroque et classicisme perdurent dans la plupart des pays jusqu'au milieu du XVIIIᵉ siècle. Baroque et rococo, rocaille et classicisme gracieux « à la française », palladianisme britannique, se mêlent dans les pays de l'Europe centrale, du Nord et de

e al ruolo educativo delle arti accompagnarono anche questa evoluzione. Si può dire che i rappresentanti dei differenti stili d'architettura dei due primi terzi del XVIII secolo si affrontarono consapevolmente tramite il disegno. E ciò in due maniere: in principio nella creazione concreta di forme nuove che l'immagine veicolava, poi attraverso l'ampiezza della diffusione dei modelli professionali. Liberi, oscillanti, flessibili, leggeri e spesso asimmetrici, queste sono le linee sulle quali si appoggia l'unità fortemente naturalista e anti-vitruviana dell'ornamento rocaille e dello stile rococò. Il ruolo degli *ornatisti* (indifferentemente pittori, architetti o scultori d'oggetti, tutti disegnatori d'ornamenti) si è trovato valorizzato da una produzione senza precedenti delle arti decorative e da una stupefacente libertà grafica. Prototipi formali apparvero spesso nel mobilio, nella decorazione del rivestimento o nelle arti applicate (oreficeria, bronzo, ferro battuto, ceramica), prima di essere trascritti nella pietra. Dopo il 1750, la reazione antichizzante, dapprima qualificata ironicamente a Parigi come "gusto alla greca", si oppone al "gusto cicoria" o rocaille; i recuperi di ornamenti antichi e nuove iconografie reintroducono strutture geometriche stabili, dalle forme pure, simmetriche, direttamente disegnate a partire dalle rovine o dagli oggetti degli scavi; tutto ciò combinato in un nuovo sincretismo dove l'Egitto e l'Etruria ritornano al modello greco iniziale. Gli antiquari, eruditi e storici come Caylus e Winckelmann, assegnarono al ruolo-testimone del disegno delle virtù comunicative ed esemplificative.

Ma è con l'architetto incisore Piranesi che sorge a Roma il genio dell'invenzione di un nuovo sistema decorativo e figurativo al quale la storia dell'arte ha assegnato i vocaboli di piranesiano e Piranesismo. La sua raccolta di progetti di camini (*Diverse maniere di ornare i cammini*, 1769), simbolo d'un eclettismo egizio-etrusco-greco trattato con efficacia grafica stupefacente, fissa l'egittomania che il Neoclassicismo della fine del secolo integra nello stile "Luigi XVI", "Direttorio" e "Impero".

Disegno e dibattito stilistico

Mentre tra gli anni 1745 e 1775 è in atto questa rivoluzione delle immagini e degli stili, Barocco e Classicismo perdurano nella maggior parte dei paesi fino alla metà del XVIII secolo. Barocco e Rococò, Rocaille e Classicismo grazioso "alla francese", Palladianesimo britannico, si mescolano nei paesi dell'Europa Centrale, del Nord e dell'Est,

Rocaille and graceful "French style" Classicism, as well as British Palladianism mixed together in the countries of central, northern and eastern Europe, while the Iberian peninsula remained faithful to the twofold influence of Italy and France. Conflicts of influence resulted in intense debates over "good taste" in intellectual circles, literary and artistic salons, academic centres, as well as in some enlightened courts. The moral regeneration of the Arts, demanded by philosophers and certain rulers, discovered a new form of critical humanism in the *antique revival*, based on the imitation of real nature.

However, certain artists who were radical in their desire for change, and inspired by architecture and history, confused Antiquity with Nature and pushed the Neo-Classicism of the last years of the eighteenth century towards a supposedly exact imitation of the Greek ideal of Beauty. The drawing of outlines, with its role as a normative blueprint, became the favoured form of expression for adepts of this new asceticism, based on examples engraved in stone, on bronze plaques or the outline drawings on Etrusco-Greek vases. A little before 1800, line drawing once more became a common way to depict architecture. Also used for sculpture and painting, it was seen as an objective, but also economical, means to produce illustrative engravings. In the field of architectural studies, the free practice of drawing became the new aim for a group of functionalists in the manner of Durand.

Training architects through drawing

It was in masters' studios that the apprenticeship of the *rendering* and the *project* of architecture was carried out, while the geometric plan, elevation and section remained essential tools. Perspective and stereotomy were also studied, and it would not be an exaggeration to say that the entirety of eighteenth-century architectural training was based on drawing. The most gifted pupils, or those who were most imaginative and did not immediately find building work, became known for their *vedute*, their architectural *caprices* and models of ornaments, luxury goods, furniture or decorations (panels, ceilings, religious decorations etc). Shaded at 45° with a graduated grey or bistre wash on India ink outlines, with watercolours of pink (for the plans and sections), blue and green (to depict

l'Est, tandis que la péninsule Ibérique demeure fidèle à la double influence italienne et française. Dans les milieux intellectuels, les salons littéraires et artistiques, les foyers académiques, comme dans certaines cours éclairées, d'intenses polémiques sur le « bon goût » illustrent les conflits d'influences. La régénération morale des arts que réclamaient les philosophes et certains édiles, trouva dans l'*antique revival* une nouvelle voie d'humanisme critique fondée sur l'imitation de la vraie nature.

Toutefois, certains artistes radicaux dans leur volonté de changement, subjugués par l'histoire et l'archéologie vivifiantes, confondirent antique et nature et orientèrent le néoclassicisme des dernières années du XVIIIᵉ siècle vers une imitation conforme, ou prétendue telle, du beau idéal grec. Le dessin des contours, avec sa valeur d'épure normative, devint l'expression privilégiée de ceux qui légitimaient ce nouvel ascétisme par l'exemple des figures gravées sur les pierres, les plaques de bronze, ou des peintures cernées des vases étrusco-grecs. Peu avant 1800, le dessin au trait redevint un des moyens courants de la représentation de l'architecture ; pratiqué également pour la sculpture et la peinture, il fut considéré comme un moyen objectif et de surcroît très économique pour l'exécution des gravures d'illustration. Dans le domaine de l'enseignement de l'architecture, l'exercice libre du dessin devint la cible de nouveaux sectateurs de l'art de bâtir, fonctionnalistes à la manière de Durand.

La formation d'architecte par le dessin

C'est dans l'agence des maîtres que se perfectionne l'apprentissage du *rendu* et du *projet* d'architecture, dont le plan, l'élévation et la coupe géométrales demeurent les instruments obligés. L'étude de la perspective et de la stéréotomie n'est pas négligée ; et on peut dire sans exagérer que tout l'enseignement de l'architecture au XVIIIᵉ siècle repose sur la pratique du dessin. Les plus doués des élèves, ou ceux qui, après une brillante formation, n'obtenaient pas d'emblée des chantiers, les plus imaginatifs, se firent connaître par leur *vedute*, leurs caprices d'architecture ou par des modèles d'ornements, d'objets de luxe, de mobilier ou de décor (lambris, plafonds, décor religieux, etc.). Ombrée à 45° par un lavis dégradé de gris ou de bistre sur tracé à l'encre de chine noire, aquarellée en rose (pour les plans et les coupes), en bleu et en vert (pour figurer l'eau et la végétation) et parfois rehaussée de gouache (pour accentuer les reliefs),

mentre la Penisola iberica resta fedele alla doppia influenza italiana e francese. Negli ambienti intellettuali, nei saloni letterari e artistici, nei centri accademici, come all'interno di certe corti illuminate, animate polemiche sul "buon gusto" manifestano questi conflitti d'influenza. La rigenerazione morale delle arti reclamata dai filosofi e da certi funzionari municipali, trovò nel revival dell'antico una nuova via d'Umanesimo critico fondato sull'imitazione della vera natura.

Tuttavia certi artisti radicali nella loro volontà di cambiamento, soggiogati dalla storia e dall'archeologia come fonte di vita, mescolarono antico e natura e orientarono il Neoclassicismo degli ultimi anni del XVIII secolo verso un'imitazione conforme, o pretesa tale, dell'ideale greco del Bello. Il disegno dei contorni, con il suo valore di disegno tridimensionale normativo, divenne l'espressione privilegiata di coloro che legittimavano questo nuovo ascetismo con l'esempio delle figure incise sulle pietre, delle lastre di bronzo, o delle pitture incise dei vasi etrusco-greci. Poco prima del 1800, il disegno al tratto ridivenne uno dei mezzi correnti di rappresentazione dell'architettura; praticato ugualmente dalla scultura e dalla pittura, esso fu considerato come un mezzo oggettivo ed in più molto economico per l'esecuzione delle incisioni d'illustrazione. Nel campo dell'insegnamento dell'architettura, l'esercizio libero del disegno divenne l'obiettivo di nuovi settori dell'arte di costruire, funzionalisti alla maniera di Durand.

La formazione dell'architetto attraverso il disegno

È nei laboratori dei maestri che si perfeziona l'apprendimento del "reso" e del "progetto" d'architettura di cui il piano, l'alzato e lo spaccato geometrico restano gli strumenti obbligati. Lo studio della prospettiva e della stereotomia non è dimenticato, e si può dire senza esagerare che tutto l'insegnamento dell'architettura nel XVIII secolo si appoggia alla pratica del disegno. Gli allievi più dotati, o quelli che, dopo una brillante formazione, non ottenevano di primo acchito dei cantieri, quelli più fantasiosi, si fecero conoscere per le loro *vedute*, i loro capricci d'architettura o per dei modelli di ornamenti, d'oggetti di lusso, di mobilia o di decoro (rivestimenti, soffitti, decorazioni religiose). Ombreggiata a 45° da un inchiostro sfumato di grigio o di bistro su tracciato d'inchiostro di china nero, acquerellata di rosa (per i piani e gli spaccati), in blu e verde (per raffigurare l'acqua e la

water and vegetation) and sometimes highlighted with gouache (to bring out the reliefs), the representation of building projects reached an impressive level in the second half of the eighteenth century. Some drawings are several metres long. They were produced to be exhibited in competitions, or kept rolled up in archives, and today they bear witness to a flourishing architectural art that was suggestive, exciting and highly conceptual.

Three bodies provided official drawing lessons during professional or pre-professional training, especially in France, where primary education had been rapidly adopted: free drawing schools, the *Ecole de l'Académie Royale d'Architecture* in Paris and, finally, the civil or military engineering schools (*Ecole Royale des Ponts et Chaussées*, set up in 1747, the *Ecole Royale du Génie* set up in Mezières in 1748, the *Ecole Polytechnique* of 1794, etc.). In 1740, the Rouen school opened a list of free establishments where children could learn to practise one of the branches of "the art of drawing". At first, these free schools were designed to provide trained workers for the royal and regional manufacturers of decorative objects made of wood, metal, textiles or ceramics. But they also encouraged the vocations of many painters, sculptors and architects. The Paris school, set up by Bachelier in 1767, (it is the ancestor of today's *Ecole des Arts Décoratifs*), as well as schools in Dijon, Lyons, Toulouse, Bordeaux, Reims and a good thirty other towns, played a vital role in giving drawing the prestige of a varied profession, but also of a means of cultural expression required by society. The same can be seen in engineering schools. Drawing lessons were not limited to the narrow technical and pragmatic demands of a particular discipline. They included work on *trompe-l'œil*, watercolours, gouache and wash, thus transforming a plate illustrating a working machine, a project for a bridge or a coloured topographical survey into a vibrant picture.

The domination of drawing at the Academy

After being in principle codified and strictly disciplined until the death in 1774 of Blondel, the famous professor of architecture, the style of drawing practised by pupils at the *Académie Royale d'Architecture* then became more openly influenced by a taste for the picturesque. Under

la figuration des projets d'édifices atteint des dimensions impressionnantes dans la seconde moitié du XVIIIᵉ siècle. Certains dessins peuvent mesurer plusieurs mètres de long. Destinés à l'exposition des concours, conservés roulés dans les archives des académies et des écoles, ils témoignent aujourd'hui de la floraison d'un art architectural suggestif, incitatif et fortement conceptuel.

Trois institutions dispensent un enseignement officiel du dessin dans la formation professionnelle, ou préprofessionnelle, notamment en France où l'instruction primaire a été très tôt favorisée : les écoles gratuites de dessin, l'École de l'académie royale d'architecture à Paris et, enfin, les écoles d'ingénieurs civils ou militaires (École royale des ponts et chaussées, fondée en 1747, École royale du génie de Mézières, 1748, École polytechnique, 1794, etc.). En 1740, l'école de Rouen inaugure la liste des établissements gratuits où les enfants peuvent se former en vue d'exercer une des branches des « arts du dessin ». D'abord destinées à fournir d'excellents ouvriers aux manufactures royales ou régionales d'arts appliqués dans le bois, les métaux, le textile et la céramique, les écoles gratuites encouragèrent bien des vocations de peintres, de sculpteurs et d'architectes. L'école de Paris, créée par Bachelier en 1767 (c'est l'ancêtre de l'actuelle École des arts décoratifs), les écoles de Dijon, Lyon, Toulouse, Bordeaux, Reims et d'une trentaine d'autres villes, eurent un rôle capital dans la reconnaissance du dessin comme exercice professionnel diversifié, mais également comme instrument d'une expression culturelle revendiquée par la société. Le constat est identique dans le rôle des écoles d'ingénieurs. L'enseignement du dessin ne s'y bornait pas aux exigences techniques et pragmatiques d'une discipline. Mais il englobait le trompe-l'œil d'objets, l'aquarelle, la gouache et le lavis, propres à transformer en tableau vivant telle planche illustrant une machine en fonctionnement, tel projet de pont ou tel relevé topographique richement coloré.

L'hégémonie du dessin à l'Académie

En principe très codifié et réellement discipliné jusqu'à la mort du célèbre professeur d'architecture Blondel en 1774, le dessin tel que le pratiquent les élèves de l'Académie royale d'architecture se laissa ensuite plus ouvertement influencer par le goût du pittoresque. Sous la conduite du nouveau professeur, piranésien et

vegetazione) e talvolta rialzata da sinistra (per accentuare i rilievi), la raffigurazione dei progetti di edifici raggiunge dimensioni impressionanti nella seconda metà del XVIII secolo. Certi disegni possono misurare parecchi metri di lunghezza. Destinati all'esposizione dei concorsi, conservati arrotolati negli archivi delle accademie e delle scuole, essi testimoniano oggi la fioritura di un'arte architettonica suggestiva, stimolante e fortemente concettuale.

Tre istituzioni dispensano un insegnamento ufficiale del disegno nella formazione professionale, o pre-professionale, in modo particolare in Francia, dove l'istruzione primaria è stata ben presto favorita: le scuole gratuite di disegno, l'*École de l'Académie Royale d'Architecture* a Parigi e, infine, le scuole d'ingegneri civili o militari (*École Royale des Ponts et Chaussées*, fondata nel 1747, *École Royale du Genie de Mézières*, 1748, *École Polytechnique*, 1794, ecc.). Nel 1740, la scuola di Rouen inaugura la lista degli istituti gratuiti dove i bambini possono formarsi in vista di esercitare uno dei rami dell'"arte del disegno". Dapprima destinate a fornire degli eccellenti operai alle manifatture reali o regionali d'arte applicata per il legno, i metalli, il tessile e la ceramica, le scuole gratuite incoraggiarono notevolmente la vocazione di pittori, scultori e architetti. La scuola di Parigi, creata da Bachelier nel 1767 (è l'antenata dell'attuale *École des Arts Décoratifs*), le scuole di Digione, Lione, Tolosa, Bordeaux, Reims e di una trentina di altre città, ebbero un ruolo capitale nel riconoscimento del disegno come strumento di un'espressione culturale rivendicata dalla società. L'analisi è identica per il ruolo delle scuole di ingegneri. L'insegnamento del disegno non si limitava qui alle esigenze tecniche e pragmatiche di una disciplina, ma inglobava il *trompe-l'œil* di oggetti, l'acquerello, la gouache e l'*inchiostro acquarellato*, atti a trasformare in *tableau vivant* una tavola illustrante una macchina in funzione, un certo progetto di ponte o una certa rilevazione topografica riccamente colorata.

L'egemonia del disegno all'Accademia

In principio molto codificato e veramente regolamentato fino alla morte del celebre professore d'architettura Blondel nel 1774, il disegno quale lo praticano gli allievi dell'*Académie Royale d'Architecture* si lasciò in seguito più apertamente influenzare dal gusto del pittoresco. Sotto la guida di Le Roy, nuovo professore,

its new director, the Piranesian archaeologist Le Roy, and thanks to the example of Academicians such as De Wailly, Peyre and above all Boullée, who trained many French and foreign pupils in their studios, the candidates for the Grand Prix (later the nineteenth century's *Prix de Rome*) excelled in virtuoso renderings. Vegetation, rocks, water, clouds, the landscape itself animated increasingly spectacular light and shade effects. At the end of the 1780s, perspective allied itself with a geometric rendering of buildings. The programme for the latter had been strictly formulated by the Academicians. But in the last third of the eighteenth century, it became over-inflated, grandiose, making any realisation of such projects highly unlikely. In an opulent orgy of colonnades, porticos and endless arcades, projects for public baths, circuses, maritime customs houses, stock exchanges, hospitals, markets, barracks, colleges, etc expressed the extraordinary projects of town planners to beautify cities, which had expanded hugely during the previous century.

The utopian dimension of architecture during this period, which is often criticised by historians, mainly derives from the contemporary urban and social utopia of the Revolution and Empire, which paved the way for the nineteenth-century megapolis. Despite certain detractors, and despite the functionalists' struggle for influence, the programmes and competitions of the Ancien Régime's Academy were to provide the industrial revolution with the essential structure of its Fine Arts system: the large brightly coloured drawing would remain the basis of architectural training until the twentieth century. Elsewhere, most of Europe's great academies, in an attempt to rival the prestige of Paris's *Académie Royale*, followed very much in its footsteps. There was an international manner of drawing for academic competitions, which can easily be seen in the archives of the Academies of Stockholm, Saint Petersburg, Berlin, Vienna and Madrid. Even Italy, which had provided the Academy with its original models, took its inspiration from the French system in Venice, Rome (Academia di San Luca), in Bologne (Academia di Clementino) and Parma. In this way, the engineers of the Directoire and the Empire thus found themselves in an already conquered country when they had to equip Italian towns… Had the eighteenth century taken architectural drawing too far?

archéologue, Le Roy, et grâce à l'exemple des académiciens, De Wailly, Peyre ou, surtout, Boullée, qui formaient dans leur agence nombre d'élèves, français et étrangers, les candidats au concours annuel du Grand Prix (futur « Prix de Rome » au XIXᵉ siècle) rivalisèrent de virtuosité dans leurs rendus. La végétation, les rochers, les eaux, les nuages, le paysage lui-même animèrent les effets d'ombre et de lumière de plus en plus spectaculaires. Et, à la fin des années 1780, la perspective s'allia elle-même, sur une seule feuille, au rendu géométral des édifices. Ces derniers, dont le programme était strictement formulé par les académiciens, connurent dans le dernier tiers du siècle une inflation de gigantisme, une mégalomanie, qui en rendait la réalisation potentielle fort peu plausible. Dans une opulente débauche de colonnades, de portiques et d'arcades sans fin, les projets de bains publics, les cirques, les douanes maritimes, les bourses, les hôpitaux, les marchés, les casernes, les collèges, etc., traduisent l'extraordinaire réflexion des urbanistes sur l'embellissement et l'équipement des villes dont la croissance s'était considérablement accélérée durant un siècle.

La dimension utopique du projet d'architecture de cette époque, trop souvent dénoncée par l'histoire, vient principalement de l'utopie urbaine et sociale contemporaine de la Révolution et de l'Empire, qui prépare la mégapole du XIXᵉ siècle. Malgré certains détracteurs, malgré la lutte d'influence des fonctionnalistes, programmes et concours de l'Académie de l'Ancien Régime légueront au Siècle de l'industrie l'essentiel de son système des beaux-arts : le grand dessin vivement coloré y demeurera la panacée de la formation d'architecte jusqu'au XXᵉ siècle. D'ailleurs, soucieuses de rivaliser avec le prestige de l'académie royale de Paris, la plupart des grandes académies d'Europe, créées à son image, avaient suivi ses traces : une manière internationale de dessiner lors des concours académiques s'observe aisément dans les fonds des académies de Stockholm, Saint-Pétersbourg, Berlin, Vienne, Madrid ; l'Italie même, qui avait donné les anciens modèles d'académie, s'inspira du système français à Venise, à Rome (académie de Saint-Luc), à Bologne (Académie clémentine) ou à Parme. Les ingénieurs du Directoire et de l'Empire se trouvèrent, de ce point de vue, en pays conquis à l'heure d'équiper les villes soumises… Le XVIIIᵉ siècle aurait-il abusé du dessin d'architecture ?

piranesiano ed archeologo e grazie all'esempio degli accademici De Wailly, Peyre o, soprattutto, Boullée, che formavano nel loro gabinetto un gran numero di allievi, francesi e stranieri, i candidati al concorso annuale del Grand Prix (futuro "premio di Roma" nel XIX secolo), gareggiarono in virtuosismo nella loro potenza espressiva. La vegetazione, le rocce, le acque le nuvole, il paesaggio stesso animarono effetti d'ombra e di luce sempre più spettacolari. E alla fine degli anni 1780, la prospettiva stessa si allea, su un solo foglio, alla resa geometrica degli edifici. Questi ultimi, il cui programma era strettamente formulato dagli accademici, conobbero nell'ultimo terzo del secolo un'inflazione di gigantismo, una megalomania, che ne rendeva la realizzazione potenziale poco plausibile. In un'opulenta orgia di colonnati, di portici e di arcate senza fine, i progetti di bagni pubblici, di circhi, di dogane marittime, di borse, di ospedali, di mercati, di caserme, di collegi, ecc. tradussero la straordinaria riflessione degli urbanisti sull'abbellimento e l'attrezzatura delle città la cui crescita si era considerabilmente accelerata in un secolo.

La dimensione utopica del progetto d'architettura di quest'epoca, troppo spesso denunciata dalla storia, ha la sua origine principalmente dall'utopia urbana e sociale contemporanea alla rivoluzione e all'Impero, che prepara la megalopoli del XIX secolo. Malgrado alcuni detrattori, malgrado la lotta d'influenza dei funzionalisti, programmi e concorsi dell'Accademia dell'Ancien Régime trasmisero al Secolo dell'Industria l'essenziale del suo sistema delle Belle Arti: il grande disegno riccamente colorato resterà la panacea della formazione dell'architetto fino al XX secolo. D'altra parte, ansiosi di rivalizzare con il prestigio dell'*Académie Royale* la maggior parte delle grandi accademie d'Europa, create a immagine di quella, ne avevano seguito le tracce: una maniera internazionale di disegnare all'epoca dei concorsi accademici si osserva facilmente nei depositi delle accademie di Stoccolma, San Pietroburgo, Berlino, Vienna, Madrid; l'Italia stessa, che aveva fornito gli antichi modelli all'*Académie*, si ispira al sistema francese a Venezia, Roma, (Accademia di San Luca), a Bologna (Accademia Clementina) o a Parma. Gli ingegneri del Direttorio e dell'impero si trovarono, da questo punto di vista, in paesi conquistati nel momento di attrezzare le ville sottomesse… il XVIII secolo avrebbe forse abusato del disegno di architettura?

In Rome: drawings of landscapes and ancient ruins

For the eighteenth century itself, and not its legacy, some of the answer to this question is to be found in another institution, the Academy of France in Rome, which was the most dynamic and most open to the cosmopolitanism of the time. Set up by Louis XIV (in 1666) it was originally a sort of finishing school for painters and sculptors who had won the Grand Prix; it then opened its doors to architects after the *Académie Royale d'Architecture* had been founded in Paris in 1671. The communal life of artists from different disciplines, their shared interest in the masterpieces of contemporary Rome and, even more, the emulation that led them to imitate the vestiges of Antiquity (in Rome itself, but also in Latium, Umbria, in Naples and Sicily), helped to create the ideal "union of artists" to serve society and a strong cultural policy. The Academy of France in Rome was the symbol of an enlightened diplomacy, an opening to international exchanges and an institution for the promotion of imitations of Antiquity. It was both a showcase for French talent and an obligatory port of call for foreigners attracted to the Eternal City. Russians, Germans, Scandinavians and Spaniards, as state pensioners, or the English, as artists or connoisseurs on the Grand Tour, all met up around the Mancini palace, which housed the Academy during the eighteenth century. The art of drawing was here practised for making copies, surveys and compositions, but also when walking round Rome and its outskirts in groups. The *veduta*, drawn *in situ*, brought together artists and amateurs in their daily occupations. In the middle of the century, the painter Natoire, then director of the Academy, recommended drawing from nature and himself took students out to the countryside of Tivoli or to places closer to the Seven Hills. The prestige of Pannini, a landscape painter and architect, and the success of Vasi, an engraver of views of Rome, show just how much Italian artists themselves cultivated the *veduta* and the *caprice*, bringing views of architecture or ruins to life with small characters and pastoral or familiar scenes.

Piranesi, or the liberation of imagination

Finally, we come to Piranesi. Given his proximity to the Academy (in 1745, he opened his studio on the Corso, facing the Mancini palace), his

À Rome : dessins de paysages et de ruines antiques

Pour le XVIIIᵉ siècle lui-même, et non pour sa postérité, les éléments de réponse à cette question sont à chercher autour d'une autre institution, la plus dynamique et la plus ouverte sur le cosmopolitisme ambiant : l'Académie de France à Rome. Créée par Louis XIV (1666), d'abord pour les peintres et les sculpteurs, comme un centre de perfectionnement de l'éducation des artistes lauréats du Grand Prix, l'Académie de France à Rome s'ouvre aux architectes à la création de l'Académie royale d'architecture de Paris (1671). La vie communautaire des artistes des différentes disciplines, leur intérêt commun pour les chefs-d'œuvre de la Rome moderne et, encore plus, l'émulation qui les porte à étudier ensemble les vestiges de l'Antiquité (à Rome même, dans le Latium, en Ombrie, puis à Naples et en Sicile), contribuent à établir l'idéale « réunion des arts » mise au service de la société et d'une politique culturelle volontariste. Symbole d'une diplomatie éclairée, école ouverte aux échanges internationaux et véritable organe de promotion de l'imitation des Antiques, l'Académie de France à Rome est à la fois une vitrine de la culture française et le lieu de passage obligé des étrangers attirés par la Ville éternelle. Russes, Allemands, Scandinaves, Espagnols, pensionnaires des institutions de leurs pays, Anglais, artistes ou *connoisseurs* effectuant le Grand Tour, tous se retrouvent dans les parages du palais Mancini, la résidence de l'Académie au XVIIIᵉ siècle. Pratiqué pour la copie, les relevés, la composition mais aussi, en commun, lors des promenades dans Rome et dans les environs, l'art du dessin, de la *veduta* exécutée *in situ*, unit les artistes et les amateurs dans leurs occupations quotidiennes. Au milieu du siècle, le peintre Natoire, directeur de l'Académie, recommande le dessin d'après nature et conduit lui-même les élèves dans la campagne de Tivoli ou des environs plus immédiats des Sept Collines. Le prestige de Pannini, peintre de paysage et d'architecture, le succès de Vasi, graveur de vues de Rome, montrent à quel point les artistes italiens eux-mêmes cultivent la *veduta* et le caprice, animant les vues d'architecture ou de ruines de petits personnages, de scènes pastorales ou familières.

Piranèse ou l'imaginaire libéré

Piranèse enfin, par sa présence à proximité de l'Académie (en 1745, il ouvre son atelier sur le Corso, face au palais Mancini), par les amitiés qu'il

A Roma: disegni di paesaggi e di rovine antiche

Per il XVIII secolo stesso, e non per quelli successivi, gli elementi di risposta a questa domanda si devono cercare intorno ad un'altra istituzione, la più dinamica e la più aperta sul cosmopolitismo ambientale: l'Accademia di Francia a Roma. Creata da Luigi XIV (1666), inizialmente per i pittori e gli scultori, come un centro di perfezionamento dell'educazione degli artisti laureati del Grand Prix, l'Accademia di Francia a Roma si apre agli architetti con la creazione dell'*Académie Royale d'Architecture* di Parigi (1671). La vita comunitaria degli artisti delle differenti discipline, il loro interesse comune per i capolavori della Roma moderna e, ancor più, l'emulazione che li porta a studiare insieme le vestigia dell'antichità (a Roma stessa, nel Lazio, in Umbria, poi a Napoli e in Sicilia), contribuirono a fissare l'ideale "riunione delle arti" messa al servizio della società e di una politica culturale volontarista. Simbolo di una diplomazia illuminata, scuola aperta agli scambi internazionali e vero organo di promozione dell'imitazione degli antichi, l'Accademia di Francia a Roma è allo stesso tempo una vetrina della cultura francese e il luogo di passaggio obbligato degli stranieri attirati dalla città eterna. Russi, Tedeschi, Scandinavi, Spagnoli, pensionanti delle istituzioni dei loro paesi, Inglesi, artisti o *connoisseurs* in giro col Grand Tour, tutti si ritrovano nei paraggi del palazzo Mancini, la sede dell'Accademia nel XVIII secolo. Utilizzato per la copia, i rilevamenti, le composizioni, ma anche, comunemente, nelle passeggiate in Roma e nei dintorni, il disegno della veduta eseguita in situ, unisce gli artisti e gli amatori nelle loro occupazioni quotidiane. A metà del secolo, il pittore Natoire, direttore dell'Accademia, raccomanda un disegno conforme alla natura e conduce lui stesso gli allievi nella campagna di Tivoli o dei dintorni più immediati dei Sette Colli. Il prestigio di Pannini, pittore di paesaggio e d'architettura, il successo di Vasi, incisore di vedute di Roma, mostrano a qual punto gli artisti italiani stessi coltivassero la veduta e il capriccio, animando le vedute d'architettura o di ruderi di piccoli personaggi, di scene pastorali o familiari.

Piranesi o l'immaginario liberato

Piranesi, infine, per la sua presenza vicina all'Accademia (nel 1745 egli apre il suo atelier sul Corso, davanti al Palazzo Mancini), per le

friendship with the young artists, and above all the aura of his highly original and polemical work, by 1750 he had managed to crystallise the various new approaches to depicting architecture. With his disobedient, entrepreneurial spirit in a city that was certainly open, yet politically nervous, and where papal authority forbade freedom of thought, Piranesi set about expressing the deepest nostalgia and the most intense introspection which a painter-architect could feel when contemplating ruins, through archaeology, history and the freedom of drawing. As an admirer and illustrator of the modern greatness of sixteenth- and seventeenth-century Rome, and a defender of the magnificence of the ancient city, Piranesi gave new life to pre-Classical (Egyptian or Etruscan) art in his personal compositions, which were generous, sometimes humoristic and often provocative.

At an artistic level, Piranesi's message, inciting us to meditate the greatness and decline of empires, freedom and slavery (I am thinking in particular of his *Carceri*, or imaginary prisons), the life in the golden ages of civilisations and the dark forebodings of death conjured up by inhospitable ruins, was a bold call for *imagination*. It is thus not surprising that a new generation of young artists, attracted by change, gravity in their art and the desire to share their emotions with an enlightened public, was guided by Piranesi's manner. The Piranesians that invented *sentimental architecture* (to use Ledoux's expression) explored and communicated it thanks to a sensualistic interpretation of the image. Drawing was the crucible of this alchemy, which it would now be vain to refute or to trivialise.

Having introduced colour, the illusion of luminous space and movement into their drawings, the architects of the Enlightenment left a legacy of expressive emotion, sensuality and the communicative generosity of a liberal art at the service of society. Once this society had been turned into their *public*, it could participate, not in the art of building, but in living out architecture.

Projected decoration of a vault, pen, brown ink and wash.

noue avec les jeunes artistes et, surtout, grâce à l'aura de son œuvre profondément original et combatif, sait cristalliser les différentes approches novatrices de l'architecture figurée autour de 1750. Esprit indocile et entreprenant dans une ville ouverte certes, mais politiquement frileuse, où l'autorité pontificale réprime la libre pensée, Piranèse choisit, à travers l'archéologie, l'histoire et l'autonomie du dessin, d'exprimer la plus forte nostalgie et la plus intense introspection qu'un architecte-peintre peut ressentir à l'observation des ruines. Admirateur et illustrateur de la grandeur romaine moderne des XVIᵉ et XVIIᵉ siècles, défenseur de la magnificence de la Rome antique, Piranèse redonne vie à l'art préclassique (égyptien, étrusque) dans des compositions personnelles généreuses, parfois humoristiques, souvent provocantes.

Incitant à méditer la grandeur et l'écroulement des empires, la liberté et l'asservissement (je pense aux fameuses *Carceri*, les prisons imaginaires), la vie à l'âge d'or des civilisations et les noirs pressentiments de la mort qui côtoient les ruines inhospitalières, le message de Piranèse, sur le plan artistique, est un formidable appel à l'*imagination*. Dès lors, rien d'étonnant à ce qu'une nouvelle génération d'artistes, jeunes, épris de changement, de gravité dans leur art et d'une volonté de partager leurs émotions avec un public éclairé, se soit laissée guider par la manière de Piranèse. Les Piranésiens qui inventent l'*architecture sentimentale* (j'emprunte l'expression à Ledoux), ont exploré et diffusé celle-ci grâce à l'interprétation sensualiste de l'image ; le dessin est le creuset de cette alchimie dont on chercherait en vain, en ce XXᵉ siècle finissant, quelque réfutation positive ou triviale.

Ayant introduit la couleur, l'illusion de l'espace lumineux et du mouvement dans leurs dessins, les architectes du Siècle des lumières quittent la scène en transmettant l'émotion, la sensualité, la générosité communicative d'un art libéral mis au service de la société. Celle-ci, éduquée, transformée en *public*, s'initie, non pas à l'art de bâtir, mais à vivre l'architecture.

amicizie che stringe con i giovani artisti e, soprattutto, grazie all'aura della sua opera profondamente originale e combattiva, sa cristallizzare i diversi approcci innovatori dell'architettura rappresentata intorno al 1750. Spirito indocile e intraprendente in una città certamente aperta, ma tentennante, dove l'autorità pontificia reprime il libero pensiero, Piranesi sceglie, attraverso l'archeologia, la storia e l'autonomia del disegno, di esprimere la più forte nostalgia e la più intensa introspezione che un architetto-pittore possa sentire con l'osservazione delle rovine. Ammiratore e illustratore della grandezza romana moderna del XVI e XVII secolo, difensore della magnificenza della Roma antica, Piranesi ridona vita all'arte pre-classica (egizia, etrusca) in composizioni personali generose, a volte umoristiche, spesso provocanti.

Invitando a meditare sulla grandezza e il crollo degli imperi, la libertà e l'asservimento (penso alle famose *Carceri*, le prigioni immaginarie), la vita all'epoca d'oro delle civiltà e i cupi presentimenti della morte che costeggia le rovine inospitali, il messaggio di Piranesi, sul piano artistico, è un formidabile richiamo all'immaginazione. Da allora, non stupisce che una nuova generazione di artisti giovani, presi dal cambiamento, da una gravità nella loro arte e da una volontà di mettere in comune le loro emozioni con un pubblico illuminato, si sia lasciata guidare dalla maniera di Piranesi. I piranesiani che inventano l'*architettura sentimentale* (prendo in prestito l'espressione da Ledoux) hanno esplorato e diffuso quest'ultima grazie all'interpretazione sensuale dell'immagine; il disegno è il crogiolo di questa alchimia di cui si cercherebbe invano, in questo XX secolo che volge alla fine, qualche confutazione positiva o triviale.

Avendo introdotto il colore, l'illusione dello spazio luminoso e del movimento nei loro disegni, gli architetti del Secolo dei Lumi abbandonano la scena trasmettendo l'emozione, la sensualità, la generosità comunicativa di un'arte liberale messa al servizio della società. Questa, educata, trasformata in pubblico, viene iniziata non all'arte del costruire, ma a vivere l'architettura.

1. *Les Beaux Arts réduits à un même principe*, 1746.
2. Preface to the translation of Vitruvius, 1684.
3. We should also mention schools in Turin, Genoa and Venice, where painters such as Tiepolo and architects such as Juvarra and Vittone added to this genre's prestige.
4. *Cours de peinture*, 1708.

1. *Les Beaux Arts réduits à un même principe*, 1746.
2. Préface de la traduction de Vitruve, 1684.
3. Il faudrait aussi évoquer les foyers de Turin, Gênes et Venise où des peintres comme Tiepolo, des architectes comme Juvarra et Vittone, s'illustrèrent dans ce genre.
4. *Cours de peinture*, 1708.

1. *Les Beaux Arts réduits à un même principe*, 1746
2. Prefazione alla traduzione di Vitruvio, 1684.
3. Bisognerebbe anche evocare i centri di Torino, Genova e Venezia dove pittori come il Tiepolo, architetti come Juvarra e Vittone, si distinguono in questo genere.
4. *Cours de peinture*, 1708.

PART I

THE EUROPE
OF THE MODERNS
A STYLISTIC PANORAMA

L'EUROPE
DES MODERNES,
PANORAMA STYLISTIQUE

L'EUROPA DEI
MODERNI, PANORAMA
STILISTICO

During the Enlightenment, the patronage of enlightened monarchs, as an instrument of power, of identity and education of the populations of new states, set off an unprecedented artistic flourishing throughout Europe. After the death of Louis XIV (1715), the fame of Versailles and European enthusiasm for the French language went hand in hand with an emulation of the art, language and ceremonies of the church. Papal Rome and the powerful congregations of the Counter-Reformation, whose Baroque militancy had triumphed in the seventeenth century, extended their influence to Austria, Bohemia and the Catholic German states, while the Iberian civilisations carried them to colonial America. During the 1720s, the most prosperous countries, France and England, contained certain groups that resisted Roman rhetoric and the hegemony of Italian art that had been in place since the Renaissance. They opposed the persuasive grandiloquence of Baroque masters with an art that was freed of academic norms, based on a totally original ornamental repertoire and structure. In the period of Watteau and Tiepolo, civil and religious Rococo architecture symbolised a new expression of Modernity.

In their concern for progress and European integration, the Scandinavian kingdoms and Russia started up prestigious building programmes. These were an opportunity to invite foreign artists, who could then train local architects on the job. Everywhere, borders were being crossed. Like artists, philosophers, men of letters and scientists, princes and certain monarchs also went on "study" tours. The circulation of works of art, the spectacular flourishing

Le mécénat des despotes éclairés, comme instrument de pouvoir, d'identité et d'éducation des peuples soumis à de nouveaux États, connaît un éclat artistique sans précédent dans l'Europe des Lumières. Après la mort de Louis XIV (1715), le mythe de Versailles et l'engouement européen pour la langue française, entretiennent une émulation avec l'art, la langue et le cérémonial de l'Église. La Rome pontificale, les puissantes congrégations de la Contre-Réforme, dont le militantisme baroque triomphe au XVIIe siècle, étendent leur influence à l'Autriche, à la Bohême, aux Pays germaniques catholiques ; à travers le rayonnement de la péninsule Ibérique, elles touchent l'Amérique coloniale. Dès les années 1720, les pays les plus prospères, la France et l'Angleterre, avec certains milieux réfractaires à la rhétorique romaine et à l'hégémonie de l'art italien affirmée depuis la Renaissance, opposent à la grandiloquence persuasive des maîtres baroques un art libéré des normes académiques, fondé sur un répertoire ornemental et une mise en œuvre structurelle, totalement inédits. À l'époque de Watteau et Tiepolo, l'architecture civile et religieuse rococo symbolise une nouvelle expression des Temps modernes.

Soucieux de progrès et d'intégration dans une perspective européenne en voie d'élargissement, les royaumes scandinaves et la Russie inaugurent une politique prestigieuse des bâtiments ; celle-ci est l'occasion d'inviter des artistes étrangers qui forment sur place des maîtres d'œuvre. Un goût sans frontières s'en trouve favorisé : comme les artistes, les philosophes, les hommes de lettres et de sciences, les princes et certains souverains eux-mêmes entreprennent des voyages d'« étude ». La circulation des œuvres d'art, l'essor du dessin, de

Il mecenatismo dei despoti illuminati, inteso come strumento di potere, d'identità e d'educazione dei popoli sottomessi a dei nuovi Stati, conosce uno splendore senza precedenti nell'Europa degli Illuministi. Dopo la morte di Luigi XIV (1715), il mito di Versailles e l'entusiasmo europeo per la lingua francese sono strettamente legati all'arte, la lingua e il cerimoniale della Chiesa. La Roma pontificia e le potenti congregazioni della Controriforma, il cui militantismo barocco trionfa nel XVII secolo, estendono la loro influenza all'Austria, alla Boemia, ai paesi germanici cattolici; attraverso l'espansione della Penisola iberica, essi raggiungono l'America coloniale. Dagli anni 1720 i paesi più prosperi, la Francia e l'Inghilterra, con alcuni ambienti refrattari alla retorica romana e all'egemonia dell'arte italiana affermatasi a partire dal Rinascimento, contrappongono alla magniloquenza dei maestri barocchi un'arte libera dalle norme accademiche, fondata su un repertorio ornamentale ed una messa in opera strutturale totalmente inedita. All'epoca di Watteau e Tiepolo, l'architettura civile e religiosa rococò rappresenta una nuova forma di espressione dei Tempi Moderni.

Ansiosi di progresso e d'integrazione in una prospettiva europea in via di espansione, i regni scandinavi e la Russia inaugurano una politica prestigiosa delle costruzioni; questa è l'occasione d'invitare degli artisti stranieri che formano sul posto dei direttori dei lavori. Un gusto senza frontiere ne esce favorito: come gli artisti, i filosofi, gli uomini di lettere e di scienza, i principi e certi stessi sovrani intraprendono dei "viaggi di studio". La circolazione delle opere d'arte, lo sviluppo del disegno, dell'incisione, del libro, con

of drawings, engravings and books with the opening of new collections, academies and schools considerably broadened the choice of available models. A certain cosmopolitan intelligentsia gathered in Paris (the home of the "Republic of Letters") the crucible of a radical change of taste. Turning its back on the solemnity of the previous century, the Régence style was based on the recognisable values of a highly cultured society: lightness, grace, flexibility, mobility, clarity.

Individualistic feelings, the art of conviviality, rational thought, and the revelation of a new urban civilisation based on exchanges were all reasons for the introduction of an astonishing freedom of invention, a large input from nature and, finally, an eclecticism that stimulated eighteenth-century architecture. The academic art of the ancient orders, still in place, had to face competition from a *modern* taste. It had partly to disappear, or else become integrated in the spatial, sculptural, coloured and capricious construction of interiors. Bourgeois art, which displays itself in towns through a refined domestic architecture, reflected the ease of a society in which tradesmen and artisans appropriated the external signs of the aristocracy and adapted them for their own use. The layouts of apartments relayed the atmosphere of public concourses offering up for enjoyment an essentially ornamental, graphic and meandering structure, always modelled on transparency and light effects. Rocaille, a free form of ornamentation, passed its character on to Rococo architecture, which was illustrated with bright gildings, transparent trellises and perforated cartouches in its vaults, and the reflections of mirrors.

France

It was in the office of Louis XIV's chief architect, J. Hardouin-Mansart, and then his successor Cotte, that the Rocaille style was created. Their disciples and imitators, in particular Oppenord, Boffrand, Lassurance, Courtonne and Aubert, produced their masterpieces in countless Parisian town houses and châteaux, but also in episcopal palaces and religious settings.

la gravure, du livre, avec l'ouverture de nouvelles collections, d'académies et d'écoles, élargissent considérablement le choix et l'usage des modèles. Une certaine intelligentsia cosmopolite trouve notamment à Paris (foyer de la République des Lettres), le creuset d'un changement de goût radical. Récusant la gravité solennelle du siècle passé, mais sans exclure son mode d'expression fastueux, le nouveau style de la Régence s'est établi sur des valeurs reconnaissables dans la société la plus cultivée : la légèreté, la grâce, la flexibilité, la mobilité, la clarté.

Le sentiment individualiste, l'art de la convivialité, le rationalisme de la pensée, la prise de conscience d'une nouvelle civilisation urbaine faite d'échanges, sont autant de causes qui introduisent une étonnante liberté d'invention, une grande imprégnation de la nature vraie et, finalement, un éclectisme stimulant dans l'architecture du XVIIIᵉ siècle. L'art savant des ordres antiques, prestigieux et toujours en usage, doit subir la concurrence de l'arbitraire d'un goût *moderne* : il doit s'intégrer, ou disparaître partiellement, dans la mise en scène spatiale, sculpturale, colorée et capricieuse des intérieurs. L'art bourgeois, qui s'extériorise en ville par une architecture domestique raffinée, reflète l'aisance d'une bonne société où le commerce et l'artisanat s'approprient les signes de l'aristocratie en les adaptant à leurs débouchés. La distribution des appartements prolonge le sentiment des espaces collectifs qui offrent à la délectation une structure essentiellement ornementale, graphique et sinueuse, toujours modelée par la transparence ou les effets de lumière. La rocaille, formule libre d'ornement, a donné son caractère à l'architecture rococo qui décline l'éclat des dorures, la transparence des grilles et des cartouches ajourés dans les voûtes, le reflet des miroirs.

La France

C'est dans l'agence du premier architecte du roi Louis XIV, J. Hardouin-Mansart, et de son successeur de Cotte, que s'est formé le style rocaille. Leurs disciples et émules, Oppenord, Boffrand, Lassurance, Courtonne, Aubert, notamment, donnent leurs chefs-d'œuvre dans

l'apertura di nuove collezioni, d'accademie e di scuole, ampliano considerevolmente la scelta e l'uso dei modelli. Una certa intellighenzia cosmopolita trova in particolare a Parigi (fulcro della repubblica delle Lettere), il crogiolo di un cambiamento di gusto radicale. Rifiutando la gravità solenne del secolo passato, ma senza escludere il suo modo di espressione fastoso, il nuovo stile Reggenza si è fondato su valori riconoscibili all'interno della società più colta: la leggerezza, la grazia, la flessibilità, la mobilità, la chiarezza.

Il sentimento individualista, l'arte della convivialità, il razionalismo di pensiero, la presa di coscienza di una nuova civiltà urbana fatta di scambi, sono altrettante cause che introducono una strabiliante libertà d'invenzione, un grande condizionamento della natura vera e, alla fine, un eclettismo stimolante all'interno dell'architettura del XVIII secolo. L'arte dotta degli ordini antichi, prestigiosa e sempre in voga, deve subire la concorrenza dell'arbitrio di un gusto moderno; si deve integrare, o sparire parzialmente, nella messa in scena spaziale, scultorea, colorata e capricciosa degli interni. L'arte borghese, che si manifesta in città attraverso un'architettura domestica raffinata, riflette il benessere di una buona società dove il commercio e l'artigianato si appropriano dei segni dell'aristocrazia e li adattano ai loro fini. La distribuzione degli appartamenti prolunga il sentimento degli spazi collettivi che offrono al piacere una struttura essenzialmente ornamentale, grafica e sinuosa, sempre modellata dalla trasparenza o i giochi di luce. Il Rocaille, formula libera di ornamento, ha dato il suo carattere all'architettura rococò che attenua lo sfarzo delle dorature, la trasparenza delle griglie e dei cartigli traforati nelle volte, il riflesso degli specchi.

La Francia

È nello studio del Primo Architetto del re Luigi XIV, J. Hardouin-Mansart, e del suo successore de Cotte, che si è formato lo stile Rocaille. I loro allievi ed imitatori, Oppenord, Boffrand, Lassurance, Courtonne, Aubert, in particolare, espongono i loro capolavori in innu-

Boffrand's Hôtel de Soubise in Paris (1737-1740) or Robert de Cotte's Palais Rohan in Strasbourg (1731-1742) remain models of this genre. Even in Versailles, the new apartments for the young Louis XV introduced the grace and refined balance of clear and gilded sculpted panels. This *Style Louis XV* was made illustrious by several internationally renowned specialists: Pineau and Le Blond, who worked in Russia; Robert de Cotte, who was consulted for work in Piedmont, Spain and the German states; Boffrand, whose influence in Germany was soon rivalled by local artists. Decorators and painters, such as Meissonnier and Lajoue, produced engravings which were rich sources of Rocaille models, firstly for interior decoration, then subsequently transferred to the façades of new or renovated buildings in Paris, Nantes, Bordeaux, Aix-en-Provence, Rouen, etc. In this context of great decorative influence, the French architects nevertheless remained faithful to the monarchical classicism, the "grand style" propagated by Hardouin-Mansart, for their civil and religious constructions. Cotte and Boffrand, as producers of Rocaille panels, varied and lightened the use of placid arrangements in numerous urban buildings. In Nancy, Héré, a disciple of Boffrand at the court of Lorraine, produced a sumptuous arrangement of public squares (1751-1760), punctuated with fountains, statues, trophies, arcades and triumphal arches, in which the antique order serves as a frame for the Rocaille ornamentation and Lamour's wrought iron work. The theme of the royal square, inherited from the seventeenth century, broadened out in the eighteenth century into a civic preoccupation. The French example, imitated in Lisbon, Berlin, Brussels and Copenhagen, became the symbol of the Enlightenment's urban art. Jacques Gabriel, a successor of Robert de Cotte, simultaneously designed the Rocaille interiors and the imposing monumental façades of the Place Louis XV in Rennes and in Bordeaux, and the Palais des Etats in Dijon. From 1733 to 1745, it was Servandoni, a Parisian by adoption, whose Saint Sulpice became the first grand church façade of a powerful dynamic Classicism, directly inspired from his own antique-style scenographies. This freedom of expression,

d'innombrables hôtels particuliers parisiens, des châteaux, mais aussi des palais épiscopaux et des décors religieux. L'hôtel de Soubise (1737-1740) à Paris, de Boffrand, ou le palais Rohan (1731-1742) de Strasbourg, de Robert de Cotte, sont restés des modèles du genre. À Versailles même, pour le jeune Louis XV, de nouveaux appartements introduisent la grâce et l'équilibre raffiné des lambris sculptés, clairs et dorés. Synonyme de *style Louis XV,* ce genre de décoration est illustré par certains spécialistes de renommée internationale : Pineau, Le Blond, séjournent en Russie ; Robert de Cotte est consulté pour des chantiers en Piémont, en Espagne et dans les Pays germaniques, tout comme Boffrand dont l'influence outre-Rhin se trouve concurrencée par des artistes autochtones. Des ornemanistes, des peintres, comme Meissonnier ou Lajoue, à travers leurs estampes, sont de féconds donneurs de modèles et l'art rocaille, d'abord réservé au décor intérieur, est bientôt transcrit sur les façades d'immeubles neufs ou rénovés, à Nantes, Paris, Bordeaux, Aix-en-Provence, Rouen... Dans ce contexte, fortement amplifié par les arts décoratifs, les architectes français restent toutefois fidèles, dans l'art monumental religieux ou civil, au classicisme monarchique, ou « grand genre », dont Hardouin-Mansart est le héraut. Auteur de lambris rocaille, de Cotte et Boffrand varient et allègent l'usage des calmes ordonnances dans de nombreuses réalisations urbaines. Disciple de Boffrand à la cour de Lorraine, Héré réalise à Nancy un somptueux décor de places (1751-1760) ponctuées de fontaines, de statues, de trophées, d'arcades et d'arc de triomphe, où l'ordre antique sert d'écrin à l'ornement rocaille et de support aux grilles de Lamour. Hérité du XVIIᵉ siècle, le thème de la place royale s'élargit au XVIIIᵉ siècle de préoccupations édilitaires : l'exemple français, suivi à Lisbonne, Berlin, Bruxelles, Copenhague, devient le symbole même de l'art urbain des Lumières. Successeurs de Robert de Cotte, Jacques V Gabriel dessine simultanément des décors intérieurs rocaille et d'imposantes façades monumentales, sur les places Louis XV de Rennes et de Bordeaux, au palais des États de Dijon. Entre 1733-1745, il appartient au Parisien d'adoption Servandoni de créer à Saint-Sulpice la

merevoli palazzi privati parigini, castelli, ma anche palazzi episcopali e ambienti religiosi. L'Hôtel de Soubise (1737-1740) a Parigi, di Boffrand, o il Palazzo Rohan (1731-1742) di Strasburgo, di Robert de Cotte, sono rimasti dei modelli del genere. A Versailles, per il giovane Luigi XV, dei nuovi appartamenti introducono la grazia e l'equilibrio raffinato dei rivestimenti scolpiti, chiari e dorati. Sinonimo di stile Luigi XV, questo genere di decorazione è rappresentato da alcuni specialisti di fama internazionale: Pineau e Le Blond soggiornano in Russia; Robert de Cotte è consultato per dei cantieri in Piemonte, in Spagna e nei Paesi germanici, esattamente come Boffrand la cui influenza Oltre-Reno si viene a trovare in concorrenza con quella degli artisti autoctoni. Degli ornatisti, dei pittori, come Meissonnier o Lajoue, con le loro stampe, sono fecondi fornitori di modelli e l'arte Rocaille, in principio riservata alla decorazione d'interni, viene presto trasposta sulle facciate di palazzi nuovi o rinnovati, a Nantes, Parigi, Bordeaux, Aix-en-Provence, Rouen... In questo contesto, fortemente amplificato dalle Arti Decorative, gli architetti francesi restano tuttavia fedeli, nell'arte monumentale religiosa o civile, al classicismo monarchico, o "gran genere", di cui Hardouin-Mansart è l'araldo. Autori di rivestimenti rocaille, de Cotte e Boffrand variano e alleggeriscono l'uso di ordini altrimenti tranquilli in numerose realizzazioni urbane. Discepolo di Boffran alla corte di Lorena, Héré realizza a Nancy una sontuosa decorazione di piazze (1751-1760) punteggiate di fontane, statue, trofei, arcate e archi di trionfo, dove l'ordine antico serve da scrigno all'ornamento rocaille e da supporto ai cancelli di Lamour. Ereditato dal XVII secolo, il tema della piazza reale si amplia al XVIII secolo con preoccupazioni di edilizia: l'esempio francese, seguito da Lisbona, Berlino, Bruxelles, Copenaghen, diviene il simbolo stesso dell'arte urbana dei Lumi. Successore di Robert de Cotte, Jacques V Gabriel disegna allo stesso tempo decorazioni da interni rocaille e imponenti facciate monumentali, nelle piazze Luigi XV di Rennes e Bordeaux, al *Palais des États* di Digione. Tra il 1733-1745, spetta al parigino d'adozione Servandoni creare

which included the royal Academy's "grand style", the elegant Classicism appreciated at the court and a widespread Rocaille, gave the French architecture of the time a flexibility of interpretation that explains its international success.

England

While English architecture was aware of these various currents, it stands rather aloof from them. The twofold influence of Roman Baroque and Versailles Classicism can certainly be seen at the end of the seventeenth century in the work of Sir Christopher Wren. But Rocaille made only a feeble late appearance in its decorative arts. Until the mid-eighteenth century, British architecture wavered between two time-honoured tendencies – a Classicism inspired by Palladio and a late Mannerism. Two artists, Hawksmoor and Vanbrugh, dominated the work done in the great aristocratic houses and in the churches during the renovation of the City of London. Having created a sort of austere Baroque, varied in its treatment of pure exterior volumes, they included certain Gothic and Elizabethan elements in their work. Vanbrugh's Castle Howard and Blenheim Palace (1705-1724), and Hawksmoor's Christ Church, Spitalfields and Saint George's in Bloomsbury are masterpieces of this insular modern genre. Gibbs, a Scottish Catholic trained by Fontana in Rome, returned to an elegant Antique style (Saint Martin's in the Fields in London, 1721-1726), while Lord Burlington, Kent and Campbell reaffirmed the pre-eminence of *Palladianism* (Chiswick House, 1720-1725), which was to spread over both the Continent and North America in the second half of the century.

Italy

Italy, from Milan to the Kingdom of the Two Sicilies, kept up its Baroque passion until the middle of the eighteenth century. However, the decorative arts did adopt the Rocaille style, which became enriched with polychrome incrustations. Meanwhile, the grand traditions

première grande façade d'église, d'un classicisme puissant et dynamique, directement inspiré de ses scénographies à l'antique. Cette liberté d'expression, du « grand goût » prôné par l'Académie royale, du classicisme élégant apprécié à la cour et de la rocaille généralisée, donne à l'architecture française de cette époque une souplesse d'interprétation qui favorise sa grande diffusion hors des frontières.

L'Angleterre

Sans les méconnaître, l'architecture anglaise échappe en partie à ces différents courants. Certes, la double influence du baroque romain et du classicisme versaillais s'y rencontre à la fin du XVIIᵉ siècle avec l'œuvre de Sir Christopher Wren. Mais la rocaille la touchera peu, ou plus tardivement, dans les arts décoratifs. Jusqu'au milieu du XVIIIᵉ siècle, l'architecture britannique oscille entre deux tendances séculaires : le classicisme inspiré de Palladio et le maniérisme tardif. Deux artistes dominent très nettement, dans les grandes demeures aristocratiques, comme dans les églises de la reconstruction de la City : Hawksmoor et Vanbrugh. Créateurs d'une sorte de baroque austère, varié dans le traitement des volumes extérieurs purs, ils intègrent dans leurs œuvres certains traits gothiques et élisabéthains. Castle Howard et Bleinheim Palace (1705-1724) de Vanbrugh, Christ Church à Spitalfields et Saint-Georges à Bloomsbury (1716-1731) de Hawksmoor, sont les chefs-d'œuvre du genre moderne insulaire. Écossais, catholique, formé à Rome chez Fontana, Gibbs illustre un retour à l'antique élégant (église Saint-Martin-in-the-Fields à Londres, 1721-1726), tandis qu'avec Lord Burlington, Kent et Campbell réaffirment la prééminence du style de Palladio ou *Palladianisme* (Chiswick House, 1720-1725) qui rayonnera sur le Continent dans la seconde moitié du siècle ainsi qu'en Amérique du Nord.

L'Italie

L'Italie, de Milan au royaume des Deux-Siciles, prolonge sa fougue baroque en plein milieu du XVIIIᵉ siècle. Les arts décoratifs adoptent

a Sant-Sulpice la prima grande facciata di chiesa, di un classicismo potente e dinamico, direttamente ispirato dalle sue scenografie all'antica. Questa libertà d'espressione, del "gran gusto" predicato dall'Accademia reale, del classicismo elegante apprezzato a corte e del rocaille generalizzato, dà all'architettura francese di questa epoca una flessibilità d'interpretazione che favorisce la sua grande diffusione oltre frontiera.

L'Inghilterra

Pur senza sottovalutarle, l'architettura inglese sfugge in parte a queste diverse correnti. Certamente, la doppia influenza del barocco romano e del classicismo di Versailles si ritrova qui alla fine del XVII secolo con l'opera di Sir Christopher Wren. Ma la Rocaille la toccherà limitatamente, o solo tardivamente, nelle arti decorative. Fino alla metà del XVII secolo l'architettura britannica oscilla tra due tendenze secolari: il classicismo ispirato da Palladio e il Manierismo tardivo. Due artisti dominano in modo indiscutibile, nelle grandi dimore aristocratiche, come nelle chiese della ricostruzione della *City*: Hawksmoor e Vanbrug. Creatori di una specie di Barocco austero, diversificato nel trattamento dei volumi esteriori puri, essi integrano nelle loro opere certi aspetti gotici ed elisabettiani. Castle Howard e Bleinheim Palace (1705-1724) di Vanbrugh, Christ Church a Spitafields e Saint-Georges a Bloomsbury (1716-1731) di Hawksmoor, sono i capolavori del genere moderno insulare. Scozzese, cattolico, formato a Roma presso Fontana, Gibbs rappresenta un ritorno all'Antico elegante (chiesa di Saint-Martin-in-the-Fields a Londra, 1721-1726), mentre con Lord Burlington, Kent e Campell si riafferma la preminenza dello stile di Palladio o *Palladianesimo* (Chiswick Hous, 1720-1725) che si diffonderà sul Continente nella seconda metà del secolo così come in America del Nord.

L'Italia

L'Italia, da Milano al Regno delle Due Sicilie, prolunga il suo impeto barocco fino alla metà del XVIII secolo. Le arti decorative adottano però

of painting in the land of the fresco reached a sort of zenith with the interiors of Tiepolo, originally from Venice. The illusionist Rococo style was combined with light painting in stucco or gilded arabesque frames, for example in the gallery of the Archbishopric of Udine (1726-1728) or in certain Venitian palaces, which created a scintillatingly bright architectural space. Elsewhere, the palaces that Tiepolo decorated in Würzburg (1751-1753) and in Madrid (1762-1766) display the profound influence of Venitian Rococo in the middle of the century. However, it was in Piedmont, in the circles round the architect Juvarra, that Italian Baroque acquired its most striking originality: the transparency of spaces and the invention of spectacular structures which added to the personal contributions of Guarini, the great Turinese architect of the end of the seventeenth century. The imposing stairwell in the Madame palace (1723), the Carmelite church in Turin and the Stupinigi palace (1729-1733) are Juvarra's best known works, along with the basilica of Superga (1715-1731) where the architect adopted a more Roman tone. Two other Piedmontese architects, Vittone and Alfieri, extended Borromini's considerable influence into the north of Italy. A similar passion marks the work of the Galli Bibiena, famous Bolognese scenographers and architects, who travelled widely in Italy and Europe and whose artistic arrangements had a decisive influence all around the Mediterranean, in Germanic countries, and as far as Lorraine. On the other hand, in Rome and Naples, Baroque was more serious, or at least more monumental. Numerous palaces and churches, such as Galilei's San Giovanni di Latran (1736) or Fuga's Santa Maria Maggiore (1741-1743), seem to carry on the grandiose influence of Bernini or Fontana, while Vantivelli rivalled the grandeur of Versailles at Caserte (begun in 1752), near Naples, whose gardens decked with statues, waterfalls and fountains are some of the finest of the century. In Rome itself, the art of water springing up from architecture enlivened with rocks and sculpted groups reached its peak with Salvi's Trevi fountain (1732-1762).

cependant la rocaille qui s'enrichit de jeux d'incrustations polychromes, mais les grands cycles de peinture, traditionnels dans ce pays de la fresque, connaissent une sorte d'apogée avec les décors intérieurs du Vénitien Tiepolo. Le style rococo illusionniste combine l'emploi de la peinture claire et d'encadrements de stucs blancs ou d'arabesques d'or, comme à la galerie de l'archevêché d'Udine (1726-1728) ou dans certains palais de Venise, et crée un espace architectural lumineux et scintillant. À l'étranger, les palais que Tiepolo décore à Würzburg (1751-1753) et à Madrid (1762-1766) montrent le rayonnement du rococo vénitien au milieu du siècle. C'est néanmoins en Piémont, autour de l'architecte Juvarra que le baroque italien acquiert alors sa plus évidente originalité : la transparence des espaces et l'invention des structures spectaculaires enrichissent encore l'apport si personnel du grand Turinois de la fin du XVIIᵉ siècle, Guarini. L'imposante cage d'escalier du palais Madame (1732) et l'église des Carmes, à Turin, le palais de Stupinigi (1729-1733), sont les œuvres les plus célèbres de Juvarra, avec la basilique de Superga (1715-1731) où l'architecte retrouve des accents plus romains. Deux autres architectes piémontais, Vittone et Alfieri, prolongent l'influence considérable de Borromini dans le nord de l'Italie. Un élan similaire distingue l'art des Galli Bibiena, fameux scénographes et architectes bolonais qui parcourent l'Italie et l'Europe, et dont l'art de la mise en scène est déterminant, à bien des égards, tant autour de la Méditerranée que dans les Pays germaniques et jusqu'en Lorraine... À Rome ou à Naples, au contraire, le baroque est plus grave, ou du moins plus monumental. De nombreux palais et façades d'églises, Saint-Jean-de-Latran (1736) de Galilei, Sainte-Marie-Majeure (1741-1743) de Fuga, semblent prolonger l'art grandiose du Bernin ou de Fontana, tandis que Vantivelli rivalise de grandeur avec Versailles, près de Naples, au château de Caserte (commencé en 1752), dont les jardins parés de statues, de cascades et de fontaines, sont parmi les plus beaux du siècle. À Rome même, l'art des eaux jaillissantes au cœur de l'architecture animée de rochers et de groupes sculptés connaît son apogée avec la fontaine de Trevi (1732-1762) de Salvi.

la rocaille che si arricchisce di giochi di incrostazioni policrome, mentre i grandi cicli della pittura, tradizionali in questo paese dell'affresco, conoscono una specie di apogeo con le decorazioni del veneziano Tiepolo. Lo stile rococò illusionista combina l'utilizzo della pittura chiara con cornici di stucchi bianchi o d'arabeschi d'oro, come nella galleria dell'arcivescovo di Udine (1726-1728) o in certi palazzi di Venezia, e crea uno spazio architettonico luminoso e scintillante. All'estero, i palazzi che il Tiepolo decora a Würzburg (1751-1753) e a Madrid (1762-1766), mostrano la diffusione del Rococò veneziano alla metà del secolo. È nondimeno in Piemonte, intorno all'architetto Juvarra, che il Barocco italiano acquisisce allora la sua più evidente originalità: la trasparenza degli spazi e l'invenzione delle strutture spettacolari arricchiscono ancora l'apporto così personale del grande Torinese della fine del XVII secolo, Guarini. L'imponente tromba delle scale di palazzo Madama (1732) e la Chiesa dei Carmini, a Torino, il Palazzo di Stupinigi (1729-1733), sono le opere più celebri di Juvarra, insieme con la Basilica di Superga (1715-1731) in cui l'architetto ritrova degli accenti più romanici. Due altri architetti piemontesi, Vittone e Alfieri, prolungano l'influenza notevole del Borromini nel Nord Italia. Uno slancio simile distingue l'arte dei Galli Bibiena, famosi scenografi e architetti bolognesi che percorrono l'Italia e l'Europa e la cui arte della messa in scena è determinante, per molti aspetti, tanto nella zona del Mediterraneo che nei paesi germanici fino in Lorena... A Roma o a Napoli, al contrario, il Barocco è più serio, o meno monumentale. Dei numerosi palazzi e facciate di chiese, San Giovanni in Laterano (1736) di Galilei, Santa Maria Maggiore (1741-1743) di Fuga, sembrano prolungare l'arte grandiosa del Bernini o di Fontana, mentre Vanvitelli gareggia in grandezza con Versailles, vicino Napoli, con la Reggia di Caserta (iniziata nel 1752), i cui giardini ornati di statue, di cascate e di fontane, sono tra i più belli del secolo. A Roma stessa, l'arte delle acque zampillanti in seno ad un'architettura animata da rocce e da gruppi scolpiti conosce il suo apogeo con la fontana di Trevi (1732-1762) di Salvi.

The Iberian peninsula

The reredos, that sumptuous gilded scene in the shadows of the choir and votive chapels, sums up the main characteristics of Iberian architecture in its Italian influence. Many Gothic churches received this new form of decoration during the eighteenth century. In Spain, two families of architects imposed their personal geniuses on a superb regional art: the Figueroa family, leaders of the Andalusian Baroque, and the Churriguera, who became a byword for Castilian Baroque. José Churriguera's altarpieces in the church of Saint Sebastian in Salamanca are some of the finest examples of this religious art that unites exuberance with an extremely harmonious formal balance. Alberto Churriguera then adapted the allure of this devotional art form to the ceremonies of city life: the Plaza Mayor (1728-1755) in Salamanca, which he planned and which was completed by García de Quiñones, is one of Europe's most beautiful squares. In Lisbon, the Square of Commerce was designed by Manuel de Maia and Eugenio dos Santos as a French style royal square. Overlooking the Tagus, it brilliantly symbolises the reconstruction of the city after the 1755 earthquake. Mateus Vincente de Oliveira and François Robillon produced a rare but perfect example of Portuguese Rococo in their royal palace of Queluz (1758-1794). Meanwhile, Spanish royal residences constituted an extraordinary blending of the Versailles style, European Rococo and Italian Baroque. The reconstruction of the huge royal palace in Madrid (1738-1764) by Rodríguez and the Italian architect Sacchetti (both pupils of Juvarra, who drew up the initial plans) consecrated the art of the Bourbons' court. Two "satellites" of Versailles, the palace of La Granja de San Ildefonso and the palace of Aranjuez, in the midst of vast regularly laid out gardens, illustrate how the French style became truly European in the eighteenth century.

Northern and Eastern Europe

If there was a clear foreign influence on the German states, by artists such as Borromini, Fontana, Juvarra, Guarini, Bibiena, Meissonnier,

La péninsule Ibérique

Le retable, somptueuse mise en scène dorée, nimbée dans l'ombre du chœur et des chapelles votives, résume les principaux caractères de l'architecture ibérique directement influencée par l'Italie. Bon nombre d'églises gothiques reçoivent cette nouvelle parure au XVIIIᵉ siècle. En Espagne, deux familles d'architectes ont imposé leur génie personnel à un art régional somptueux : les Figueroa, chefs de file du baroque andalou, et les Churriguera, dont le nom devient synonyme de baroque castillan. Les retables de l'église Saint-Sébastien de Salamanque, de José Churriguera, sont une des plus parfaites réalisations de cet art religieux qui allie l'exubérance à l'équilibre formel le plus harmonieux. Alberto Churriguera sait adapter les séductions de cet art culturel aux cérémonies de la vie urbaine : la Plaza Mayor (1728-1755) de Salamanque, dont il donne les plans, et qu'achève Garcia de Quiñones, est une des plus belles places d'Europe. À Lisbonne, la place du Commerce est conçue par Manuel de Maia et Eugenio dos Santos comme une place royale à la française : ouverte sur le Tage, elle symbolise avec éclat la reconstruction de la ville, après le tremblement de terre de 1755. Au palais royal de Queluz (1758-1794), Mateus Vincente de Oliveira et le Français Robillon donnent un rare, mais parfait exemple de rococo portugais. Les résidences royales espagnoles font l'objet d'une étonnante synthèse entre le goût versaillais, le rococo européen et le baroque italien. La reconstruction de l'immense palais royal de Madrid (1738-1764) par l'Italien Sacchetti et Rodriguez (deux élèves de Juvarra, qui a d'ailleurs conçu les premiers plans), consacre l'art de cour des Bourbons ; deux « satellites » de Versailles, le palais de La Granja de San Ildefonso et celui d'Aranjuez, au cœur de vastes jardins réguliers, illustrent l'adoption d'un thème français, devenu européen au XVIIIᵉ siècle.

Pays du nord et de l'est de l'Europe

En Pays germaniques, si l'on comprend bien ce que l'art doit à l'influence étrangère des Borromini, Fontana, Juvarra, Guarini, Bibiena,

La Penisola iberica

Il retablo, sontuosa messa in scena dorata, splendente nell'ombra del coro e delle cappelle votive, riassume i principali caratteri dell'architettura iberica direttamente influenzati dall'Italia. Un buon numero di chiese gotiche ricevono questo nuovo ornamento nel XVIII secolo. In Spagna, due famiglie di architetti hanno imposto il loro genio personale ad una sontuosa arte regionale: i Figueroa, capifila del Barocco andaluso e i Churriguera, il cui nome diventa sinonimo di barocco castigliano. I retabli della chiesa San Sebastiano di Salamanca, di José Churriguera, sono una delle più perfette realizzazioni di quest'arte religiosa che abbina l'esuberanza all'equilibrio formale più armonioso. Alberto Churriguera sa adattare la seduzione di quest'arte culturale alle cerimonie della vita urbana: la Plaza Major (1728-1755) di Salamanca, di cui egli fa i progetti, e che completerà Garcia de Quiñones, è una delle piazze più belle d'Europa. A Lisbona, la piazza del Commercio è ideata da Manuel de Uraia e Eugenio dos Santos come una piazza reale alla francese: aperta sul Tago, essa simboleggia con slancio la ricostruzione della città, dopo il terremoto del 1755. Al Palazzo Reale di Queluz (1758-1794), Mateus Vincente de Oliveira e il francese Robillon donano un raro ma perfetto esempio di Rococò portoghese. Le residenze reali spagnole sono l'oggetto di una stupefacente sintesi tra il gusto di Versailles, il Rococò europeo e il barocco italiano. La ricostruzione dell'immenso Palazzo Reale di Madrid (1738-1764) ad opera di Rodriguez e dell'italiano Sacchetti (due allievi di Juvarra che ha d'altra parte ideato i primi progetti), consacrano l'arte di corte dei Borboni; due "satelliti" di Versailles, i palazzi di La Granja di San Ildefonso e quello d'Aranjuez, al centro di ampi e regolari giardini, illustrano l'adozione di un tema francese, divenuto europeo nel XVIII secolo.

Paesi del Nord e dell'Est Europa

Nei paesi germanici, se si comprende bene ciò che l'arte deve all'influenza straniera dei Borromini, Fontana, Juvarra, Guarini, Bibiena,

Boffrand and Cuvilliés, we can nevertheless wonder at the metamorphosis of their architecture. Local characteristics, resulting from the political and religious divisions of the country, explain the extraordinary diversity of German architecture which was principally influenced by the Italian, Austrian or French styles, depending on the particular court. Rocaille ornamentation, imported by Cuvilliés from France to Bavaria during the 1730s, was to impose itself on luxurious apartments and the famous theatre of the residential palace in Munich, as well as in Nymphenburg (1734-1739), before spreading to religious art in the Catholic states. Creators of sculpture, stucco and frescoes competed in fantastic inventions. With what are often turbulent forms, they modelled the luminous and highly unified architectural spaces in their churches. Neumann, in the abbey of Neresheim (1745-1798) and in Vierzehnheiligin (1745-1772), Zimmermann in the pilgrims' sanctuary in Wies (1745-1750), the Asams in Munich, Regensburg and in Freising, Schmuzers in Ettal and the Fischers in Ottobeuren are, with Thumb's abbey church of Saint Gall, the best examples of this highly original art. Based on contrasts between elegant exterior volumes (though deprived of any decorative attraction apart from clock-towers crowned with cupolas) with luxurious interior decoration, these Rococo buildings are based on extremely varied plans. The double plan, both centred and circular, of the abbey church in Ettal, for example, is reminiscent of Roman or Turinese models, while the plans in the nave correspond more closely to examples from the north. What is more, the walls vanish behind a transparent effect, created by a continuous interchange between heavily sculpted supports and *trompe-l'œil* painted vaults, dominated by arabesques.

If the apartments in princes' palaces generally contain French models, the conception of banqueting rooms and the arrangement of façades owe more to Italian Baroque. The huge stairwells and vestibules dotted with vigorous telamons, the throne rooms, galleries, ballrooms and reception areas were inspired by a brilliant

Meissonnier, Boffrand et Cuviliés, on ne peut que constater la métamorphose de l'architecture outre-Rhin. Les particularismes locaux dus au morcellement politique et religieux du pays expliquent l'extrême diversité de l'architecture allemande soumise, selon les différentes cours princières, à l'influence prépondérante des modes italiennes, autrichiennes ou françaises. L'ornement rocaille, importé par le Français Cuvilliés en Bavière, dans les années 1730, va s'imposer aux grands appartements et au célèbre théâtre du palais de la résidence à Munich, ainsi qu'au Nymphenburg (1734-1739), avant de se répandre dans l'architecture religieuse des états catholiques. Sculpteurs, stucateurs et fresquistes rivalisent de fantaisie: dans des formes souvent remuantes, ils modèlent l'espace architectonique lumineux et volontairement très unitaire des églises. Neumann à l'abbaye de Neresheim (1745-1798) et à celle de Vierzehnheiligen (1745-1772), Zimmermann au sanctuaire de pèlerinage de Wies (1745-1750), les Asam à Munich, à Regensburg ou à Freising, Schmuzers à Ettal et les Fischer à Ottobeuren sont, avec Thumb à l'abbatiale de Saint-Gall, les meilleurs représentants de cet art profondément original. Fondé sur les contrastes entre les volumes extérieurs élégants, mais privés de séduction décorative autre que de hauts clochers couronnés de bulbes, et d'une ornementation luxuriante à l'intérieur, ces édifices rococo adoptent les plans les plus variés. Le double plan centré, circulaire, de l'église abbatiale d'Ettal, par exemple, se souvient des modèles romains ou turinois, tandis que les plans à nef unique se conforment davantage à la tradition septentrionale. Mais, dans tous les cas, le mur plastique s'efface derrière des effets de transparence qui lient en toute continuité les supports extrêmement sculptés aux voûtes peintes en trompe l'œil où domine l'arabesque.

Si les petits appartements des résidences princières se rapprochent davantage des exemples français, la conception des espaces d'apparat et l'ordonnance des façades s'inscrivent dans le courant du baroque italien. Les immenses cages d'escalier et les vestibules ponctués d'atlantes puissants, les salles du trône, galeries, salles de bal et réception, s'inspirent d'une scénographie

Meissonnier, Boffrand e Cuvilliés, non si può che costatare la metamorfosi dell'architettura d'Oltre-Reno. I particolarismi locali dovuti alla frammentazione politica e religiosa del paese spiegano l'estrema diversità dell'architettura tedesca sottomessa, secondo le varie corti principesche, all'influenza preponderante delle mode italiane, austriache o francesi. L'ornamento rocaille, importato dal francese Cuvilliés in Baviera, negli anni 1730, è destinato ad imporsi nei grandi appartamenti e al celebre teatro del palazzo della residenza a Monaco, così come al Nymphenburg (1734-1739), prima di diffondersi nell'architettura religiosa degli stati cattolici. Scultori, stuccatori e affrescatori entrano in competizione per la fantasia. In forme spesso irrequiete, essi modellano lo spazio architettonico luminoso e volontariamente molto unitario delle chiese. Nuemann nell'abbazia di Nereshieim (1745-1798) e in quella di Vierzehnheiligen (1745-1772), Zimmermann nel santuario di Wies (1745-1750), di Asam a Monaco, a Regensburg o a Freising, Schmuzers a Ettal e i Fischer a Ottobeuren sono, con Thumb alla chiesa abbaziale di Saint-Gall, i migliori rappresentanti di quest'arte profondamente originale. Fondati sui contrasti tra i volumi esterni eleganti, ma privi di seduzione decorativa all'infuori di alti campanili coronati da cupole bulbeiformi, e un ornamento lussuoso all'interno, questi edifici rococò adottano le piante più svariate. La doppia pianta centrale, circolare, della chiesa abbaziale d'Ettal, per esempio, si richiama ai modelli romani e torinesi, mentre le piante a navata unica rimandano principalmente alla tradizione settentrionale. Ma in ogni caso, il muro plastico si annulla dietro gli effetti di trasparenza che legano in tutta continuità i supporti estremamente scolpiti alle volte dipinte a *trompe-l'œil* dove domina l'arabesco.

Se i piccoli appartamenti delle residenze principesche si avvicinano in particolar modo agli esempi francesi, la concezione degli spazi d'apparato e delle facciate s'iscrive nella corrente del Barocco Italiano. Le immense trombe delle scale o i vestiboli punteggiati di atlanti potenti, le sale del trono, gallerie, sale da ballo e da ricevimento, si ispirano ad una scenografia

scenography, suited to the ostentation of the Bishops, Electors or Margraves. The famous Zwinger (1709-1736) in Dresden, which is Pöppelmann's masterpiece, the residences in Mannheim, Ansbach, Postdam, Augsburg or Schleissheim compete in richness and daring with their distant model in Versailles. But it is undoubtedly the residence in Würzburg (1720-1740), the plans for which Neumann submitted to Boffrand and Robert de Cotte, that marks the zenith of civil German architecture.

Austria, Bohemia and Hungary were just as rich at a time when artists such as Hildebrandt, Prandtauer and above all Fischer von Erlach, were working for the church and the imperial court. The churches of Vienna, Salzburg and Prague, and certain abbeys such as the one in Melk (1709-1711), which overlooks the Danube from the top of its rocky spur, show the striking influence of Roman Baroque. The culmination of this was without doubt the sumptuous Karlskirche (1715-1723) which Fischer von Erlach built in Vienna. This artist, who was famous for his theories and published engravings, shared with Hildebrandt the construction of the grand Viennese residences of Schönbrunn and the Belvedere (1721).

Apart from in Russia, where the momentum created by Peter the Great gave rapid results, architectural creation in northern and eastern Europe only really took off in the second half of the eighteenth century. It was expressed in a not particularly original eclecticism, with formal tendencies resulting from a mixture of local traditions with French or Italian influences filtered through German-Austrian examples. In the Netherlands, domestic architecture kept up its time-honoured originality, with a construction style using wood, bricks and high gables. But in aristocratic and religious architecture, there was a clear contrast between the Catholic south and the Protestant north. Flanders remained under the spell of Italian Baroque exuberance, for example in the cathedral of Namur, built by Pizzoni (1751). Meanwhile, in an austere Holland, weakened by the Treaty of Utrecht (1713), there was an eclipse of aristocratic patronage. Tilman van

brillante, propre à magnifier le goût d'ostentation des princes-évêques, électeurs ou margraves. Le fameux Zwinger (1709-1736) de Dresde, chef-d'œuvre de Pöppelmann, les résidences de Mannheim, d'Ansbach, de Postdam, d'Augsburg ou de Schleissheim rivalisent de richesses et d'audace avec le lointain modèle versaillais. Mais c'est sans doute la résidence de Würzburg (1720-1740), dont B. Neumann soumit les plans à Boffrand et Robert de Cotte, qui marque l'apogée de l'architecture civile germanique.

L'Autriche, mais aussi la Bohême et la Hongrie, ne sont pas moins riches à cette époque où des artistes comme Hildebrandt, Prandtauer et, surtout, Fischer von Erlach travaillent pour l'Église et la cour impériale. Les églises de Vienne, de Salzbourg et de Prague, certaines abbayes comme celle de Melk (1709-1711), qui domine le Danube du haut de son éperon rocheux, montrent une influence frappante du baroque romain. Il culmine sans doute à la somptueuse église Saint-Charles-Borromée (1715-1723), édifiée à Vienne par Fischer von Erlach. Cet artiste, fort connu pour ses théories et ses publications gravées, se partage avec Hildebrandt la réalisation des grandes résidences viennoises de Schönbrunn et du Belvédère (1721).

Sauf en Russie, où l'impulsion donnée par Pierre le Grand s'est concrétisée rapidement, la création architecturale dans les pays de l'Europe nordique et orientale s'épanouira surtout dans la seconde moitié du XVIIIᵉ siècle. Elle s'exprime dans un éclectisme assez peu novateur, avec des tendances formelles issues d'un mélange de tradition locale et d'apports italiens ou français, filtrés par l'exemple germano-autrichien. Aux Pays-Bas, l'architecture domestique conserve son originalité séculaire, avec son système constructif qui fait appel au bois et à la brique et ses hauts pignons sur rue. Dans l'architecture noble et religieuse, les contrastes s'affirment entre le Sud catholique et le Nord protestant. La Flandre demeure soumise à l'exubérance du baroque italien, comme à la cathédrale de Namur construite par Pizzoni (1751); tandis que la Hollande, austère et affaiblie par le traité d'Utrecht (1713), connaît une éclipse du mécénat aristocratique. Un des meilleurs architectes hollandais, Tilman van

brillante, atta a magnificare il gusto d'ostentazione dei principi-vescovi, elettori o margravi. Il famoso Zwinger (1709-1736) di Dresda, capolavoro di Pöppelmann, le residenze di Mannheim, d'Ansbach, di Postdam, d'Augsburg o di Schleissheim gareggiano in ricchezza ed audacia con Versailles loro lontano modello. Ma è senza dubbio la resídenza di Würzburg (1720-1740), di cui B. Neumann sottopone i progetti a Boffrand e Robert de Cotte, che segna l'apogeo dell'architettura civile germanica.

L'Austria, ma anche la Boemia e l'Ungheria, non sono meno ricche in questo periodo in cui degli artisti come Hildebrandt, Prandtauer e, soprattutto, Fischer von Erlach lavorano per la Chiesa e la corte imperiale. Le chiese di Vienna, Salisburgo e Praga, certe abbazie come quella di Melk (1709-1711), che domina il Danubio dall'alto del suo sperone roccioso, mostrano un'influenza sorprendente del Barocco romano. Esso culmina senza dubbio nella sontuosa chiesa di San Carlo Borromeo (1715-1723), costruita a Vienna da Fischer von Erlach. Questo artista, molto conosciuto per le sue teorie e per le sue pubblicazioni incise, condivide con Hildebrandt la realizzazione delle grandi residenze viennesi di Schönbrunn e del Belvedere (1721).

Ad eccezione della Russia, dove l'impulso dato da Pietro il Grande si è concretizzato rapidamente, la creazione architettonica nei paesi dell'Europa settentrionale ed orientale sboccerà soprattutto nella seconda metà del XVIII secolo. Essa si esprime in un eclettismo abbastanza poco innovatore, con tendenze formali nate da una fusione della tradizione locale con apporti italiani o francesi, filtrati dall'esempio tedesco-austriaco. Nei Paesi Bassi, l'architettura domestica conserva la sua originalità secolare, con il suo sistema costruttivo che ricorre al legno e al mattone e ai suoi alti timpani sulla strada. Nell'architettura nobile e religiosa, i contrasti si affermano tra il sud cattolico ed il nord protestante. Le Fiandre restano sottomesse all'esuberanza del barocco italiano, come nella cattedrale di Namur costruita da Pizzoni (1751); mentre l'Olanda, austera e indebolita dal trattato di Utrecht (1713), conosce un'eclissi del mecenatismo aristocratico. Uno dei migliori architetti olandesi, Tilman van

Gameren, one of Holland's finest architects, worked in Poland, particularly in Warsaw and Krakow, which were traditionally close to Saxon Baroque. The German-Dutch influence, which was strongly present in Scandinavia and eastern Europe during the seventeenth century, now gave way to the French influence. In Sweden, the Tessins, a famous family of architects, contributed to the beautification of Stockholm, in particular the royal palace. In Drottningholm, Tessin the Elder and his son placed a French style château and gardens. After the piazza theme had been built in Amalienburg, the architects Harsdorff and Eigtved were rivalled by Jardin, a French Piranesian who built the royal church of Frederik V (1755). In Russia, Italian Baroque was faithfully imported by Trezzini to Saint Petersburg, where he built the Peter and Paul basilica (1712-1733) and, above all, by Rastrelli, who had been trained by his father in Robert de Cotte's studio, and who built the Winter Palace (1732-1736), the Smolny monastery and numerous residences for the Tsarina Elizabeth (Tsarskoïe-Selo, the Strogonov Palace, etc). The Venice of the Neva, which was to turn towards international Neo-Classicism with Catherine II, was also drawn to Parisian Rococo. Nicolas Pineau, the famous decorator of apartments, stayed for a long time in Saint Petersburg with Le Blond, the architect. His panels of sculpted oak in the Peterhof, as well as his statues and fountains in the gardens around the residence, are shining examples of the Régence style outside France. Michetti, the garden designer and decorator, competed with Le Blond and helped to train a generation of Russian architects who, in the last third of the eighteenth century, went to study directly in Paris or Rome under the direction of Saint Petersburg's imperial academy.

Gameren, construit en Pologne, à Varsovie et à Cracovie notamment, villes traditionnellement proches du baroque saxon. Très présente au XVIIᵉ siècle dans les Pays scandinaves et en Europe orientale, l'influence germano-hollandaise fait place au XVIIIᵉ siècle à l'influence française. En Suède, une célèbre famille d'architectes, les Tessin, contribue aux embellissements de Stockholm avec, notamment, la reconstruction du palais royal; à Drottningholm, Tessin l'Ancien et son fils introduisent le type du château et du jardin français. Avec le thème de la place royale concrétisé à Copenhague par l'Amalienbourg, les architectes danois Harsdorff et Eigtved seront concurrencés par un piranésien français, Jardin, qui entreprend l'église royale de Frédérik V (1755). En Russie, à Saint-Pétersbourg, le baroque italien est fidèlement implanté par Trezzini, l'architecte de la basilique de Pierre et Paul (1712-1733) et, surtout, par Rastrelli, formé par son père dans l'agence de Robert de Cotte, auteur du palais d'Hiver (1732-1736), du couvent de Smolny et de nombreuses résidences pour la cour de la tzarine Elisabeth (château de Tsarskoïe-Sélo, palais Strogonov). La Venise des rives de la Néva, qui va avec Catherine II se tourner vers le néoclassicisme international, n'ignore pas non plus le rococo parisien. Nicolas Pineau, fameux décorateur d'appartements, fait un long séjour à Saint-Pétersbourg, en compagnie de l'architecte Le Blond : ses lambris de chêne sculpté à Péterhof, ainsi que les statues des fontaines du parc de ce château, illustrent avec éclat le style Régence hors de France. Michetti, architecte et décorateur de jardins, en concurrence avec Le Blond, contribue à former une génération d'architectes russes qui, dans le dernier tiers du XVIIIᵉ siècle, viennent étudier directement à Paris ou à Rome sous l'égide de l'académie impériale de Saint-Pétersbourg.

Gajmeren, costruisce in Polonia, a Varsavia e a Cracovia in particolare, città tradizionalmente vicine al barocco sassone. Molto presente nel XVIII secolo nei Paesi Scandinavi e in Europa orientale, l'influenza germano-olandese fa posto nel XVIII secolo all'influenza francese. In Svezia, una celebre famiglia di architetti, i Tessin, contribuiscono ad abbellire Stoccolma, in particolare con la ricostruzione del Palazzo reale; a Drottningholm, il vecchio Tessin e suo figlio introducono il tipo di castello e di giardino francese. Con il tema della piazza reale concretizzata nell'Amalienbourg, gli architetti Harsdoff e Eigtved troveranno la concorrenza di un piranesiano francese, Jardin, che intraprende la costruzione della chiesa reale di Federico V (1755). In Russia, a San Pietroburgo, il barocco italiano è fedelmente impiantato da Trezzini, l'architetto della basilica di Pietro e Paolo (1712-1733) e, soprattutto, da Rastrelli, formato dal padre nel gabinetto di Robert de Cotte, autore del palazzo d'inverno (1732-1736), del convento Smolny e di numerose residenze per la corte della zarina Elisabetta (castello di Tsarskoïe-Sélo, palazzo Strogonoff). La Venezia delle rive della Neva, che con Caterina II si volgerà verso il neoclassicismo internazionale, non ignora più il Rococò parigino. Nicolas Pineau, famoso decoratore di appartamenti, fa un lungo soggiorno a San Pietroburgo, in compagnia dell'architetto Le Blond: il suo rivestimento di quercia scolpita a Péterhof, così come le statue delle fontane del parco di questo castello, illustrano splendidamente lo stile Reggenza fuori dalla Francia. Michetti, architetto e decoratore di giardini, in concorrenza con Le Blond, contribuisce a formare una generazione di architetti russi che, nell'ultimo terzo del XVIII secolo, si recarono a studiare direttamente a Parigi o a Roma sotto l'egida dell'accademia imperiale di San Pietroburgo.

FILIPPO JUVARRA (1678-1736)

Elevation of a projected church with a cupola.
Pen, brown ink and grey wash on brown paper.

Élévation d'un projet d'église à coupole.
Plume, encre brune et lavis gris sur papier brun.

Alzato di un progetto di chiesa a cupola.
Penna, inchiostro bruno e inchiostro acquarellato grigio su carta scura, 950 x 615/578 mm.

Berlin, Bildarchiv Preussischer Kulturbesitz.

Toises

ROBERT DE COTTE (1656-1735)

*Project for the decoration of the high altar
in the chapel of the château of Versailles.*
Pen, wash and watercolour.

**Projet de décoration pour le maître-autel
de la chapelle du château de Versailles.**
Plume, lavis et aquarelle.

*Progetto di decorazione per l'altare principale
della cappella del castello di Versailles.*
Penna, inchiostro acquarellato ed acquerello,
337 x 568 mm.

Saint-Pétersbourg, musée de l'Ermitage.

31

JUSTUS HEINRICH DIENTZENHOFER (1702-1744)

Longitudinal section of the abbey church of Amorbach.
Pen, brown ink, grey wash and red Indian ink.

Coupe longitudinale de l'église abbatiale d'Amorbach.
Plume, encre brune, lavis gris et encre de chine rouge

Spaccato longitudinale della chiesa abbaziale d'Amarbach.
Penna, inchiostro bruno, inchiostro acquarellato grigio
e inchiostro di china rosso, 438 x 645 mm.

Berlin, Bildarchiv Preussischer Kulturbesitz.

NICOLAUS-FRIEDRICH HARBEL (1724)

Design for lateral section of a church (1723).
Pen, wash and watercolour.

Projet d'élévation latérale d'une église (1723).
Plume, lavis et aquarelle

Progetto di alzato laterale di una chiesa (1723).
Penna, inchiostro acquarellato e acquarello,
515 x 480 mm.

Saint-Pétersbourg, musée de l'Ermitage.

▲ FLAMINO INNOCENZO MINOZZI (1735-1817)

(attributed to) *Design for ceiling.*
Pen, wash and watercolour.

(attribué à) *Projet de plafond.*
Plume, lavis, aquarelle.

(attribuito) *Progetto di soffitto.*
Penna, inchiostro acquarellato, acquerello, 254 x 297 mm.

New York, The Metropolitan Museum of Art.

► GERMAIN BOFFRAND (1667-1754)

Elevation of the façade of La Merci church in Paris.
Pen, ink and wash.

Élévation de la façade de l'église de la Merci à Paris.
Plume, encre et lavis.

Alzato della facciata della chiesa della Mercede a Parigi.
Penna, inchiostro e inchiostro acquarellato.

Stockholm, Statens Kunstmuseer.

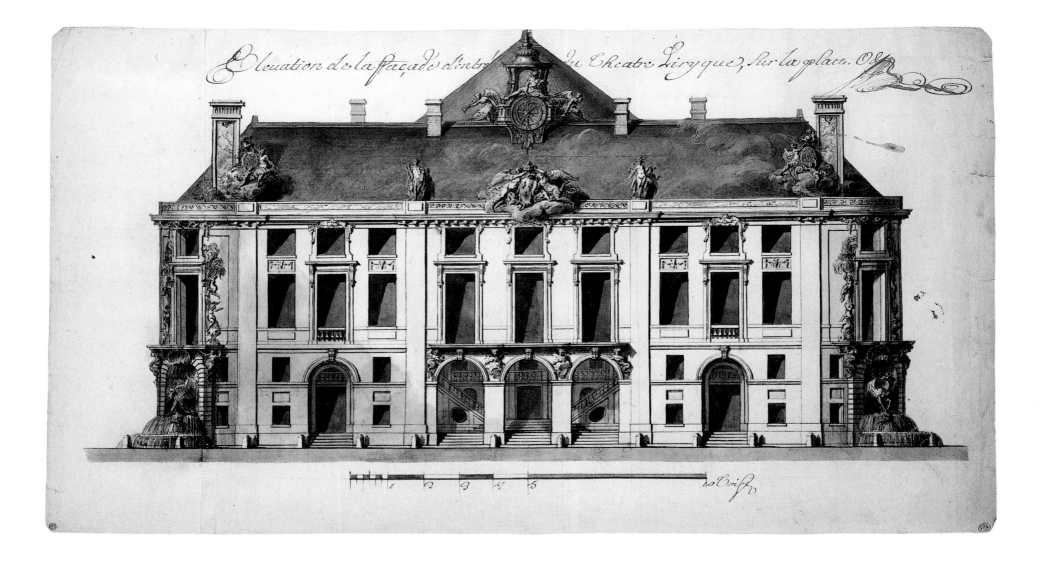

GILLES-MARIE OPPENORD (1676-1742)

Elevation of the façade of an opera house for Paris,
(second project), 1734.
Pen, black ink, grey wash and watercolour highlights.

Élévation de la façade d'un théâtre lyrique pour Paris
(second projet), 1734.
Plume, encre noire, lavis gris et rehauts d'aquarelle.

Alzato della facciata di un teatro lirico per Parigi,
(secondo progetto), 1734.
Penna, inchiostro nero, inchiostro acquarellato grigio e
lumeggiatura di acquerello.

Paris, École nationale supérieure des Beaux-Arts.

GILLES-MARIE OPPENORD (1676-1742)

Fragment of an elevation of the façade of an opera house for Paris, (first project), 1734.
Pen, red-brown ink.

Fragment d'élévation de la façade d'un théâtre lyrique pour Paris (premier projet), 1734.
Plume, encre brun-rouge.

Frammento di alzato della facciata di un teatro lirico per Parigi (primo progetto), 1734.
Penna, inchiostro bruno-rosso.

Paris, École nationale supérieure des Beaux-Arts.

▲ NICCOLO MICHETTI

(attributed to) *Perspective view of a fountain and cascades in front of a palace*, circa 1720.
Pen, ink and watercolour.

(attribué à) *Vue perspective d'une fontaine et de cascades devant un palais*, vers 1720.
Plume, lavis et aquarelle.

(attribuito a) *Vista prospettica di una fontana e di cascate davanti ad un palazzo*, intorno al 1720.
Penna, inchiostro acquarellato ed acquerello, 179 x 215 mm.

Saint-Pétersbourg, musée de l'Ermitage.

► JEAN-BAPTISTE LE BLOND (1679-1741)

Project for "the château on water" of Strelna, section, elevation and plan, 1717.
Pen, black ink, wash and watercolour.

Projet pour « le château sur l'eau » de Strelna, coupe, élévation et plan, 1717.
Plume, encre noire, lavis et aquarelle.

Progetto per "Il castello sull'acqua" di Strelna, spaccato, alzato e pianta, 1717.
Penna, inchiostro nero, inchiostro acquarellato ed acquerello, 1278 x 677 mm.

Saint-Pétersbourg, musée de l'Ermitage.

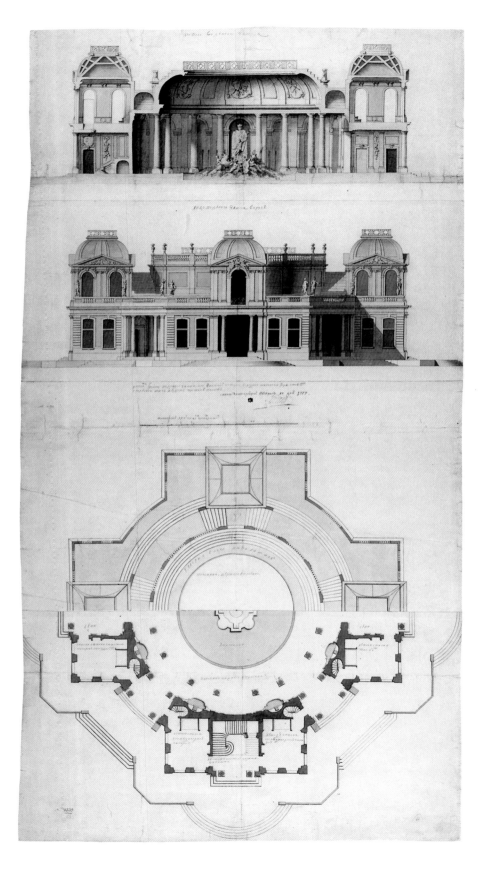

JAMES GIBBS (1682-1754)

Project for the vestibule of Kedleston Hall, Derbyshire, 1726.
Pen, ink, wash and watercolour.

Projet pour le vestibule de Kedleston Hall, Derbyshire, 1726.
Plume, encre, lavis et aquarelle.

Progetto per il vestibolo di Kedleston Hall, Derbyshire, 1726.
Penna, inchiostro, inchiostro acquarellato e acquerello, 368 x 514 mm.

London, National Trust.

GERMAIN BOFFRAND (1667-1754)

Ink, graphite and wash.

Plume, mine de plomb et lavis.

Penna, mina di piombo e inchiostro acquarellato.

Berlin, Bildarchiv Preussischer Kulturbesitz.

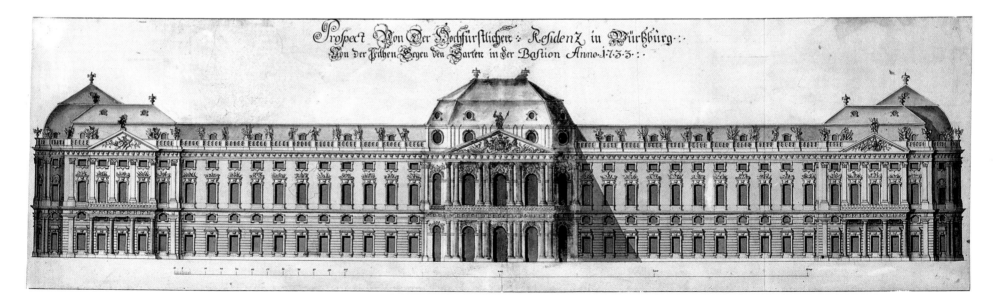

BALTHASAR NEUMANN (1687-1753)

Ink, graphite and wash.

Plume, mine de plomb et lavis.

Penna, mina di piombo e inchiostro acquarellato.

Berlin, Bildarchiv Preussischer Kulturbesitz.

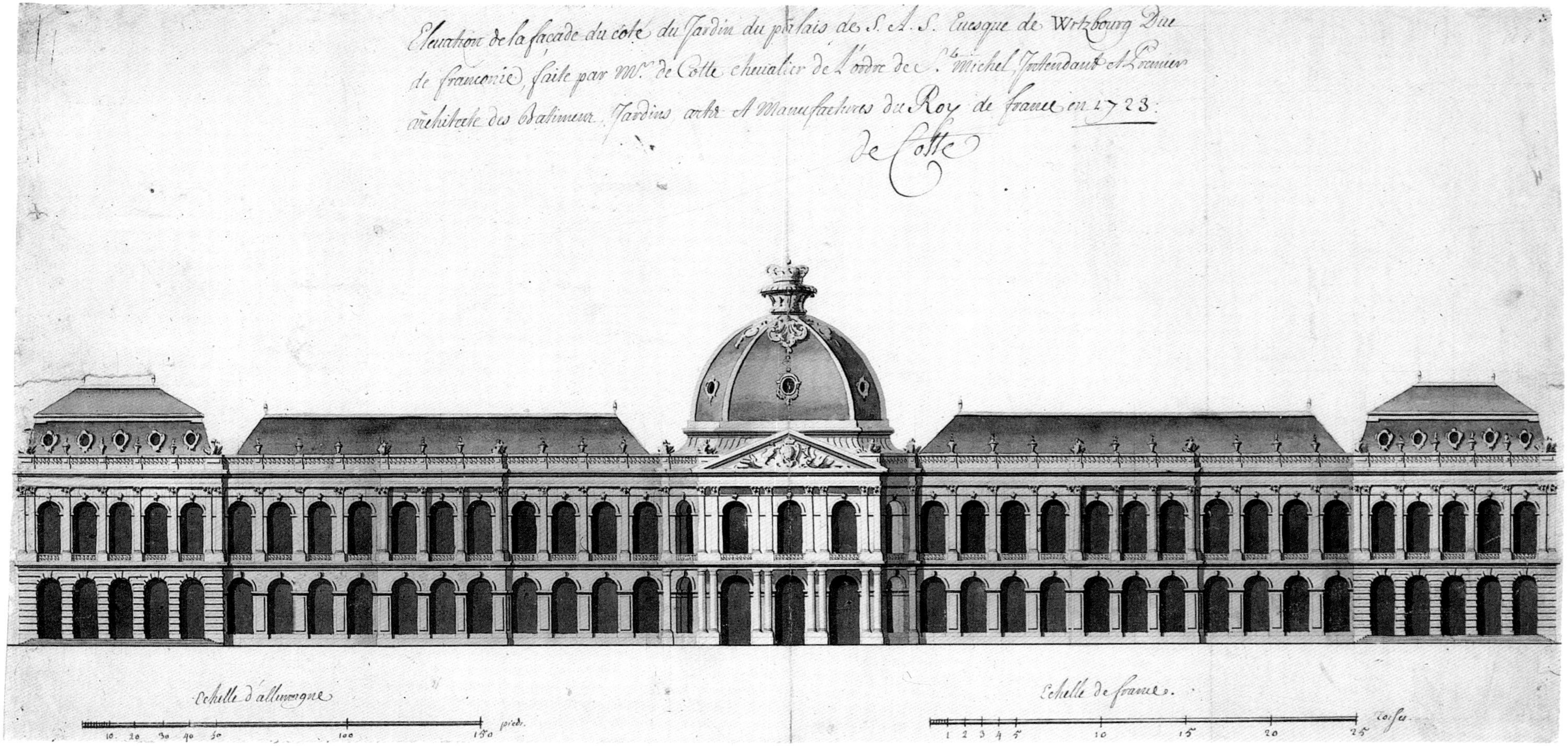

Elevation de la façade du côté du Jardin du palais de S. A. S. Euesque de Wirzbourg Duc de franconie, faite par Mr. de Cotte chevalier de l'ordre de St. Michel Jntendant et Premier architecte des batimens Jardins arts et Manufactures du Roy de france en 1723.

de Cotte

Echelle d'allemagne

10. 20. 30. 40. 50.   100.   150.   pieds.

Echelle de france.

1 2 3 4 5   10   15   20   25   toises

ROBERT DE COTTE (1656-1735)

Ink, graphite and wash.
Plume, mine de plomb et lavis.
Penna, mina di piombo e inchiostro acquarellato.

Berlin, Bildarchiv Preussischer Kulturbesitz.

Three elevations of projects for the façade of the Residence at Würzburg, 1723-1733.
Trois élévations des projets de la façade de la Résidence de Würzburg, 1723-1733.
Tre elevazioni dei rispettivi progetti della facciata della Residenza di Würzburg, 1723-1733.

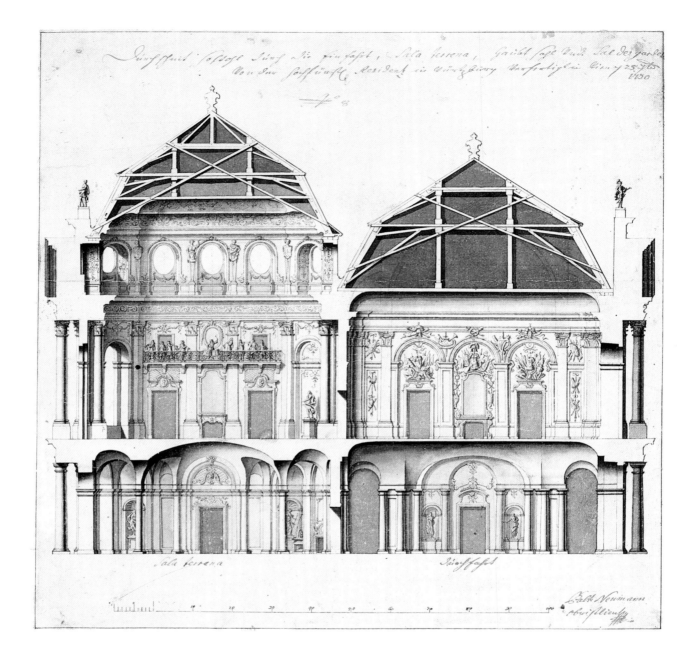

BALTHASAR NEUMANN (1687-1753)

Transversal section of a projected Residence at Würzburg, 1730.
Pen, graphite, brown ink, Indian ink and wash.

Coupe transversale du projet de Résidence de Würzburg, 1730.
Plume, mine de plomb, encre brune, encre de chine et lavis.

Spaccato trasversale del progetto di Residenza di Würzburg, 1730.
Penna, mina di piombo, inchiostro bruno, inchiostro di china
e inchiostro acquarellato, 418 x 416 mm.

Berlin, Bildarchiv Preussischer Kulturbesitz.

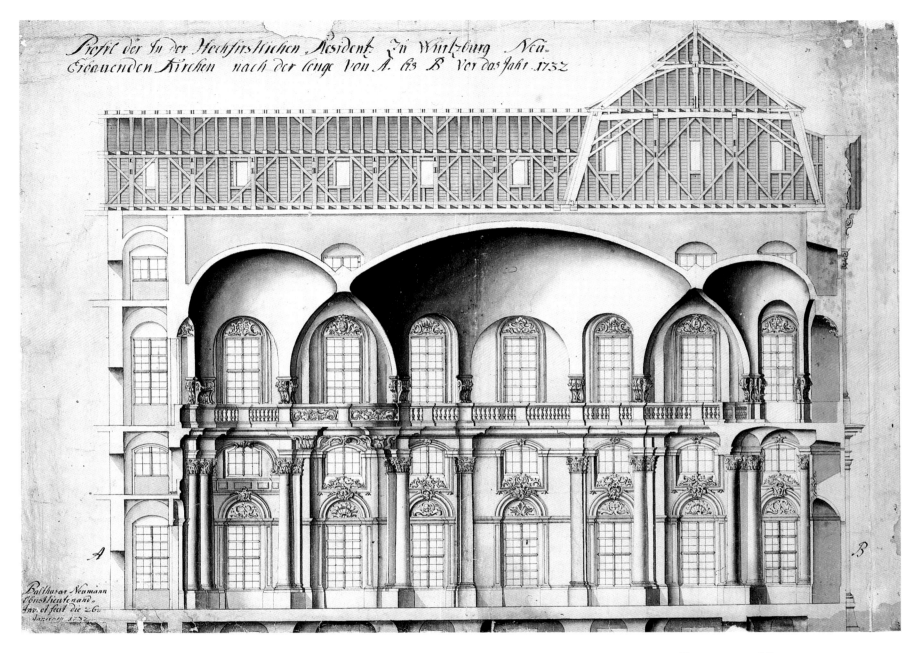

BALTHASAR NEUMANN (1687-1753)

Section of the Hofkirche in Würzburg, 1732.
Pen and graphite, grey wash.

Coupe de l'Hofkirche à Würzburg, 1732.
Plume et mine de plomb, lavis gris.

Spaccato dell'Hofkirche a Würzburg, 1732.
Penna e mina di piombo, inchiostro acquarellato grigio, 487 x 683 mm.

Berlin, Bildarchiv Preussischer Kulturbesitz.

▲ **GERMAIN BOFFRAND** (1667-1754)

*Decoration project for the salon of the
Arsenal in Paris.*
Pen, ink, wash and watercolour.

*Projet de décoration pour le salon
de l'Arsenal à Paris.*
Plume, encre, lavis et aquarelle.

*Progetto di decorazione per il salone
dell'arsenale a Parigi.*
Penna, inchiostro, inchiostro acquarellato
e acquerello.

Berlin, Bildarchiv Preussischer Kulturbesitz.

▶ **GERMAIN BOFFRAND** (1667-1754)

*Projected completion of the mural decorations
of a hunting lodge.*
Pen, ink, wash and watercolour.

*Projet d'achèvement du décor mural d'un
pavillon de chasse.*
Plume, encre, lavis et aquarelle.

*Progetto di compimento della decorazione murale
di un casino da caccia.*
Penna, inchiostro, inchiostro acquarellato
e acquerello, 251 x 230 mm.

Saint-Pétersbourg, musée de l'Ermitage.

▲ JACQUES V GABRIEL (1667-1742)

*Élévation of the banisters and railings of the Palais des États
de Bourgogne in Dijon, 1735.*
Pen, ink, wash and watercolour.

*Élévation des rampes et gardes-corps de l'escalier du
palais des États de Bourgogne à Dijon, 1735.*
Plume, encre, lavis et aquarelle.

*Alzato delle rampe e parapetti della scala del Palais des États
di Borgogna a Dijon, 1735.*
Penna, inchiostro, inchiostro acquarellato e acquerello.

Dijon, Archives départementales de la Côte-d'Or.

► JACQUES V GABRIEL (1667-1742)

*Section of the staircase of the Palais des États de
Bourgogne in Dijon, 1731.*
Pen, ink, wash and watercolour.

*Coupe de l'escalier du palais des États de
Bourgogne à Dijon, 1731.*
Plume, encre, lavis et aquarelle.

*Spaccato di scala del Palais des États di Borgogna
a Dijon, 1731.*
Penna, inchiostro, inchiostro acquarellato e acquerello.

Dijon, Archives départementales de la Côte-d'Or.

◄ **NICOLAS PINEAU (1684-1754)**

Projected fireplace with sculpted panels.
Pen, graphite, Indian ink, wash.

Projet d'une cheminée et de lambris sculptés
Plume, mine de plomb, encre de chine, lavis.

Progetto di un camino e di rivestimenti scolpiti.
Penna, mina di piombo, inchiostro di china,
inchiostro acquarellato, 297 x 234 mm.

Berlin, Bildarchiv Preussischer Kulturbesitz.

▲ **NICOLAS PINEAU (1684-1754)**

Project for five panels of sculpted wood.
Graphite and red chalk.

Projet pour cinq panneaux de boiserie sculptée.
Mine de plomb et sanguine.

*Progetto per cinque pannelli di rivestimento di
legno scolpito.*
Mina di piombo e sanguigna, 290 x 300 mm.

Saint-Pétersbourg, musée de l'Ermitage.

▲ BERNARDO-ANTONIO VITTONE (1702-1770)

Project for the fountain of the Quatre Fleuves, with an equestrian statue of an emperor, Clementino competition of 1732.
Pen, brown ink and wash.

Projet de fontaine des Quatre Fleuves, avec la statue équestre d'un empereur, Concours Clementino de 1732.
Plume, encre brune et lavis.

Progetto di fontana dei quattro fiumi, con la statua equestre di un imperatore, Concorso Clementino del 1732.
Penna, inchiostro bruno e inchiostro acquarellato.

Roma, Accademia nazionale di San Luca, Archivio storico.

◄ DENIS BRUCKET

Plan of the first project for the garden at Ekateringoff, circa 1717.
Pen, ink, wash and watercolour.

Plan d'un premier projet du jardin de Ekateringoff, vers 1717.
Plume, encre, lavis et aquarelle

Piano di un primo progetto del giardino di Ekateringoff, verso il 1717.
Penna, inchiostro, inchiostro acquarellato ed acquerello, 805 x 410 mm.

Saint-Pétersbourg, musée de l'Ermitage.

► JOHANN-CHRISTOPH KNOFFEL (1678-1736)

Section of the salon of the Count of Brühl's palace in Nischvitz.
Graphite, pen, ink and coloured wash.

Coupe de la salle du palais du comte de Brühl, à Nischvitz.
Mine de plomb, plume, encre et lavis de couleur.

Spaccato della sala del Palazzo del Conte di Brühl a Nischvitz.
Mina di piombo, penna, inchiostro e inchiostro acquarellato di colore, 427 x 584 mm.

Berlin, Bildarchiv Preussischer Kulturbesitz.

Coupe de la Salle du Pallais du Comte de Brühl à Nischwitz.

Der Plaße des so genandten steineren Tisches in dem garten. | La place de la table, comunement apellé de pierre,
Zu Hellbrun nächst Salzburg. | dans le jardin de Hellbrun.

behr. par Fr. L. Danreiter

▲ FRANZ-ANTON DANREITER

*View of the "table square" in the garden of
Helbrunn, near Salzburg, 1720.*
Pen, ink and wash.

*Vue de la « place de la table » dans le jardin
d'Helbrunn, près de Salzbourg, 1720.*
Plume, encre et lavis.

*Veduta della "piazza della tavola" nel giardino
d'Helbrunn, vicino a Salisburgo, 1720.*
Penna, inchiostro e inchiostro acquarellato,
237 x 339 mm.

Berlin, Bildarchiv Preussischer Kulturbesitz.

► JACQUES-FRANÇOIS BLONDEL (1705-1774)

*(after) Temporary decoration of the Porte Saint-Martin, for the ceremonial
entrance into Paris of Louis XV in 1745.*
Pen, brown ink, coloured wash and gouache on beige paper.

*(d'après) Décor éphémère de la porte Saint-Martin pour l'entrée de
Louis XV à Paris, en 1745.*
Plume, encre brune, lavis de couleur et gouache sur papier beige.

*(secondo) Decorazione effimera della porta Saint-Martin per l'entrata
di Luigi XV a Parigi, nel 1745.*
Penna, inchiostro bruno, inchiostro acquarellato di colore e gouache
su carta beige, 278 x 352 mm.

Montréal, Centre Canadien d'Architecture.

PAOLO POSI (1706-1776)

Villa flanked by obelisks in a garden.
Pen, brown ink, grey, green and brown wash.

Villa flanquée d'obélisques, dans un jardin.
Plume, encre brune, lavis gris, vert et brun.

Villa fiancheggiata di obelischi, in un giardino.
Penna, inchiostro bruno, inchiostro acquarellato
grigio, verde e bruno, 365 x 598 mm.

New York, Cooper Hewitt Museum.

PART II

Figurative Innovation:
THE BIBIENA FAMILY AND PIRANESI

L'innovation figurative :
LES BIBIENA ET PIRANÈSE

L'Innovazione Figurativa:
I BIBIENA E PIRANESI

The triumph of the architectural picture (*veduta*), the caprice (imaginary architecture) and views of ruins or of towns, from Pannini to Hubert Robert, and from Ricci to Canaletto or Vernet (his series of *Ports de France*) led to the establishment of a distinctly independent genre in the eighteenth century. This triumph over historical painting, practised by the great seventeenth-century landscape painters (for example Poussin, Le Lorrain, or Rosa), was based on the curiosity of an extremely broad educated public. The important role played by illustration in the *Encyclopédie*, that epitome of Enlightenment knowledge, cannot be understated. In the same way, a taste for travel souvenirs, in the form of engravings, drawings and paintings, increased the interest in architectural views. Private collections and libraries, which were readily available to artists and sometimes to the public, were not the only means of conveying the figurative architecture of the eighteenth century. The theatre, the exhibitions of the Louvre Salons, competition shows, temporary decorations for festivities and optical devices offered similar advantages. In the contemplation of a transposed space, they even associated an awakening urban consciousness with the pleasure of being a witness or participant. This collective escape into history, the mirror of civilisations, and into a nature associated with the industrious presence of mankind (either abroad or else projected into an imaginary world) extended the realm of the onlooker towards infinite horizons!

For example, the beginning of the great fashion for optical devices occurred between the years 1740 and 1750. Paris was one of the main European centres that produced the engravings that were displayed inside. Perspective views of architecture were commonly used. They were almost invariably views of famous ancient or modern sites, evocative of capitals or well-known landmarks (Vesta's temple at Tivoli was a typical example), "French" gardens, church

Le triomphe du tableau d'architecture (*veduta*), caprice (architecture imaginaire), vue de ruines ou de ville, de Pannini à Hubert Robert, de Ricci à Canaletto ou Vernet (série des *Ports de France*), distingue un genre devenu franchement autonome au XVIIIe siècle. Ce triomphe sur la peinture d'histoire, où se situent les grands peintres du paysage du XVIIe siècle (Poussin, Gellée dit Le Lorrain, Rosa, par exemple), s'appuie sur la curiosité et l'éducation d'un public très large. On se rappelle l'importance du rôle de l'illustration dans cette formidable somme des Lumières qu'est l'*Encyclopédie* ; de même, le goût pour les souvenirs de voyages favorise, à travers l'estampe, le dessin et la peinture, l'attrait pour la vue d'architecture. La collection d'amateur, la bibliothèque, facilement ouvertes aux artistes et parfois au public, ne sont pas les seuls moyens *médiatiques* qui permettent la sensibilisation à l'architecture figurée au XVIIIe siècle : la scène de théâtre, les cimaises des Salons du Louvre, les expositions des concours, le décor éphémère des fêtes et la boîte d'optique offrent les mêmes avantages. Mieux, ils associent, dans la contemplation de l'espace transposé, et l'éveil d'une conscience urbanisée, et le plaisir d'en être le témoin ou l'acteur. L'évasion collective dans l'histoire, miroir des civilisations, dans la nature associée à la présence industrieuse de l'homme, dans des pays étrangers, ou projetée dans l'imaginaire, étendent vers d'infinis lointains le règne du voyeur !

Les débuts de la grande vogue des boîtes d'optique, par exemple, se situent précisément dans les années 1740-1750. Paris est un des principaux centres européens de production des gravures qu'on y montre. La vue perspective d'architecture est fréquente, sous forme d'une typologie quasi invariable : vues de monuments connus, anciens ou modernes, qui évoquent les capitales ou les sites fameux (le temple de Vesta à Tivoli est un poncif du genre, par exemple), jardins « à la française », intérieurs d'église, nefs de temple ou vestibules à l'antique, prisons, etc. Les deux

Il trionfo del quadro di architettura (veduta), capriccio (architettura immaginaria), veduta di rovine o di città, da Pannini a Hubert Robert, Ricci, Canaletto o Vernet (serie dei porti di Francia), contraddistingue un genere divenuto senza dubbio autonomo nel XVIII secolo. Questo trionfo sulla pittura storica, in cui si situano i grandi paesaggisti del XVII secolo (Poussin, Gellée detto Le Lorrain, Rosa, per esempio) si appoggia sulla curiosità e sull'educazione di un pubblico molto ampio. Si ricorda l'importanza dell'illustrazione in quella formidabile *summa* dell'Illuminismo che è l'*Enciclopedia* e, nello stesso tempo, il gusto per i ricordi di viaggio favorisce, attraverso la stampa, il disegno e la pittura, l'attrattiva per la veduta d'architettura. La collezione d'amatore e la biblioteca, facilmente aperte agli artisti e qualche volta al pubblico, non sono i soli mezzi *mediatici* che permettono la sensibilizzazione per la rappresentazione di architettura nel XVIII secolo: la scena di teatro, le cimase dei saloni del Louvre, le esposizioni dei concorsi, la decorazione effimera delle feste e la scatola ottica offrono gli stessi vantaggi. O meglio, essi associano, nella contemplazione dello spazio trasposto, sia il risveglio di una coscienza urbana, sia il piacere di esserne il testimone o l'attore. L'evasione collettiva nella storia, specchio delle civiltà, nella natura associata alla presenza costruttiva dell'Uomo, nei paesi stranieri, o proiettata nell'immaginario, estende all'infinito lontano il regno dell'osservatore.

Gli inizi della gran moda delle scatole ottiche, per esempio, si collocano negli anni 1740-1750. Parigi è uno dei principali centri europei di produzione delle incisioni qui poi esposte. La vista prospettica dell'architettura è frequente, sotto forma di una tipologia quasi invariabile: vedute di monumenti conosciuti, antichi o moderni, che evocano le capitali o i siti famosi (il tempio di Vesta a Tivoli è un motivo del genere, per esempio), giardini "alla francese", interni di chiese, navate di templi o vestiboli

interiors, naves of temples or antique-style vestibules, prisons, etc. The last two subjects, in bad copies that had been gaudily stencilled, were even illustrated by Piranesi himself, in his collection *Prima Parte* (1743). The few experts of this sort of popular engraving have noted a spreading of this "amusement" from aristocratic circles, to the comfortable bourgeoisie, and finally to the lower classes thanks to itinerant displays in fairs. The theatre provides an analogy of this development of the architectural image as an attraction. In less than a century, we pass from Servandoni's dumb-shows, which were such a success in the *Salle des Machines* in the Tuileries under Louis XV, to the famous *Eidophusikon* which the French painter Loutherbourg created in London (it represented natural phenomena or visions inspired by Milton, by mechanical means, changing lights, transparencies, etc), then to the optical theatre of Carmontelle, and finally to the dioramas and panoramas on the *Grands Boulevards* in the 1800s. The pull of the image, becoming increasingly illusive, a panoramic, more luminous and modelled with an atmospheric mood in which the gaze seems to move about as though taking a stroll, was well summed up by Marmontel when discussing Servandoni, in his article on "Decoration" in the *Encyclopédie*: "To leave the imagination free is a basic principle in all of the arts: we are always losers if we circumscribe its space; thus it is that general ideas, having no determined limits, are the most sublime sources".

The aesthetics of the *sublime*, of which the British were the first theorists (their landscape artists produced physical illustrations of poetic and moral virtues around country houses), seeks to capture the eye through areas of shadow. It fosters deep feelings through the meditation or the shock of extraordinary effects from masses, distant shortcuts and emphatic contrasts. Hidden or suspended ruins, cypress trees, smoke, dense groves, caves and vaults pierced to allow in the light create this chiaroscuro décor. This is true in the serene authority of the wash tint which, first damp, then luminous, in one trace plays with the potential thickness of the white sheet of paper. It is true in the ink of an engraving, which runs down into ever darker incisions. Some architects adapted such shadowplay into cut stone with extraordinary bosses. Piranesi and Ledoux were the two geniuses of this genre, thus sealing the osmosis between drawings of fictional architecture and the poetic emotion of actual constructions.

derniers thèmes, à travers de mauvaises copies vivement coloriées au pochoir. véhiculent certaines images publiées par Piranèse lui-même dans son recueil *Prima Parte* (1743). Les rares spécialistes de ce type d'estampes populaires ont noté la progression de cet « amusement », des milieux aristocratiques aux salons bourgeois aisés et, finalement, jusqu'au petit peuple grâce aux montreurs itinérants des foires. Ce phénomène *spectaculaire* de l'image d'architecture est analogue sur la scène de théâtre : en moins d'un siècle, on passe des spectacles muets de Servandoni qui firent sensation dans l'ancienne salle des Machines des Tuileries sous Louis XV, au fameux *Eidophusikon* que le peintre français Loutherbourg crée à Londres (y sont reproduits des phénomènes de la nature, ou des visions inspirées de Milton, à l'aide de savantes mécaniques, d'éclairages changeants, de transparents...), au théâtre d'optique de Carmontelle pour arriver aux dioramas et aux panoramas des Boulevards, autour de 1800. L'emprise de l'image sans cesse plus illusionniste, panoramique, lumineuse, modelée avec un semblant d'atmosphère, dans laquelle l'œil semble évoluer comme au cours d'une promenade, a été joliment analysé par Marmontel, précisément à propos de Servandoni, dans l'article « Décoration » de l'*Encyclopédie* : « C'est dans tous les arts un grand principe que de laisser l'imagination en liberté : on perd toujours à lui circonscrire un espace ; de là vient que les idées générales n'ayant point de limites déterminées sont les sources les plus sublimes. »

L'esthétique du *sublime,* dont les Anglais sont les premiers théoriciens (leurs paysagistes illustrent concrètement ses vertus poétiques et morales autour des *country houses*), recherche la captation du regard par les zones d'ombre ; elle prédispose aux sentiments profonds par la méditation ou le choc des effets démesurés de masses, de lointains raccourcis, de contrastes appuyés. Ruines enfouies ou suspendues, cyprès, fumées, bosquets compacts, cavernes et voûtes percées à contre-jour, campent le décor du clair-obscur. C'est vrai dans l'autorité sereine du lavis qui, en une seule trace, se joue de l'épaisseur potentielle de la feuille blanche, d'abord humide, puis lumineuse ; c'est vrai dans l'encre de l'estampe qui fouille les incisions toujours plus noires. Certains architectes adapteront l'effet d'ombre recherché dans la pierre taillée en bossages fracassants : Piranèse et Ledoux sont les

all'antica, prigioni, ecc. I due ultimi temi, attraverso delle cattive copie vivamente colorate con sagome forate, veicolano certe immagini pubblicate da Piranesi stesso nella sua raccolta *Prima Parte* (1743). I rari specialisti di questo tipo di stampa popolare hanno notato la progressione di questo "divertimento", dagli ambienti aristocratici ai saloni borghesi agiati e, alla fine, fino al popolo minuto grazie agli espositori temporanei delle fiere. Questa trasposizione spettacolare dell'immagine dell'architettura è analoga sulla scena di teatro: in meno di un secolo, si passa dagli spettacoli muti di Servandoni che suscitarono impressione nell'antica sala delle Macchine delle Tuileries sotto Luigi XV, al famoso Eidophusikon che il pittore francese Loutherbourg crea a Londra (qui sono riprodotti i fenomeni della natura, o delle visioni ispirate da Milton, con l'aiuto di complessi meccanismi, di illuminazioni mutevoli, di trasparenze...), al teatro ottico di Carmontelle per arrivare ai diorama e ai panorami dei Boulevards, intorno al 1800. L'influenza dell'immagine senza sosta più illusionista, panoramica, luminosa, modellata con un sembiante d'atmosfera, nella quale l'occhio sembra evolvere come nel corso di una passeggiata, è stata felicemente analizzata da Marmontel, precisamente a proposito di Servandoni, nell'articolo "Decorazione" dell'*Enciclopedia*: "C'è in tutte le arti un gran principio clu è quello di lasciare l'immaginazione in libertà: si perde sempre nell'asseguar loro uno spazio; per questa ragioree le idee generali, non avendo dei limiti determinati, sono le fonti più sublimi."

L'estetica del sublime, di cui gli inglesi sono i primi teorici (i loro paesaggisti illustrano concretamente le loro virtù poetiche e morali intorno alle *country houses*) cerca di captare lo sguardo attraverso le zone d'ombra; essa predispone ai sentimenti profondi attraverso la meditazione o lo choc degli effetti smisurati di masse, di lontane scorciatoie, dell'accostamento di contrasti. Rovine nascoste o sospese, cipressi, fumi, folti boschetti, caverne e volte traforate in controluce, caratterizzano la decorazione del chiaro scuro. È vero nell'autorità serena dell'inchiostro acquarellato che, in una sola traccia, si burla dello spessore potenziale del foglio bianco, in principio umido, poi luminoso; è vero nell'inchiostro della stampa che scava le incisioni sempre più nere. Certi architetti adattarono l'effetto d'ombra ricercata nella pietra tagliata in bugne strepitose: Piranesi e Ledoux sono i due

Scenic illusions: the Bibiena family

Italy, that great cradle of scenographers, decorators and theatrical architects since the Renaissance, opened European sensibilities to displays of the marvellous, in particular thanks to its operas. It kept this pre-eminence during the eighteenth century, and not a single country escaped Italian influence, either in music or in decoration. Even France, which set up a national opera in the tradition of its great seventeenth-century tragic theatre, also called in artists who had studied in Italy: Servandoni, Galliari and Brunetti all decorated Parisian theatres. As for architecture, the scenographic image provided suggestive solutions to the arrangement of space, surprising decorative effects and a great freedom in the interpretation of structures. Stage design itself, freed of any constraint of verisimilitude which would, for example, reveal the difference between what had been painted and what "built" into the frame of the set, turned towards an increasingly ornamental vision, reinforced by virtuoso sketches. Thanks to a system of improvisation or variations, which was technically dominated by a reduced form of the *quadratura*, the wash tint stage sketch became marvellously spontaneous.

Juvarra was the absolute master of this genre, but also of the architectural caprice, which brought together colonnades, vases, ruins, tombs and pyramids. This great Piedmontese architect, originally from the south of Italy and at first a skilled ornamenter and designer, studied in Rome. A disciple of Fontana, he won the Academia di San Luca prize, became a member of the same academy, then obtained his first commissions (1708) for religious decorations, festivities and ceremonies, before turning to stage work with the Ottoboni theatre. As Chief Architect of the Court of Savoy (1714), Juvarra then had a sparkling career in building work. Turin and Piedmont, then Madrid where he died in 1736, were to see his projects come to life. Then his countless disciples perpetuated his style long into the eighteenth century. One of them, Vittone, displayed just as great a talent as a decorator of the churches in and around Turin, as well as in his rather didactic fondness for caprices.

Between Milan, Parma, Bologna and Venice, several schools of scenographers, painters of

---

Illusion scénique : les Bibiena

L'Italie, grande pourvoyeuse de scénographes, de décorateurs et d'architectes de théâtre depuis la Renaissance, a sensibilisé l'Europe au spectacle du merveilleux, notamment grâce à l'opéra. Elle conserve cette prééminence au cours du XVIIIᵉ siècle et pas un seul pays n'échappe au style italien, tant en musique qu'en décoration. Cas unique, la France qui crée un opéra national, dans la lignée de son théâtre tragique du XVIIᵉ siècle, fait appel également aux artistes de formation italienne : Servandoni, Galliari et Brunetti illustrent la scène à Paris. Sur le plan de l'architecture, l'image scénographique montre des solutions d'aménagement de l'espace suggestives, des effets décoratifs surprenants et une grande liberté d'interprétation des structures constructives. Le dessin de scène lui-même, libéré de toute contrainte de vraisemblance qui ferait apparaître, par exemple, la différence entre ce qui est peint ou « bâti » sur châssis dans le décor, s'oriente vers une vision purement ornementale que renforce la virtuosité de l'esquisse. Dans l'esprit d'un système d'improvision ou de variations, techniquement dominé par la science de la *quadratura* en réduction, le croquis de scène acquiert grâce au lavis une spontanéité captivante.

Dans ce genre, mais également dans celui du caprice d'architecture où se mêlent colonnades, vases, ruines, tombeaux et pyramides, Juvarra s'impose avec l'autorité d'un maître qui fait école. Le grand architecte piémontais, originaire d'Italie du Sud, d'abord ornemaniste et habile dessinateur, s'est formé à Rome. Disciple de Fontana, lauréat puis membre de l'académie de Saint-Luc, il reçoit ses premières commandes (1708) dans le domaine du décor religieux, décor de fêtes et de cérémonies, avant d'aborder l'espace de la scène au théâtre Ottoboni. Premier architecte de la cour de Savoie (1714), Juvarra connaît ensuite une carrière de constructeur éblouissante ; Turin et le Piémont, avant Madrid où il meurt en 1736, verront ses projets se concrétiser et ses nombreux disciples prolonger son style tard dans le XVIIIᵉ siècle. L'un d'entre eux, Vittone, auteur de plusieurs églises à Turin et dans ses

---

Illusione scenica: i Bibiena

L'Italia, grande fornitrice di scenografi, di decoratori e di architetti di teatro a partire dal Rinascimento, ha sensibilizzato l'Europa allo spettacolo del meraviglioso, in particolare grazie all'opera. Essa conserva questa supremazia nel corso del XVIII secolo e non un solo paese sfugge allo stile italiano, tanto nel campo della musica che in quello della decorazione. Caso unico è la Francia che crea un'opera nazionale, nella tradizione del suo teatro tragico del XVII secolo, ma fa appello ugualmente agli artisti di formazione italiana: Servandoni, Galliari e Brunetti illustrano la scena a Parigi. Sul piano dell'architettura, l'immagine scenografica mostra delle soluzioni di allestimento dello spazio suggestive, degli effetti decorativi sorprendenti e una grande libertà di interpretazione delle strutture costruttive. Il disegno di scena stesso, liberato da ogni vincolo di verosimiglianza che farebbe apparire, per esempio, la differenza tra ciò che è dipinto o "costruito" sull'intelaiatura all'interno della decorazione, si orienta verso una visione puramente ornamentale che rinforza il virtuosismo dello schizzo. Nello spirito di un sistema di improvvisazione o di variazioni, tecnicamente dominato dalla scienza della quadratura in riduzione, il bozzetto di scena acquista, grazie all'inchiostro acquarellato una spontaneità accattivante.

In questo genere, ma allo stesso modo in quello del capriccio d'architettura in cui si mescolano colonnati, vasi, rovine, tombe e piramidi, Juvarra s'impone con l'autorità di un maestro che fa scuola. Il grande architetto piemontese, originario dell'Italia del Sud, in principio ornatista e abile disegnatore, ha compiuto la sua formazione a Roma. Discepolo di Fontana, laureato poi membro dell'Accademia di San Luca, riceve le sue prime commissioni (1708) nel settore della decorazione religiosa, decorazione di feste e di cerimonie, prima di intraprendere lo spazio della scena al teatro Ottoboni. Primo Architetto della corte dei Savoia (1714), Juvarra conosce successivamente una sfolgorante carriera di costruttore; Torino e il Piemonte, prima di Madrid dove morirà nel 1736, vedranno concretizzarsi i suoi progetti e numerosi suoi discepoli prolungare il suo stile sino al XVIII

quadratura and architects multiplied models, scenic or festive productions, as well as constructions of theatres, palaces and churches. The most famous of these schools is identified with a dynasty of artists: the Galli Bibiena, whose studio productions cannot always be reliably attributed from their autographs. The eldest, Fernandino (1657-1743), was also the most illustrious and was himself the son of a Bolognese painter. He worked in Bologna, Parma, Barcelona and Vienna. As the inventor of the *scena per angola*, which he adapted to a system of multiple vanishing points, he succeeded in conveying with the required grandeur and pomp the fantasy, mobility and the dynamism of fragmentary and intermediate spaces in the actual space of the stage and in its virtual extensions. Sinuous arcades held up by consoles, arrangements of grouped caryatids, wreathed columns decked with garlands or sculpted bosses of geometric ornaments alongside medallions, curvilinear pedestals and a profusion of balustrades. This elaborate decorative approach fixed the illusionary space of a vestibule, a huge stairwell or gallery leading out into a garden, but without limiting it.

All of the Bibiena family enchanted Europe and their designs, which were sometimes engraved, bear witness to a civilisation that was in love with the theatre. Francesco Galli Bibiena (1649-1739) built the court opera houses in Nancy and Vienna. Allessandro (1687-1769) employed his talents in Mannheim. Giuseppe (1696-1756) studied in Vienna, designed festive decorations in Prague and built theatres in Florence, Mantua and Bologna (1756-1763). Giovanni-Carlo (1700-1760) designed the royal theatre in Lisbon. Finally, Carlo (1725-1780) worked in the court of the king of Prussia, before travelling to Paris, London, The Hague and Saint Petersburg. Other dynasties of scenographers, also from the north of Italy, became equally famous. For example, the Galliari, who were active in Milan, and whose activities in Innsbruck, Berlin and Vienna pay witness to their success. Righini, attached to the Parma court, produced decors for the Teatro Reggio of Turon and the San Carlo of Naples. His style, more measured than his colleagues from Bologna, signals the change from a deep perspective vision to a "tableau" stage system, closer to the *vedutistas*.

environs, montre un égal talent de décorateur, avec un penchant, plus didactique peut-être, pour le caprice.

Entre Milan, Parme, Bologne et Venise, plusieurs écoles de scénographes, peintres de la *quadratura* et architectes, vont multiplier les modèles, les réalisations scéniques ou festives, les constructions de théâtres, de palais ou d'églises. La plus célèbre s'identifie à une dynastie d'artistes : les Galli Bibiena dont la production d'atelier ne facilite pas toujours l'identification autographe des dessins. Fernandino (1657-1743), l'aîné, le plus illustre, fils lui-même d'un peintre bolonais, œuvre à Bologne, Parme, Barcelone et Vienne. Inventeur de la *scena per angolo,* qu'il adapte au système des points de fuite multiples, il sait traduire, avec la grandeur et la pompe requises, la fantaisie, la mobilité et le dynamisme des espaces fragmentaires et intermédiaires dans l'ouverture concrète de la scène et ses prolongements virtuels. Arcades sinueuses portées par des consoles, ordonnances de cariatides groupées, colonnes torses ornées de guirlandes ou de bossages sculptés d'ornements géométriques associés à des médaillons, piédestaux curvilignes et balustrades à profusion : c'est tout l'appareil décoratif, hypertrophié, qui concrétise, sans le limiter, l'espace illusionniste d'un vestibule, d'une immense cage d'escalier, d'une galerie ouverte sur jardin.

Tous les Bibiena enchantèrent l'Europe et leurs dessins, parfois gravés, témoignent d'une civilisation soumise à l'optique frénétique du théâtre. Francesco Galli Bibiena (1649-1739) construit les opéras de cour de Nancy et de Vienne ; Allessandro (1687-1769) exerce ses talents à la cour de Mannheim ; Giuseppe (1696-1756), formé à Vienne, est l'auteur de décors de fêtes à Prague et constructeur de théâtres à Florence, Mantoue et Bologne (1756-1763) ; Giovanni-Carlo (1700-1760) réalise le théâtre royal de Lisbonne ; et Carlo (1725-1780) est à la cour du roi de Prusse avant de voyager à Paris, Londres, La Haye et Saint-Pétersbourg. D'autres dynasties de scénographes s'illustrent tout autant, toujours à partir de l'Italie du Nord : par exemple, les Galliari, actifs à Milan, mais dont le passage à Innsbruck, à Berlin ou Vienne, atteste leur succès. Righini, attaché à la cour de Parme, donne des décors pour le Teatro Reggio de Turin et le San Carlo de Naples : son style, plus mesuré que celui de ses confrères bolonais, marque le passage de la vision à perspective profonde au système de la scène « tableau », plus proche des védutistes.

secolo inoltrato. Uno di questi, Vittone, autore di parecchie chiese a Torino e nella vicinanze, dimostra un pari talento di decoratore, con un'inclinazione, forse più didattica, per il capriccio.

Tra Milano, Bologna e Venezia, parecchie scuole di scenografi, pittori della quadratura e architetti, moltiplicheranno i modelli, le realizzazioni sceniche o festive, le costruzioni di teatri, di palazzi o di chiese. La più celebre si identifica in una dinastia di artisti: i Galli Bibiena la cui produzione d'atelier non facilita sempre l'identificazione autografa dei disegni. Fernandino (1657-1743), il maggiore, egli stesso figlio di un pittore bolognese, lavora a Bologna, Parma, Barcellona e Vienna. Inventore della "scena per angolo", che adatta al sistema dei punti di fuga multipli, egli sa tradurre, con la grandezza e la pompa richiesti, la fantasia, la mobilità e il dinamismo degli spazi frammentari e intermedi nell'apertura concreta della scena e i suoi prolungamenti virtuali. Arcate sinuose sorrette da mensole, disposizioni di cariatidi raggruppate, colonne tortili ornate da ghirlande o da bugne scolpite d'ornamenti geometrici associati a medaglioni, piedistalli curvilinei e balaustre a profusione: è tutto l'apparato decorativo, ipertrofico, che concretizza, senza limitarlo, lo spazio illusionista di un vestibolo, di un'immensa tromba delle scale, di una galleria aperta sul giardino.

Tutti i Bibiena incantarono l'Europa e i loro disegni, a volte incisi, testimoniano di una civiltà sottomessa all'ottica frenetica del teatro. Francesco Galli Bibiena (1649-1739) costruisce i teatri dell'opera della corte di Nancy e di Vienna; Alessandro (1687-1769) esercita i suoi talenti alla corte di Mannheim; Giuseppe (1696-1756), formatosi a Vienna, è l'autore delle decorazioni di feste a Praga e costruttore di teatri a Firenze, Mantova e Bologna (1756-1763); Giovanni-Carlo (1700-1760) realizza il Teatro reale di Lisbona; e Carlo (1725-1780) è alla corte del re di Prussia prima di viaggiare a Parigi, Londra, La Haye e San Pietroburgo. Altre dinastie di scenografi si distinsero ugualmente, sempre a partire dell'Italia del Nord: per esempio, i Galliari, attivi a Milano, ma il cui passaggio a Innsbruck, a Berlino o a Vienna, attesta il loro successo. Righini, funzionario alla corte di Parma, realizza le decorazioni per il teatro regio di Torino e il San Carlo di Napoli: il suo stile, più misurato di quello dei suoi colleghi bolognesi, segna il passaggio dalla visione della prospettiva profonda al sistema della scena "quadro", più prossima dei vedutisti.

Piranesi: antique visions and architectural fictions

Venice certainly did not escape from this craze for the theatre. The city, which is so spectacular in itself, became the subject of a style of *veduta* that increased its fame. Landscape painters, trained in the schools of quadraturists, scenographers, perspective and architectural draughtsmen easily exported their work. Ricci, who was greatly appreciated in England and painted pictures of ruins and tormented seascapes, seems to have transmitted his taste for the Elements to an entire generation. Zuccarelli, a founder member of the Royal Academy in London, painted Palladian British architecture, at the same time that Canaletto, Venice's most famous *vedutista*, was enjoying a ten-year stay in England (1746-1756). From views of the Grand Canal, and the squares and palaces that enliven the laguna, to the banks of the Thames, and from the land of Palladio to the kingdom of the landscaped garden, a new artistic sensibility for "inhabited" nature emerged in these "portraits" of architecture and of cities.

When a love of history and of dramatic ruins is added, we arrive at an explanation for the revolutionary vocation of a young Venetian who was profoundly to transform the *vision* of architecture. Piranesi lived out his destiny in Rome, another cosmopolitan centre, while his artistic heritage took root in Paris, the City of Light. He learnt the rules of perspective in décor studios and was introduced to archaeology by Temanza, the famously learned Palladian engineer and architect. Though born in Mestre, he always called himself a "Venetian architect". When part of the suite of the Venetian ambassador to Rome, he satisfied his vocation as a *vedutista* after discovering the works of Pannini and the engraving studio of Vasi. Having studied *quadratura* in Emilia, he made his reputation in Rome as a palace decorator. Then, as Cardinal de Polignac's protégé, he became the most prestigious painter of ruins, caprices and *vedute* in the Eternal City, and his work was collected by numerous artistic patrons passing through Rome. Vasi was equally successful in the inferior medium of etchings, and Piranesi was to benefit from this fact at the start of his career. Devoted to archaeology and the meditation of ruins, and inspired by the example of Fischer von Erlach's *Historical Architecture*, this "Venetian architect" visited Naples and

Piranèse : visions antiques et fictions architecturales

Venise n'échappe pas, bien au contraire, à cette théâtromanie ambiante : la ville, si spectaculaire en elle-même, devient le sujet d'un style de *veduta* qui augmente sa renommée. Les peintres paysagistes, formés à l'école des quadraturistes, scénographes, dessinateurs de perspective et d'architecture, exportèrent aisément leurs œuvres. Très apprécié en Angleterre, Ricci (il peint des tableaux de ruines, des marines tourmentées) semble avoir transmis son goût pour l'expression des éléments à toute une génération. Zuccarelli, membre fondateur de la Royal Academy de Londres, peint l'architecture *palladienne* britannique, au moment où Canaletto, le plus célèbre vedudiste de Venise, effectue lui-même un séjour de dix années outre-Manche (1746-1756). Des vues du Grand Canal, des places et des palais qui animent la lagune, aux berges de la Tamise, de la patrie de Palladio à celle du jardin paysager, c'est une nouvelle sensibilité pour la nature habitée qui se dégage des « portraits » d'architecture et de ville.

La passion pour l'histoire et la dramaturgie ruiniste, ajoutée à ce contexte, explique la vocation révolutionnaire d'un jeune Vénitien appelé à transformer en profondeur la *vision* de l'architecture : Piranèse, dont le destin s'accomplira dans une autre aire cosmopolite, Rome, et la descendance dans la ville des Lumières, Paris. Né à Mestre, formé à la pratique de la perspective dans des ateliers de décors et initié à l'archéologie par le célèbre érudit, ingénieur et architecte palladien Temanza, Piranèse se nommera lui-même, toute sa vie, « architecte vénitien ». Participant à la suite de l'ambassadeur de Venise à Rome (1740), il satisfait sa vocation de vedutiste au contact des œuvres de Pannini et dans l'atelier du graveur Vasi. Pannini, formé à la *quadratura* en Émilie, a acquis sa réputation à Rome comme décorateur de palais ; protégé par le cardinal de Polignac, collectionné par de nombreux mécènes de passage à Rome, il est devenu le peintre par excellence des ruines, des caprices et des *vedute* de la Ville éternelle. Vasi, dans le genre inférieur de l'eau-forte, connaît un égal succès, dont Piranèse profite dans les débuts de sa carrière. Voué à l'archéologie et à la méditation des ruines, stimulé par l'exemple de *L'Architecture historique* de Fischer von Erlach, l'« architecte vénitien », après avoir visité

Piranesi: visioni antiche e finzioni architettoniche

Venezia non sfugge, tutt'altro, a questa teatromania ambientale: la città, così spettacolare in se stessa, diventa soggetto di uno stile di veduta che aumenta la sua fama. I pittori ambientalisti, formati alla scuola dei quadraturisti, degli scenografi, dei disegnatori di prospettiva e d'architettura, esportano facilmente le loro opere. Molto apprezzato in Inghilterra, Ricci (dipinge dei quadri di rovine, di marine sotto la tormenta) sembra avere trasmesso il suo gusto per l'espressione degli Elementi a tutta una generazione. Zuccarelli, membro fondatore della Royal Academy di Londra, dipinge l'architettura palladiana britannica, nel momento in cui lo stesso Canaletto, il più celebre vedutista di Venezia, effettua un soggiorno di dieci anni oltremanica. (1746-1756). Dalle vedute del Canal Grande, dalle piazze e dai palazzi che animano la laguna, alle sponde del Tamigi, dalla patria del Palladio a quella del giardino paesaggistico, c'è una nuova sensibilità per la natura abitata che si svincola dai "ritratti" d'architettura e di città.

La passione per la storia e la drammaturgia rovinista, aggiunta a questo contesto, spiega la vocazione rivoluzionaria di un giovane veneziano chiamato a trasformare dal profondo la *visione* dell'architettura: Piranesi, il cui destino si compirà in un'altra area cosmopolita, Roma, e la discendenza nella città dei Lumi, Parigi. Nato a Mestre, formato alla pratica della prospettiva negli atelier di decorazione e iniziato all'archeologia dal celebre erudito, ingegnere e architetto palladiano Temanza, Piranesi stesso si chiamerà per tutta la vita "architetto veneziano". Unitosi al seguito dell'ambasciatore di Venezia a Roma (1740), soddisfa la sua vocazione di vedutista a contatto con opere di Pannini e nell'atelier dell'incisore Vasi. Pannini, formato alla *quadratura* in Emilia, ha conquistato la sua reputazione a Roma come decoratore di palazzo; protetto dal cardinale di Polignac, collezionato da diversi mecenati di passaggio a Roma, è diventato per eccellenza il pittore delle rovine, dei capricci e delle *vedute* della Città Eterna. Vasi, nel genere minore dell'acquaforte, conosce un uguale successo, da cui Piranesi trae profitto all'inizio della sua carriera. Votato all'archeologia e alla meditazione delle rovine, stimolato dall'esempio de *L'architecture historique* di Fischer von Erlach, l'"architetto veneziano", dopo aver visitato

Herculaneum, before settling in Rome for good at the age of twenty-five (1745).

Long before discovering Greek sites at the end of his life, he started digs in Hadrian's villa. Antique objects and fragments, observed *in situ* were drawn, engraved and restored before enriching the collections of the great Roman art lovers, such as Cardinal Albani, or else British ones, such as G. Hamilton. Piranesi's role as an *antiquarian* (as both a scholar and a dealer) was clearly the basis of his creative drive. His views of the buildings of modern Rome reveal an undeniable continuity with the pomp of the Eternal City, which the patronage of the Popes had regenerated. Then, to counter the idea of Greek artistic supremacy, promulgated by certain German and French scholars such as Winckelmann, Caylus, Mariette and Le Roy, Piranesi defended and celebrated the magnificence of the Romans through their Etruscan origins. The sumptuous engraved plates, which militate for a complete renewal of ancient inspiration in contemporary creation, include views of famous ruins, inventive restitutions of the ancient layout of Rome, decorative compositions which integrate the forms and hieroglyphs of Egyptian art and free compositions of caprices. If his *Prima Parte di Architettura e Prospettive* (1743) presents canonical models of intellectual architecture, occasionally of a Palladian inspiration, his *Antichità Romane* (1756), *Campo Marzio* (1762) and *Magnifizenza ed Architettura de'Romani* (1761) are intense reveries based on the emotions created by the Romans' vigorous stone constructions. In his *Parere su l'Architettura* (1765) and his *Carceri*, or "prisons", which are based on a contrast between chiaroscuro and the illusion of an unreal space whose depicted structure reveals a constructive and imaginative daring, a new poetics of architectural fiction has been set against academic norms. Piranesi's example was a timely liberation of individual creative drives, though initially only on paper.

Though already extremely famous, Piranesi had to wait for the accession of a Venetian, Clement XIII (1758-1769), to the papal throne. This member of the Rezzonico family protected him, and at last he received some commissions: the decoration of the apartments of Monte Cavallo and Castel Gandolfo, as well as a projected choir for San Giovanni de Latran. In fact, only the Egyptian decoration of the English coffee-shop (now destroyed) on the

Naples et Herculanum, se fixe définitivement à Rome à l'âge de vingt-cinq ans (1745).

Bien avant de découvrir, à la fin de sa vie, les sites grecs de la Péninsule, il établit des fouilles à la villa d'Hadrien : objets et fragments d'antiques observés *in situ*, dessinés, gravés, restaurés, vont enrichir les collections de grands amateurs romains, comme le cardinal Albani, ou britanniques, comme G. Hamilton. Le rôle d'*antiquaire* (au double sens du mot, érudit et marchand) de Piranèse se révèle être le substrat de son inspiration créatrice. Ses vues des édifices de la Rome moderne témoignent d'abord d'une continuité indéniable des fastes de la Ville éternelle que le mécénat des papes a regénérés. Puis, contre l'idée d'une suprématie de l'art grec dans l'histoire de la civilisation occidentale, comme l'affirment certains savants allemands et français, Winckelmann, Caylus, Mariette, Le Roy, Piranèse défend et illustre la magnificence des Romains à travers ses origines étrusques. Les somptueuses planches gravées qui militent pour un renouveau total de l'inspiration antique dans la création contemporaine, comptent des vues de ruines célèbres, des restitutions inventives du plan antique de Rome, des compositions décoratives qui intègrent les formes et les hiéroglyphes de l'art égyptien et des compositions libres sous forme de caprices. Si la *Prima Parte di Architettura e Prospettive* (1743) propose des modèles canoniques d'architecture savante, parfois d'inspiration palladienne, les *Antichità Romane* (1756), le *Campo Marzio* (1762) et la *Magnifizenza ed Architettura de'Romani* (1761), s'apparentent à d'intenses rêveries sur l'émotion que suscitent les puissantes constructions maçonnées des Romains. Avec le *Parere su l'Architettura* (1765) et les *Carceri* ou *Prisons,* qui s'appuient sur l'art contrasté du clair-obscur et l'illusion d'un espace irréel dont la structure figurée exprime l'audace constructive et imaginative, une nouvelle poétique de la fiction architecturale s'oppose à toute norme académique : l'exemple de Piranèse arrive à point pour libérer les pulsions créatrices individuelles, dans un premier temps, sur le papier.

Déjà très célèbre, Piranèse doit attendre l'accès au pontificat d'un Vénitien, Clément XIII (1758-1769), de la famille Rezzonico qui le protège, pour être gratifié de quelques commandes : décors d'appartements au Monte Cavallo, à Castel Gandolfo, projet de chœur pour Saint-Jean-de-Latran. En fait, seuls le décor égyptien

Napoli ed Ercolano, si fissa definitivamente a Roma all'età di venticinque anni (1745).

Molto prima di scoprire, alla fine della sua vita, i siti greci della Penisola, egli avvia degli scavi alla villa Adriana: oggetti e frammenti antichi osservati in situ, disegnati, incisi, restaurati, arricchiranno le collezioni dei grandi amatori romani, come il cardinale Albani, o britannici, come G. Hamilton. Il ruolo di antiquario (nel doppio senso della parola, erudito e mercante) di Piranesi si rivela essere il sostrato della sua ispirazione creatrice. Le sue vedute degli edifici della Roma moderna testimoniano in principio una continuità innegabile dei fasti della città eterna che il mecenatismo dei papi ha rigenerato. Inoltre, contro l'idea di una supremazia dell'arte greca nella storia della civiltà occidentale, come affermano certi eruditi tedeschi e francesi, Winckelmann, Caylus, Mariette, Le Roy, Piranesi difende e illustra la magnificenza della civiltà romana attraverso le sue origini etrusche. Le sontuose tavole incise che depongono per un rinnovo totale dell'ispirazione antica nella creazione contemporanea, contano delle viste di rovine celebri, delle restituzioni inventive della pianta antica di Roma, delle composizioni decorative che integrano le forme e i geroglifici dell'arte egizia e delle composizioni libere sotto forma di capricci. Se la *Prima Parte di Architettura e Prospettive* (1743) propone dei modelli canonici d'architettura colta, a volte d'ispirazione palladiana, le *Antichità Romane* (1756), il *Campo Marzio* (1762) e la *Magnificenza ed Architettura de' Romani* (1761) sono simili alle intense fantasticherie sull'emozione suscitate delle potenti costruzioni edificate dai Romani. Con il *Parere sull'Architettura* (1765) e le *Carceri o prigioni*, che si basano sull'arte del chiaroscuro e dell'illusione di uno spazio irreale la cui struttura raffigurata esprime l'audacia costruttiva ed immaginativa, una nuova poetica della finzione architettonica si oppone ad ogni norma accademica: l'esempio di Piranesi arriva a proposito per liberare le pulsioni creatrici individuali, in un primo tempo, sulla carta.

Già molto celebre, Piranesi deve attendere l'arrivo al pontificato di un veneziano, Clemente XIII (1758-1769), della famiglia Rezzonico che lo protegge, per ottenere qualche commissione: decorazione di appartamenti a Monte Cavallo, a Castel Gandolfo, progetto di coro per San Giovanni in Laterano. In effetti, solo la decorazione egiziana del Caffè Inglese (distrutto), a piazza

Piazza di Spagna and the restoration of the grand priory of Malta, for which he designed and built the church of Santa Maria on the Aventine, really display his talent as a builder. After his death, in 1778, his son Francesco went to Paris where he opened the Chalcographie Piranesi Frères. Acquired by Firmin-Didot, his copper plates were still used to print the master's work as late as the 1830s.

The English and French Piranesians

The direct influence of Piranesi on young painters or architects, some of whom had come to study in Rome, was a European phenomenon affecting Paris and London first of all. In the tradition of the *antiquarians*, some British architects became friends with Piranesi or else participated in the learned debates that his archaeological work inspired. Wood, a future member of the Society of Dilettanti, left Rome for Syria in 1750. On his return, he produced superb publications on the ruins of Palmyra (1753) and Baalbek (1757). Adam, who introduced the *Graeco-Pompeian* style into England, was a friend of Clérisseau, a Piranesian who published a widely acclaimed collection based on the ruins of Diocletian's palace in Spalato (1764). Chambers, after frequenting Blondel's classes in Paris, stayed for five years in Rome, where he and his compatriot Mylne successfully took part in the competition of the Academia di San Luca. Dance the Younger arrived in Rome in 1758. Wyatt and Harrisson also stayed there, whereas Soane, destined to become the most Piranesian of them all, was sent to Rome on a scholarship by George III, but reached there only in 1778, the year of Piranesi's death. All of these artists, architects, archaeologists, designers and theorists were at the origin of the second wave of British Classicism that mingled picturesque chiaroscuro, spatial effects of distribution and the purity of ancient forms with their time-honoured Palladianism.

Their French friends, rivals and sometimes competitors were to display even more variety and above all were to give yet greater prestige to the art of Piranesian design. For example, Hubert Robert, who was an internationally successful painter and active garden designer, directly influenced many architects. His imaginary views of Rome, his caprices, his views of Provence, of

du Café Anglais (détruit), place de l'Espagne, et la restauration du grand prieuré de Malte pour lequel il dessine et réalise l'église de Sainte-Marie-sur-l'Aventin (1765), témoignent du talent de constructeur de Piranèse. Après sa mort, en 1778, son fils Francesco gagne Paris où il ouvre la Chalcographie Piranesi Frères ; acquis par Firmin-Didot, les cuivres servent encore à diffuser l'œuvre du maître jusque dans les années 1830.

Les Piranésiens anglais et français

L'influence de Piranèse, directe auprès des jeunes artistes, peintres ou architectes, venus parfaire leur formation à Rome, est un phénomène européen dont Paris et Londres, d'abord, ont particulièrement bénéficié. Certains architectes britanniques, à la suite des *antiquaires*, se lient d'amitié avec Piranèse ou participent à l'émulation érudite que ses travaux archéologiques suscitent. Wood, futur membre de la Society of Dilettanti, quitte Rome pour la Syrie en 1750 : il en rapporte de précieuses publications, sur les ruines de Palmyre (1753) et de Balbek (1757). Adam, introducteur du style *helléno-pompéien* en Angleterre, lié d'amitié avec le piranésien Clérisseau, publie un recueil très admiré sur les ruines du palais de Dioclétien à Spalato (1764). Chambers, après avoir fréquenté le cours de Blondel à Paris, séjourne cinq ans à Rome où il participe avec succès, comme son compatriote Mylne, aux concours de l'académie de Saint-Luc. Dance le Jeune arrive à Rome en 1758 ; Wyatt et Harrisson y séjournent également, tandis que celui qui deviendra le plus piranésien d'entre eux, le jeune Soane, envoyé comme boursier par George III, n'atteint Rome qu'en 1778, l'année de la mort de Piranèse. Tous ces artistes, architectes, archéologues, dessinateurs et théoriciens sont à l'origine d'une seconde vague de classicisme britannique qui intègre au palladianisme séculaire, le pittoresque du clair-obscur, les effets de mise en scène spatiale et l'épuration des formes dessinées à l'antique.

Leurs amis, émules et, parfois, concurrents français, montreront davantage de variété encore et, surtout, gagneront un plus grand prestige dans l'art du dessin piranésien. Dans la peinture, comme dans l'art des jardins, où il s'implique concrètement, Hubert Robert, par exemple, connaît un succès international qui n'est pas sans influencer les architectes. Ses vues imagi-

di Spagna, e il restauro del grande priorato di Malta per il quale disegna e realizza la chiesa di Santa Maria sull'Aventino (1765), sono testimonianza del talento di costruttore di Piranesi. Dopo la sua morte, nel 1778, il figlio Francesco conquista Parigi dove apre la calcografia Fratelli Piranesi; acquisite da Firmin-Didot, le matrici di rame servono ancora a diffondere l'opera del maestro fino agli anni 1830.

I Piranesiani inglesi e francesi

L'influenza di Piranesi, diretta su giovani artisti, pittori o architetti, venuti a perfezionare la loro formazione a Roma, è un fenomeno europeo di cui Parigi e Londra, in principio, hanno beneficiato in modo particolare. Certi architetti britannici, al seguito degli antiquari, divennero amici di Piranesi o parteciparono all'emulazione erudita suscitata dai suoi lavori. Wood, futuro membro della Società dei dilettanti, lascia Roma per la Siria nel 1750: da là riporta preziose pubblicazioni, sulle rovine di Palmira (1753) e di Balbek (1757). Adam, introduttore dello stile elleno-pompeiano in Inghilterra, amico del parigino Clérisseau, pubblica una raccolta molto ammirata sulle rovine del palazzo di Diocleziano a Spalato (1764). Chambers, dopo aver frequentato il corso di Blondel a Parigi, soggiorna cinque anni a Roma dove partecipa con successo, come il suo compatriota Mylne, ai concorsi dell'accademia di San Luca. Il giovane Dance arriva a Roma nel 1758; Wyatt e Harrisson parimenti vi soggiornano, mentre quello che tra loro diventerà il più piranesiano, il giovane Soane, inviato come borsista da Giorgio III, non raggiunge Roma che nel 1778, anno della morte di Piranesi. Tutti questi artisti, architetti, archeologi, disegnatori e teorici sono all'origine di una seconda ondata di classicismo britannico che integra al palladianesimo secolare il pittoresco del chiaroscuro, gli effetti della messa in scena spaziale e la purificazione delle forme disegnate all'antica.

I loro amici, emuli e, qualche volta, concorrenti francesi, mostreranno ancora più varietà e, soprattutto, guadagneranno un più grande prestigio nell'arte del disegno piranesiano. In pittura, come nell'arte dei giardini, dove si impegna concretamente, Hubert Robert, per esempio, conosce un successo internazionale che non può non influenzare gli architetti. Le sue vedute immaginarie di Roma o di Parigi, i suoi capricci, le sue vedute di monumenti della Provenza, di

manufactories set in a vibrant nature and his luminous ruins exalted the progressive sensibilities of the Antiquarians. His projects for the grand gallery, when Louis XVI commissioned him to set up the Louvre, are symptomatic of the effects of Piranesianism on the architecture of the future. Challe and Le Lorrain, also with backgrounds as painters, stayed in Rome for several years and, before the arrival of Clérisseau and Adam, became well known for their designs for the architecture that was erected during festivities at the Mancini palace (1744) or the *Chinea* (1745-1748). Challe, who was made professor of perspective at the *Académie Royale* in 1758, became the King's royal designer and, as such, produced the decors for the plays and festivities at Louis XV's court. At the end of his life, he started translating Piranesi's works, thus reviving memories of a deep friendship. When Le Lorrain returned to Paris, he started exhibiting at the Salon in 1753. Close to Caylus and Le Roy, he was one of the first to contribute to the "Greek" revival of the decorative arts. He was invited to Russia, to direct the Academy of Arts, and died in Saint Petersburg in 1758, just a few months after his arrival there.

A good ten or twenty French Piranesians could be cited for their remarkable Parisian or international careers as working architects during the second half of the eighteenth century. Petitot, a disciple of Soufflot, a correspondent of the *Académie Royale* and author of *Raisons sur la perspective* (1758) as well as the amusing *Suite de vases* with animal patterns, was attached to the Bourbon court in Parma and worked in every decorative field, from organising festivities to building and town-planning. De la Guêperie worked in Stuttgart, Jardin drew the plans for the royal church in Copenhagen, Desprez (a prestigious illustrator and engraver who participated in the Abbé de Saint Non's famous *Voyage pittoresque* in Italy) won renown in the Swedish court of Gustav III as the King's Head Architect and as a theatre designer. In the field of theatrical decors, in which large numbers of Parisian artists were involved, the local influence of Servandoni merged with that of Piranesi and his followers. De Machy, for example, who was best known for his *vedute* of Paris which he exhibited alongside Hubert Robert, produced the décor for the 1760 revival of Rameau's *Dardanus* at the Opera; the prison scene exactly reproduced the first plate of Piranesi's *Carceri*.

This fact is attested by a commentary in the *Avant-coureur* that congratulates the artist for this allusion and also for a coloured engraving in an optical device.

Delafosse, a prolific designer and ornamenter, constructed several town houses and gave drawing lessons at the Académie de Saint-Luc in Paris. A visionary and moralistic architect, he expressed himself above all in small vignettes. His mordant drawings, enriched with wash tints and watercolours, often convey a satirical or even grotesque vision of the symbols of art and of society. Legeay, whom several great architects of the second half of the century considered as the master of figurative invention (with Servandoni) shared Piranesi's taste for satire and took it as far as caricature. After working in Rome, where he stayed from 1738 to 1742 before Piranesi arrived. Legeay returned to Paris where he taught the art of the *veduta* and the caprice, thus preparing students at the *Académie royale* for a graphic as well as thematic freedom of expression. His views of ruins, smothered by menacing vegetation which was itself absorbed by chiaroscuro, express a dream-like vision, which was openly sentimental, and sometimes fantastical, of architectural motifs and effects most often associated with sculpture. Despite several important building projects which attest his fame outside France (the Catholic church of Saint Edwige in Berlin, 1747-1773, the new plans for Potsdam and settlements around Sans-Souci), and despite the title of Head Architect of the King of Prussia, which Frederick II gave him for a time, Legeay did not have a great career as a builder. This was not the case for the best of his pupils, the *painter-architects* who won prizes at the *Académie royale d'architecture* and went to Rome on scholarships in the 1750s: such as Peyre, Moreau-Desproux and especially De Wailly, whose international career as an illustrator, architect, stage designer, town planner and teacher was associated with an original and permanent display of his projects in the Salon of the Louvre and in the supplementary volume of plates for the *Encyclopédie* (1777).

duit trait pour trait la première planche des *Carceri* de Piranèse. Le fait est attesté par un commentaire du journal *L'avant-coureur* qui félicite le peintre pour son emprunt, ainsi que par une gravure coloriée de boîte d'optique.

Grand décorateur et ornemaniste fécond, Delafosse construit plusieurs hôtels particuliers et enseigne le dessin à l'académie de Saint-Luc à Paris. Architecte visionnaire et moraliste, c'est souvent dans de petites vignettes qu'il s'exprime : son dessin, au trait mordant, enrichi de lavis et d'aquarelle, transmet souvent une vision satirique, parfois hallucinée des symboles de l'art et de la société. Legeay, que plusieurs grands architectes de la seconde moitié du siècle considèrent comme leur maître en inventions figuratives (avec Servandoni), partage avec Piranèse ce goût de la satire qu'il pousse, lui, jusqu'à la caricature. Actif à Rome où il s'est établi avant Piranèse, entre 1738 et 1742, Legeay rentre à Paris où il enseigne l'art de la *veduta* et du caprice, préparant ainsi les élèves de l'Académie royale à une liberté d'expression tant graphique que thématique : ses vues de ruines, soumises à l'étouffement d'une végétation menaçante, elle-même absorbée par le clair-obscur, traduisent une vision onirique, franchement sentimentale, parfois fantastique, des motifs et des effets architecturaux le plus souvent associés à la sculpture. Malgré quelques chantiers importants qui témoignent de sa célébrité hors de France (l'église catholique Sainte-Edwige de Berlin, 1747-1773, les nouveaux plans pour Postdam et les communs de Sans-Souci), malgré le titre de premier architecte du roi de Prusse que lui attribua, pour un temps, Frédéric II, Legeay ne connaît pas une grande carrière de constructeur. Ce n'est pas le cas de ses meilleurs élèves, ces *peintres-architectes*, lauréats de l'Académie royale d'architecture et pensionnaires à Rome dans les années 1750 : Peyre, Moreau-Desproux et surtout De Wailly, dont la carrière internationale de dessinateur, d'architecte, de décorateur de théâtre, d'urbaniste et de professeur, s'accompagne d'une diffusion permanente et originale de ses projets, sur les cimaises du Salon du Louvre et dans le supplément du volume de planches de l'*Encyclopédie* (1777).

del Piranesi. Il fatto è attestato da un commento del giornale *L'Avant-coureur* che si congratula con il pittore per il suo prestito, così come per una incisione colorata della scatola ottica.

Grande decoratore e fecondo ornatista, Delafosse costruisce numerosi palazzi privati e insegna disegno all'accademia di San Luca a Parigi. Architetto visionario e moralista, egli si esprime spesso attraverso piccole vignette: il suo disegno dal tratto mordente, arricchito di inchiostro acquarellato e di acquerello, trasmette spesso una visione satirica, a volte allucinata dei simboli dell'arte e della società. Legeay, che parecchi grandi architetti delle seconda metà del secolo considerano il loro maestro in invenzioni figurative (con Servandoni), condivide con Piranesi questo gusto per la satira che egli spinge fino alla caricatura. Attivo a Roma dove si era stabilito prima di Piranesi, tra il 1738 e il 1742, Legeay rientra a Parigi dove insegna l'arte della veduta e del capriccio, preparando così gli allievi dell'accademia reale ad una libertà di espressione tanto grafica che tematica: le sue vedute di rovine, sottoposte al soffocamento di una vegetazione incombente, essa stessa assorbita dal chiaroscuro, traducono una visione onirica, decisamente sentimentale, a volte fantastica, dei motivi e degli effetti architettonici il più delle volte associati alla scultura. Nonostante qualche cantiere importante testimoni la sua celebrità fuori dalla Francia (la chiesa cattolica Santa Edvige di Berlino, 1747-1773, le nuove piante per Postdam e le "dépendences" di sans-Souci), nonostante il titolo di Primo Architetto del re di Prussia a lui attribuito, per qualche tempo, da Federico II, Legeay non conosce una grande carriera di costruttore. Non è il caso dei suoi migliori allievi, questi pittori-architetti, laureati all'*Académie Royale d'Architecture* e pensionanti a Roma negli anni 1750: Peyre, Moreau-Desproux e, soprattutto, De Wailly, la cui carriera internazionale di disegnatore, di architetto e di decoratore di teatro, di urbanista e di professore, si accompagna ad una diffusione permanente ed originale dei suoi progetti, sulle cimase del Salone del Louvre e nel supplemento del volume di tavole dell'*Encyclopédie* (1777).

FILIPPO JUVARRA (1678-1736)

(workshop of) *Hall and stairwell of a palace.*
Pen, brown ink and wash.

(atelier de) *Vestibule et cage d'escalier d'un palais.*
Plume, encre brune et lavis.

(atelier di). *Vestibolo e tromba delle scale di un palazzo.*
Penna, inchiostro bruno e inchiostro acquarellato,
203 x 159 mm.

London, Royal Institute of British Architects.

▶ ### PIETRO RIGHINI (1683-1742)

Sketch of the hall of a palace.
Pen, brown ink and wash.

Vestibule d'un palais, esquisse.
Plume, encre brune et lavis.

Vestibolo di un Palazzo, schizzo.
Penna, inchiostro bruno e inchiostro
acquarellato, 159 x 203 mm.

London, Royal Institute of British Architects.

▲ GIOVANNI CARLO GALLI BIBIENA (1728-1787)

(after) *Porticoes and palace for Act II of La Clemenza di Tito.*
Pen, brown and black inks and wash.

(d'après) *Portiques et palais pour l'acte II de La Clémence de Titus.*
Plume, encres brune et noire, lavis.

(secondo) *Portici e palazzi per l'atto II della Clemenza di Tito.*
Penna, inchiostri bruni e neri, inchiostro acquarellato, 152 x 216 mm.

London, Royal Institute of British Architects.

► GIUSEPPE GALLI BIBIENA (1696-1757)

(attributed to) *Perspective with a semicircular colonnade.*
Pen, brown ink and grey and brown wash.

(attribué à) *Perspective avec une colonnade en hémicycle.*
Plume, encre brune, lavis gris et brun.

(attribuito a) *Prospettiva con un colonnato in emiciclo.*
Penna, inchiostro bruno, inchiostro acquarellato
grigio e bruno, 622 x 843 mm.

Paris, musée du Louvre, cabinet des Arts graphiques.

▲ GIOVANNI PAOLO PANINI (1691/92-1765)

Architectural caprice.
Pen, brown ink and grey wash.

Caprice d'architecture.
Plume, encre brune et lavis gris.

Capriccio d'architettura.
Penna, inchiostro bruno e inchiostro acquarellato grigio,
190 x 260 mm.

London, Royal Institute of British Architects.

► ANTONIO GALLI BIBIENA (1700-1774)

Hall of a palace opening on to a garden, circa 1728.
Pen, brown ink and grey and brown wash.

Zum Garten hin offene Halle eines Schlosses, um 1728.
Feder, braune Tusche, graue und braune Lavur.

Hall d'un palais ouvert sur un jardin, vers 1728.
Plume, encre brune, lavis gris et bruns,
375 x 384 mm.

London, Royal Institute of British Architects.

FERDINANDO GALLI BIBIENA (1657-1743)

Interior volumes of a church, perspective,
compositional lined diagram.
Pen, brown ink and wash.

Volumes intérieurs d'une église, perspective,
schéma de composition des tracés.
Plume, encre brune et lavis.

Volumi interni di una chiesa, prospettiva,
schema di composizione dei tracciati.
Penna, inchiostro bruno e inchiostro acquarellato,
368 x 260 mm.

München, Staatliche Graphische Sammlung.

GIOVANNI-BATTISTA PIRANESI (1720-1778)

Architecture and fantasy, circa 1750.
Pen, brown ink and wash on beige paper.

Architecture de fantaisie, vers 1750.
Plume, encre brune, lavis sur papier beige.

Architettura di fantasia, verso il 1750.
Penna, inchiostro bruno, inchiostro acquarellato
su carta beige, 196 x 274 mm.

Montréal, Centre Canadien d'Architecture.

◀ GIOVANNI-BATTISTA PIRANESI (1720-1778)

View of the Temple of Juno in Paestum.
Red chalk, graphite, pen, brown and black inks and wash.

Vue du temple de Junon à Paestum.
Sanguine, mine de plomb, plume, encres brune et noire, lavis.

Veduta del tempio di Giunone.
Sanguigna, mina di piombo, penna, inchiostro bruno e nero,
inchiostro acquarellato, 465 x 675 mm.

Amsterdam, Rijksmuseum.

▲ GIOVANNI-BATTISTA PIRANESI (1720-1778)

Triumphal bridge.
Pen and wash.

Pont triomphal.
Plume et lavis.

Ponte di trionfo.
Penna e inchiostro acquarellato.

London, British Museum.

GIOVANNI-BATTISTA PIRANESI (1720-1778)

Imaginary prison (preparatory sketch).
Pen and wash.

Prison imaginaire (dessin préparatoire).
Plume et lavis.

Carcere d'invenzione (disegno preparatorio).
Penna e inchiostro acquarellato.

Edinburgh, National Gallery.

GIOVANNI-BATTISTA PIRANESI (1720-1778)

Part of a grandiose port for the ancient Romans (study).
Pen and wash.

Partie d'un Port magnifique à l'usage des anciens Romains (étude).
Plume et lavis.

Parte di un porto magnifico in uso presso gli antichi romani (studio).
Penna e inchiostro acquarellato.

Copenhagen, Statens Museum for Kunst.

GIOVANNI-BATTISTA PIRANESI (1720-1778)

Palace interior.
Pen and wash.

Intérieur de palais.
Plume et lavis.

Interno di palazzo.
Penna e inchiostro acquarellato.

Paris, musée du Louvre, cabinet des dessins.

LOUIS-JOSEPH LE LORRAIN (1715-1759)

Architectural caprice.
Pen, black chalk, brown ink and grey wash.

Cabrice d'architecture.
Plume, pierre noire, encre brune, lavis gris.

Capriccio di architettura.
Penna, pietra nera, inchiostro bruno,
inchiostro acquarellato grigio, 279 x 225 mm.

New York, Cooper Hewitt Museum.

▲ JEAN-LAURENT LEGEAY (vers 1710-1786)

Architecture and fantasy.
Pen, brown and black inks, wash and watercolour.

Architecture de fantaisie.
Plume, encres brune et noire, lavis et aquarelle.

Architettura di fantasia.
Penna, inchiostro bruno e nero, inchiostro acquarellato
ed acquerello.

Cambridge, Fitzwilliam Museum.

► HUBERT ROBERT (1733-1808)

Ruined colonnade, 1780.
Pen, black chalk and watercolour.

Colonnade en ruine, 1780.
Plume, pierre noire et aquarelle.

Colonnato in rovina, 1780.
Penna, pietra nera e acquerello,
800 x 770 mm.

Lille, musée des Beaux-Arts.

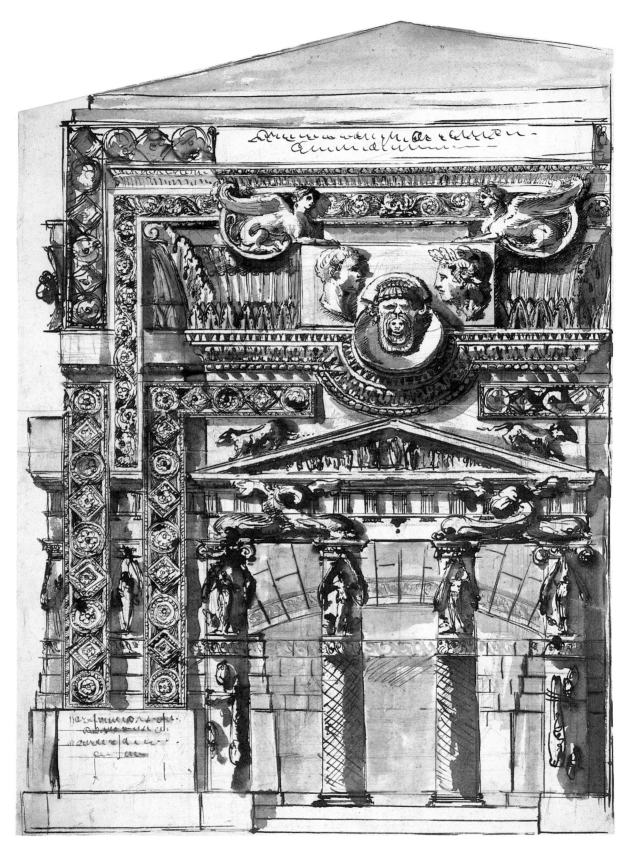

GIOVANI-BATTISTA PIRANESI
(1720-1778)

Composition of architecture and sculpture.
Pen, sepia, wash or pen, red chalk and watercolour.

Composition d'architecture et de sculpture.
Plume, sépia, lavis, ou plume, sanguine et aquarelle.

Composizione di architettura e di scultura.
Penna, seppia, inchiostro acquarellato, o penna,
sanguigna ed acquerello, 662 x 467 mm.

London, British Museum.

ENNEMOND-ALEXANDRE PETITOT (1727-1801)

*Project for a fountain with two mermaids against
a colonnade decorated with statues.*
Pen, brown ink, brown and grey wash.

*Projet de fontaine avec deux sirènes sur un fond
de colonnade ornée de statues.*
Plume, encre brune, lavis bruns et gris.

*Progetto di fontana con due sirene con sfondo
di colonnato ornato di statue.*
Penna, inchiostro bruno, inchiostro acquarellato
bruno e grigio, 505 x 415 mm.

Parma, muséo Lombardi.

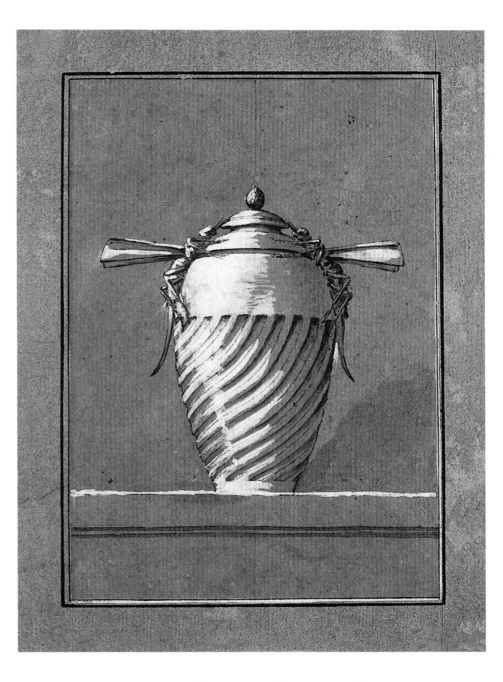

ENNEMOND-ALEXANDRE PETITOT (1727-1801)

Project for a vase decorated with grasshoppers.
Pen, red-brown ink, wash and watercolour.

Projet de vase décoré de sauterelles.
Plume, encre brun-rouge, lavis et aquarelle.

Progetto di vaso decorato con cavallette.
Penna, inchiostro bruno rosso, inchiostro acquarellato
ed acquerello, 199 x 138 mm.

Parma, muséo Lombardi.

BERNARDO ANTONIO VITTONE (1702-1770)

Architectural caprice.
Pen, black ink and wash.

Caprice d'architecture.
Plume, encre noire et lavis.

Capriccio d'architettura.
Penna, inchiostro nero e inchiostro acquarellato.

Paris, musée des Arts Décoratifs, cabinet des Dessins.

PART III

THE CLASSICAL REVIVAL AND ENLIGHTENMENT ART

LE RENOUVEAU CLASSIQUE ET L'ART DES LUMIÈRES

IL RINNOVAMENTO CLASSICO E L'ARTE DEGLI ILLUMINISTI

In the name of reason and morality, Enlightenment philosophy placed mankind at the centre of the universe. With the emphasis put on individual sentiment, the social organisation that governed our insertion in the natural order thus displayed a system of thought tending towards happiness and progress. Among the Fine Arts, which were to contribute to the expression of the dignity, identity and well-being of the civilised peoples, architecture was invested with a mission to educate the public, that same "enlightened" *public* which educated itself in the theatres and salons and which was informed by the press of progress in the sciences, arts and literature.

Relativism, experimentalism and autonomy of perception (science's militant values) dominated political, economic and civic thought, thus breaking with the hitherto dominant religious ideologies. Such, at least, was the situation in around 1750 in the rich, stable states of northern Europe (a liberal, entrepreneurial Britain, and a France open to the propaganda of the *Encyclopédistes*) and in states governed by "enlightened despots" who were directly influenced by French philosophers (for example the role played by Voltaire in the court of Frederick II of Prussia, and that of Diderot in the court of Catherine II). Later on, Josef II in Vienna and Charles III in Naples and Madrid would try to apply these new ideas, but without disturbing the cultural supremacy of the church. In the Catholic states of southern Europe, and their colonies, religious patronage continued to favour the Baroque art of the Counter-Reformation, or Rococo which was its more modern manifestation (see Part I). It

Au nom de la raison et de la morale, la philosophie des Lumières place l'homme au centre de l'univers. L'organisation sociale qui régit son insertion dans l'ordre de la nature devient, avec la mise en valeur du sentiment individuel, le révélateur d'une pensée tendue vers l'idée de bonheur et de progrès. Parmi les beaux-arts, qui doivent contribuer à exprimer la dignité, l'identité et le bien-être des peuples civilisés, l'architecture s'est vue investie d'une mission d'éducatrice du *public,* ce même public « éclairé » qui se forme au théâtre, dans les salons, et que la presse fait participer aux progrès des sciences, des arts et des lettres.

Relativisme, expérimentalisme, autonomie de l'entendement (valeurs militantes de la science) imprègnent la pensée politique, économique et édilitaire, qui se sépare des idéologies religieuses jusqu'alors dominantes. Telle est du moins, vers 1750, la situation dans les pays septentrionaux riches et stables (l'Angleterre libérale, entreprenante, la France perméable à la propagande des Encyclopédistes), dans les États soumis à des « despotes éclairés » sous l'influence directe des philosophes français (on pense au rôle de Voltaire près de Frédéric II en Prusse, à celui de Diderot près de Catherine II en Russie). Plus tardivement dans le siècle, Joseph II à Vienne, Charles III à Naples puis à Madrid, s'efforceront d'appliquer les idées nouvelles sans ébranler toutefois l'hégémonie culturelle de l'Église. Le mécénat religieux, dans les pays catholiques de l'Europe du Sud et du Centre, comme dans les colonies, continue de favoriser l'art baroque issu de la Contre-Réforme ou le rococo qui apparaît comme son illustration la plus *moderne* (on l'a vu au chapitre Ier). C'est avec le sentiment de combattre cette esthétique de l'extase, libératrice de structures et de

In nome della ragione e della morale, la filosofia degli Illuministi colloca l'Uomo al centro dell'Universo. L'organizzazione sociale che registra la sua inserzione nell'ordine della natura diviene, con la valorizzazione del sentimento individuale, l'elemento rivelatore di un pensiero teso verso l'idea della fortuna e del progresso. Tra le Belle Arti, che devono contribuire ad esprimere la dignità, l'identità e il benessere dei popoli civili, l'architettura si è vista investire di una missione d'educatrice del pubblico, quello stesso pubblico "illuminato" che si forma a teatro, nei saloni e che la stampa rende partecipe dei progressi delle scienze, delle arti e delle lettere.

Relativismo, sperimentalismo, autonomia dell'intelletto (valori militanti della scienza) impregnano il pensiero politico, economico e edile che si separa dalle ideologie religiose fino ad allora dominanti. Tale è almeno, verso il 1750, la situazione nei paesi settentrionali ricchi e stabili (l'Inghilterra liberale, intraprendente, la Francia permeabile alla propaganda degli Enciclopedisti), negli Stati sottomessi a dei "despoti illuminati" sotto l'influenza diretta dei filosofi francesi (si pensi al ruolo di Voltaire presso Federico II di Prussia, a quello di Diderot presso Caterina II di Russia). Più avanti nel secolo, Giuseppe II a Vienna, Carlo III a Napoli poi a Madrid, si sforzeranno di applicare le nuove idee senza tuttavia far vacillare l'egemonia culturale della Chiesa. Il mecenatismo religioso, nei paesi cattolici dell'Europa del Sud e del Centro, come nelle colonie, continua a favorire l'arte barocca legata alla Controriforma o il Rococò che appariva come la sua illustrazione più *moderna* (come si è visto nel capitolo I). E' con l'intenzione di combattere questa

was with the idea of combating this aesthetic of religious ecstasy, producing uncontrolled arbitrary unstable and exuberant forms, that Diderot, for one, demanded that municipal authorities regenerate the arts so as to make them of civic use. "To bring consideration of the Fine Arts into the governance of peoples is to give them an importance that must be seen in their productions" (Grimm, *Literary correspondence*, 15 January 1763).

"Classical" morals and Liberal Arts

In their search for new models and an easily attainable consensus, philosophers and artists hunted out new lessons in the works of Antiquity. The important archaeological movement relativised the time-honoured domination of Roman civilisation in its publications and travels, as well as by means of digs in Pompeii, Herculaneum, Hadrian's villa, Etruscan tombs and Greek temples. As we have seen from the influence of Piranesi and his followers, Rome remained the geographical centre of *Antiquarianism*, the place where collections of art works and copies of archaeological artefacts were created and then exported, and where new theories concerning the history of Greek art were exchanged in the circles around Winckelmann and the painter Mengs. However, the Eternal City, though as flourishing as ever, was now merely the crucible of a huge artistic reform whose most tangible, precocious and durable examples were to be found in England and France.

In about 1750, the London-Paris-Rome axis dominated the history of the Classical revival of art and architecture. By means of a sort of creative mimesis, and thanks to a novel concept of civilisation, artists experimented with new formal combinations based on a modern appropriation of ancient sources. Not only had these become diversified (for example Doric, Etruscan and Egyptian forms were added to the Graeco-Roman tradition), but their perception as ruins or fragments allowed for imaginative reconstructions or else for visionary worlds to be founded

formes incontrôlées, arbitraires, instables et exubérantes, que Diderot, par exemple, engage les édiles de son temps à *régénérer* les arts afin de les rendre utiles à la vie civique : « Faire entrer la considération des beaux-arts dans l'art de gouverner les peuples, c'est leur donner une importance dont il faut que les production se ressentent » (Grimm, *Correspondance littéraire*, 15 janvier 1763).

Morale et arts libéraux « à l'antique »

En quête de nouveaux modèles et d'un consensus aisément compréhensible, philosophes et artistes vont chercher de nouvelles leçons dans les productions des Anciens. Le vaste mouvement archéologique qui, au bénéfice des voyages et des publications, accompagne les fouilles de Pompéi, d'Herculanum, de la villa d'Hadrien, des tombes étrusques et les relevés des temples grecs, relativise désormais l'autorité séculaire de la civilisation romaine. Certes, comme on l'a vu avec le rôle de Piranèse et de ses émules, Rome demeure le cœur géographique de l'*Anticomanie*, le lieu où se forment et d'où s'exportent les collections d'œuvres d'art, de copies et d'objets archéologiques, où s'échangent autour de Winckelmann et du peintre Mengs les nouvelles théories sur l'histoire de l'art grec. Mais la Ville éternelle, alors bien moins florissante qu'autrefois, n'est plus que le creuset d'une vaste réforme des arts dont l'expression la plus tangible, précoce et durable, s'observe en Angleterre et en France.

Autour de 1750, un axe Londres-Paris-Rome domine l'histoire du renouveau classique des arts et de l'architecture. Par une sorte de mimétisme de création, à travers le concept naissant de civilisation, les artistes vont expérimenter de nouvelles combinaisons formelles dont l'idée s'appuie sur l'appropriation moderne des sources antiques ; non seulement celles-ci apparaissent diversifiées (au gréco-romain s'ajoute le dorique, l'étrusque, l'égyptien…), mais leur perception sous forme de ruines, de fragments, autorise des restitutions imaginatives ou des visions imaginaires, pétries de sentiments. La moralisation souhaitée par les philosophes et les édiles, à travers l'exemple d'Athènes ou de Rome, se formule dans la théorie du progrès d'un ordre urbain

estetica dell'estasi, liberatrice di strutture e di forme incontrollate, arbitrarie, instabili ed esuberanti, che Diderot, per esempio, esorta le autorità municipali del suo tempo a rigenerare le arti al fine di renderle utili alla vita civica: "Fare entrare la considerazione delle Belle Arti nell'arte di governare i popoli, vuol dire dare loro un'importanza di cui bisogna che le produzioni portino le conseguenze." (Grimm, *Correspondance Littéraire*, 15 gennaio 1763).

Morale ed arti liberali "all'antica"

In cerca di nuovi modelli e di un consenso facilmente comprensibile, filosofi ed artisti cercheranno delle nuove lezioni nella produzione degli Antichi. Il vasto movimento archeologico che, con beneficio dei viaggi e delle pubblicazioni, accompagna gli scavi di Pompei, di Ercolano, della Villa di Adriano, delle tombe etrusche e dei resti dei templi greci, relativizza ormai l'autorità secolare della civiltà romana. Certamente, come si è visto con il ruolo di Piranesi e dei suoi seguaci, Roma resta il cuore geografico dell'*Anticomania*, il luogo dove si formano e dove si esportano le collezioni di opere d'arte, di copie e di oggetti archeologici, dove si scambiano intorno a Winckelmann e al pittore Mengs le nuove teorie sulla storia dell'arte greca. Ma la Città Eterna, allora certamente meno fiorente che un tempo, non è nient'altro che il crogiolo di una vasta riforma delle arti la cui espressione più tangibile, precoce e duratura, si osserva in Inghilterra e in Francia.

Intorno al 1750, un asse Londra-Parigi-Roma domina la storia del rinnovamento classico delle arti e dell'architettura. Attraverso una sorta di mimetismo di creazione, attraverso il concetto nascente di civiltà, gli artisti sperimenteranno delle nuove combinazioni formali la cui idea si fonda sull'appropriazione in chiave moderna delle fonti antiche; non solo quelle appaiono diversificate (al greco-romano si aggiunge il dorico, l'etrusco, l'egizio…), ma la loro percezione sotto forma di rovine, di frammenti, autorizza delle ricostruzioni fantastiche o delle visioni immaginarie, intrise di sentimenti. La moralizzazione auspicata dai filosofi e dalle autorità municipali, attraverso gli esempi di Atene o di Roma, trova

on sentiment. The moralisation desired by philosophers and politicians, from Roman and Greek examples, was expressed as a progress of urban order by means of the *Liberal Arts*. To quote the prospectus for the *Encyclopédie Méthodique*, devoted to the "Fine Arts" (1788): "For the Greeks and the Romans, these arts took their name from *liberty* the first and greatest good, because only free men learnt about them". The *beautification* of cities became a topical concern because their populations rapidly increased in wealthy countries during the eighteenth century. Already, at the height of the Rococo period, Voltaire exclaimed when, like Colbert, he deplored the abandonment of Paris for Versailles: "Those who come after me will do that which I only imagined … Your theatres will be worthy of the immortal works presented there. New squares and public markets built below colonnades will decorate Paris like ancient Rome." (*Le Temple du Goût*, 1733.)

For the last fifty years, art historians have called this revival *Neo-Classicism*. They refer to the continuation of this so-called "style" into the nineteenth century. This is explained, in certain countries, by how long it took Baroque to die out; in other countries, by the new influence of scientific archaeology on the generalised eclecticism of the Industrial Revolution. Despite its success, the adjective "Neo-Classical" keeps its pejorative connotation, which derives from a gross simplification of how Antiquity was *imitated*. An idea of pastiche predominates. On the contrary, the Enlightenment era displays an astonishing diversity of formal research and expression, created by the exploration of sentiments (symbolic characters), the observation of nature (geometry of a simple, balanced language) and numerous urban projects (well-being and civic morals). The introduction of the landscape (walkways, parks and gardens with panoramas and picturesque manufactories) is the corollary of this civic hold on architectural creativity. This desire for a Classical harmony clearly expressing its social function was first seen in a change of tastes in the decorative arts and in a greater figurative freedom in drawings, before opening out on to revolutionary or utopian perspectives.

à promouvoir avec l'exercice des *Arts libéraux* : « Chez les Grecs et les Romains, ces arts tirèrent leur dénomination du premier et du plus grand de tous les biens, la liberté. Ils furent appelés *libéraux*, parce qu'ils faisaient partie de l'éducation des seuls hommes libres », lit-on dans le prospectus de l'*Encyclopédie Méthodique*, consacré aux *Beaux-Arts* (1788). L'*embellissement* des villes dont la population augmente à un rythme accéléré au XVIIIᵉ siècle, dans les pays prospères, est à l'ordre du jour. Déjà, en plein épanouissement du rococo, alors qu'il déplore, comme l'a fait Colbert, l'abandon de Paris pour Versailles, Voltaire s'exclame : « Ceux qui viendront après moi feront seulement ce que j'ai imaginé (…). Les salles de vos spectacles seront dignes des ouvrages immortels qu'on y présente. De nouvelles places et des marchés publics construits sous des colonnades décoreront Paris comme l'ancienne Rome » (*Le Temple du Goût*, 1733).

Les historiens de l'art, depuis un bon demi-siècle, ont dénommé ce renouveau classique du XVIIIᵉ siècle *Néoclassicisme*. Ils tiennent compte des prolongements de ce prétendu « style » jusqu'au milieu du XIXᵉ siècle. Ceux-ci s'expliquent, pour certains pays, par le retard avec lequel le baroque s'est estompé ; pour d'autres pays, par de nouvelles incidences de l'archéologie scientifique sur l'éclectisme généralisé du Siècle de l'industrie. Malgré son succès, l'adjectif « néoclassique » conserve une connotation péjorative qui provient de la simplification extrême avec laquelle est envisagé le concept d'*imitation* de l'Antiquité. L'idée de pastiche prédomine. À l'inverse, le Siècle des lumières montre l'étonnante diversité des recherches formelles et expressives auxquelles ont donné lieu l'exploration des sentiments (caractères symboliques), l'observation de la nature (géométrie d'un langage simple, équilibré) et la multiplication des programmes urbains (bien-être et morale civile). L'introduction du paysage (promenades, jardins et parcs ornés de « points de vue » et de fabriques pittoresques) est le corollaire de cette emprise de l'édilité sur la création architecturale. Celle-ci, aspirant à une harmonie classique clairement signifiante dans son rôle social, s'exprime d'abord par un changement de goût dans les arts décoratifs et par une grande liberté de figuration dans le dessin, avant d'ouvrir des perspectives révolutionnaires et

formulazione nella teoria del progresso di un ordine urbano da promuovere con l'esercizio delle arti liberali: "Presso i Greci e i Romani, queste arti derivano la loro denominazione dal primo e più grande di tutti i beni, la libertà. Esse furono chiamate liberali, perché facevano parte dell'educazione dei soli uomini liberi" si legge nel prospetto dell'*Encyclopédie Méthodique*, consacrata alle *Belle Arti* (1788.) L'abbellimento delle città la cui popolazione aumenta a un ritmo accelerato nel XVIII secolo, nei paesi prosperi, è all'ordine del giorno. Già, durante la piena fioritura del Rococò, quando deplora l'abbandono di Parigi per Versailles, Voltaire esclama: "Quelli che verranno dopo di me faranno solamente ciò che io ho immaginato (…). Le sale dei vostri spettacoli saranno degne delle opere immortali che vi si rappresentano. Delle nuove piazze e dei mercati pubblici costruiti sotto delle colonne percorreranno Parigi come l'antica Roma" (Il Tempio del Gusto, 1733).

Gli storici dell'arte, dopo un buon mezzo secolo, hanno chiamato questo rinnovamento classico del XVIII secolo, Neoclassicismo. Essi tengono conto dei prolungamenti di questo preteso "stile" fino alla metà del XIX secolo. Questi si spiegano, per certi paesi, con il ritardo col quale il Barocco è stato attenuato, per altri paesi, attraverso i nuovi influssi dell'archeologia scientifica sull'eclettismo generalizzato del secolo dell'Industria. Nonostante il suo successo, l'aggettivo neoclassico conserva una connotazione peggiorativa che proviene dalla semplificazione estrema con la quale è esaminato il concetto di *imitazione* dell'Antichità. Predomina l'idea di pastiche. Al contrario, il Secolo dei Lumi mostra la strabiliante diversità delle ricerche formali ed espressive originate dall'esplorazione dei sentimenti (caratteri simbolici), l'osservazione della natura (geometria di un linguaggio semplice, equilibrato) e la moltiplicazione dei programmi urbani (benessere morale e civile). L'introduzione del paesaggio (passeggiate, giardini e parchi ornati di "punti di vista" e di fabbriche pittoresche) è il corollario di questa impresa dell'edilizia sulla creazione architettonica. Questa, aspirante a un'armonia classica chiaramente dotata di significato nel suo ruolo sociale, si esprime in principio attraverso un cambiamento del gusto nelle arti decorative e attraverso una grande libertà figurativa

However it is examined, the new theory of *the art of building* included a desire for poetic expression to be among the basic elements of any concept of architecture. The ancient order and its system of architectural ornamentation, as with history and mythology for painting, sculpture, literature and opera, became ever more strongly seen as a re-invention of the natural beauty of the world. Germain Boffrand, one of the greatest architects of the first half of the century, acted as the prophet of this *poetic architectural art*, whose precepts were based on ancient literary traditions. He wrote: "Architecture, even though it seems that it aims merely to use material things, can offer different genres which can make its parts animated, so to speak, by the different characters that it conveys. In its composition, an edifice expresses, as the theatre shows whether a scene is pastoral or tragic, that it is a temple or palace, a public edifice for certain uses or a private house. By means of their decoration, these different edifices must inform the spectator of their purpose; if they do not, they sin against expression and are not what they should be." (*Livre d'Architecture*, 1745.)

Palladian and antiquarian Britain

Proud of its insularity, Great Britain was politically stable in the eighteenth century and dominated by an entrepreneurial aristocracy which based its power not only on foreign trade and fledgling industries, but also on the exploitation of its large country properties. The golden age of noble rural habitations saw the development of sumptuous country houses. Cultivated gentlemen equated these administrative centres and places of prestige with the "antique" villas that Palladio (1508-1580) had built on the terra firma of Venezia in the middle of the sixteenth century. This British *Palladianism*, founded by Inigo Jones at the beginning of the seventeenth century, flourished in the eighteenth century and in turn influenced world architecture from Russia to the Americas. A Scotsman, Cameron, and two Americans, Jefferson and Latrobe, were among the most famous practitioners of this worldwide trend. Palladio's style, which was

utopiques. Dans tous les cas de figure, une nouvelle théorie de l'*art de bâtir* intègre la volonté d'expression poétique parmi les composantes initiales de la conception de l'architecture. L'ordre antique et son système d'ornementation dans le domaine de l'architecture, comme l'histoire ou la mythologie dans le domaine de la peinture, de la sculpture, de la littérature ou de l'opéra, s'affirment plus que jamais comme une émanation des beautés naturelles du monde, réinventées. Un des grands architectes de la première moitié du siècle, Germain Boffrand, joue le rôle de prophète de cet *art poétique* architectural dont les préceptes s'appuient sur la tradition littéraire antique : « L'architecte, dit-il, quoiqu'il semble que son objet ne soit que l'emploi de ce qui est matériel, est susceptible de différents genres qui rendent ses parties pour ainsi dire animées par les différents caractères qu'elle fait sentir. Un édifice par sa composition exprime, comme sur un théâtre, que la scène est pastorale ou tragique, que c'est un temple ou un palais, un édifice public à certains usages, ou une maison particulière. Ces différents édifices, par la manière dont ils sont décorés, doivent annoncer au spectateur leur destination ; et s'ils ne le font pas, ils pèchent contre l'expression, et ne sont pas ce qu'ils devraient être. » (*Livre d'Architecture*, 1745).

L'Angleterre palladienne et anticomane

L'Angleterre fière de son insularité, politiquement équilibrée, est dominée au XVIIe siècle par une aristocratie entreprenante qui fonde sa puissance, non seulement sur le commerce international et l'industrie naissante, mais aussi sur l'exploitation des grands domaines fonciers. L'âge d'or de l'habitat rural noble voit se développer de somptueuses *country houses*, centres administratifs et lieux de prestige que les gentilshommes cultivés identifient aux villas « à l'antique » dont Palladio (1508-1580) avait orné la terre ferme de Vénétie au milieu du XVIe siècle. Ce *Palladianisme* britannique, introduit au début du XVIIe siècle par Inigo Jones, s'épanouit au XVIIIe siècle et influence à son tour l'architecture mondiale, de la Russie au Nouveau Monde : l'Écossais Cameron, les Américains Jefferson et Latrobe, figurent parmi les plus célèbres représentants de ce courant international. Le style de Palladio, architecte

nel disegno, prima di aprire delle prospettive rivoluzionarie ed utopiche. In tutti i casi una nuova teoria dell'arte del costruire integra la volontà d'espressione poetica tra le componenti iniziali della concezione di architettura. L'ordine antico e il suo sistema d'ornamento nel dominio dell'architettura, come la storia o la mitologia nel dominio della pittura, della scultura, della letteratura o dell'opera, si affermano più che mai come un'emanazione delle bellezze naturali del mondo, reinventate. Uno dei grandi architetti della prima metà del secolo, Germain Boffrand, riveste il ruolo del profeta di questa arte poetica architettonica i cui precetti si appoggiano sulla tradizione letteraria antica: "L'architettura, per quanto sembri che il suo oggetto non sia che l'impiego di questo o quel materiale, può adottare diversi generi che rendono le parti da essa create per così dire animate da differenti caratteri che essa fa sentire. Come un teatro può rivelare che la scena è pastorale o tragica, così un edificio, attraverso la sua composizione, manifesta se si tratta di un tempio o di un palazzo, di un edificio pubblico destinato a certi usi, o di una casa privata. Questi differenti edifici, attraverso la maniera in cui sono decorati, devono annunciare allo spettatore la loro destinazione; e se non lo fanno, sono in difetto di espressione, e non sono ciò che dovrebbero essere" (*Livre d'Architecture*, 1745).

L'Inghilterra palladiana e anticomane

L'Inghilterra, fiera della sua insularità, politicamente equilibrata, è dominata nel XVIII secolo da un'aristocrazia intraprendente che fonda la sua potenza non solo sul commercio internazionale e l'industria nascente, ma anche sullo sfruttamento dei grandi domini fondiari. L'epoca d'oro degli edifici rurali nobili vede svilupparsi delle sontuose *country houses*, centri amministrativi e luoghi di prestigio che i gentiluomini dotti assimilano alle ville "all'antica" di cui Palladio (1508-1580) aveva ornato la terraferma di Venezia nella metà del XVI secolo. Questo Palladianesimo britannico, introdotto all'inizio del XVII secolo da Inigo Jones, si espande nel XVIII secolo e influenza a sua volta l'architettura mondiale, dalla Russia al Nuovo Mondo: lo scozzese Cameron, gli americani

supposed to have been an attempt to approach as closely as possible the mythical architecture of the Greeks (as described by Vetruvius), could easily absorb new archaeological ornamentation and new structural combinations suited to rural or urban dwellings or else new public monuments. While London, Edinburgh and Dublin were experiencing a deliberate if inconsistent antiquarian development, the finest example of classical unity was produced in Bath, a town modelled by roundabouts, semicircles and snaking streets that are both leafy and monumental, which are the masterpieces of John Wood senior and junior (between 1754 and 1770).

Encouraged by the Grand Tour around Europe and especially Italy, which was an obligatory part of any young gentleman's education, and backed up by study tours made by British artists in Rome, *Antiquarianism* became part of the theoretical preoccupations that typified the Enlightenment, especially in the dialectic of the imitation of art and of nature. Following the work of Colen Campbell (*Vitruvius Britannicus*, 1715), of Lord Burlington, William Kent or John Wood, numerous architects, theorists and archaeologists opened the way to the precocious eclecticism that characterises British architecture during the second half of the eighteenth century. For example, Roger Morris stands out as a precursor of standardised methods of geometric compositions (*Lectures on Architecture*, 1734) which were to be such a success in the nineteenth century. Stuart and Revett, the rivals of Le Roy, published images of a squat, baseless Greek Doric (*The Antiquities of Athens*, 1762). Meanwhile, British Piranesians back from Rome (but also from other lands such as Dalmatia, Sicily, Syria, even China!) successfully combined theory with practice. The two greatest architects of the time, William Chambers (1723-1796) and Robert Adam (1728-1792), opened up an eclectic current that was at once faithful to native traditions, soaked with French aesthetics and underpinned by archaeological discoveries. Chambers travelled widely in his youth, was a founder member of the Royal Academy (1768), the official architect of George III, studied under Blondel in Paris and was a disciple of Laugier. In

réputé pour avoir cherché à s'approcher au plus près de l'architecture mythique des Grecs à la Renaissance (selon ce qu'en transmettait Vitruve), peut sans dommage s'enrichir de formes ornementales archéologiques, de nouvelles combinaisons structurelles adaptées à l'habitat rural, urbain et aux nouveaux monuments publics. Tandis que Londres, Edimbourg, Dublin connaissent un urbanisme à l'antique volontaire, mais encore décousu, le plus bel exemple d'unité classique se réalise à Bath, ville modelée en ronds-points, hémicycles et rues serpentines verdoyantes et monumentales à la fois, chef-d'œuvre des John Wood, père et fils (entre 1754-1770).

Favorisée par le « Grand Tour » (voyage sur le Continent et principalement en Italie), indispensable à l'éducation de tous les jeunes Lords, relayée par les séjours de formation à Rome des artistes britanniques, l'*Anticomanie* s'inscrit dans des préoccupations théoriques qui signalent l'esprit des Lumières, notamment à travers la dialectique de l'imitation de l'art des origines et de la nature. Poursuivant l'œuvre des Cohen Campbell (*Vitruvius Britannicus*, 1715), Lord Burlington, William Kent ou John Wood, de nombreux architectes, théoriciens ou archéologues, vont ouvrir la voie à un éclectisme précoce qui caractérise l'architecture anglaise de la seconde moitié du XVIIIᵉ siècle. Roger Morris, par exemple, apparaît comme un précurseur des méthodes standardisées de compositions géométriques (*Lectures on Architecture,* 1734) qui connaîtront un grand succès au XIXᵉ siècle. Stuart et Revett, rivaux du Français Le Roy, diffusent outre-Manche les images du dorique grec, trapu et sans base (*The Antiquities of Athens*, 1762), tandis que les piranésiens britanniques, de retour de Rome (mais aussi d'autres contrées : Dalmatie, Sicile, Syrie, Chine même !), conjuguent avec succès la théorie et la pratique. Les deux plus grands architectes de l'époque, William Chambers (1723-1796) et Robert Adam (1728-1792), s'ouvrent aux courants éclectiques, à la fois respectueux des traditions autochtones, imprégnés des théories esthétiques françaises et subjugués par le renouveau archéologique. Grand voyageur dans sa jeunesse, fondateur de la Royal Academy (1768), architecte officiel de George III, élève à Paris de Blondel et disciple de Laugier, Chambers publie notamment ses dessins

Jefferson e Latrobe, figurano tra i più celebri rappresentanti di questa corrente internazionale. Lo stile del Palladio, architetto famoso per aver cercato di avvicinarsi maggiormente all'architettura mitica di Greci nel Rinascimento (secondo l'insegnamento di Vitruvio), può senza pericolo arricchirsi delle forme ornamentali archeologiche, di nuove combinazioni strutturali adattate all'habitat rurale, urbano e ai nuovi monumenti pubblici. Mentre Londra, Edimburgo, Dublino conoscono un urbanesimo all'antica volontario, ma ancora incoerente, il più bell'esempio di unità classica si realizza a Bath, città moderna a rondò, emicicli e vie serpentine verdeggianti e monumentali allo stesso tempo, capolavori dei John Wood, padre e figli (tra il 1754-1770).

Favorita dal "Gran Tour" (viaggio sul Continente e principalmente in Italia), indispensabile all'educazione di tutti i giovani Lords, rafforzata dai soggiorni di formazione a Roma degli artisti britannici, l'Anticomania si iscrive nelle preoccupazioni teoriche che segnalano lo spirito degli Illuministi, in particolare attraverso la dialettica dell'imitazione dell'arte delle origini e della natura. Proseguendo l'opera dei Colen Campbell (*Vitruvius Britannicus*, 1715), Lord Burlington, William Kent o John Wood, numerosi architetti, teorici o archeologi apriranno la via ad un eclettismo precoce che caratterizza l'architettura inglese della seconda metà del XVIII secolo. Roger Morris, per esempio, appare come un precursore dei metodi standardizzati di composizioni geometriche (*Lecture on Architecture*, 1734) che conosceranno un grande successo nel XIX secolo. Stuart e Revett, rivali del francese Le Roy, diffondono oltremanica le immagini del dorico greco, tozzo e senza base (*The Antiquities of Athens*, 1762), mentre i piranesiani britannici, di ritorno da Roma (ma anche da altre contrade: Dalmazia, Sicilia, Siria, perfino la Cina), coniugano con successo teoria e pratica. I due più grandi architetti dell'epoca, William Chambers (1723-1796) e Robert Adam (1728-1792), si aprono alle correnti eclettiche, allo stesso tempo rispettosi delle tradizioni autoctone, impregnate di teorie estetiche francesi e soggiogate dal rinnovamento archeologico. Grande viaggiatore nella sua giovinezza, fondatore della Royal Academy (1768), architetto ufficiale di Giorgio III, allievo a Parigi

particular, he published architectural models taken down in China (1757), a *Treatise on Civil Architecture* (1759) and the plans and designs for Kew Gardens (1763), a seminal work of landscape gardening, which the French term "Anglo-Chinese". This Piranesian, who became a Palladian at the start of his career, introduced into Britain the French version of "Greek" taste (Casino, Marino, near Dublin, 1758), not only in architecture, but also in furniture and in the applied arts, for which he designed models for the royal family. His masterpiece, Somerset House (1776-1786), a huge government office building dominating the banks of the Thames, swarms with powerful arrangements, arcades and bossed ornamentation, reminiscent of Piranesi's repertoire and here used for State architecture. Robert Adam and his brother James tirelessly adapted ancient mansions to "modern taste", mixing together ancestral values on the exterior (sometimes Gothic or Elizabethan) with the Classical revival. They published many of their designs in *Works in Architecture* (1773-1779). Adapting the *Pompeian* (or else "Etruscan") style to walls, ceilings and to the furnishings of sumptuous salons, galleries and halls, the Adams brothers provided a lightened, elegant, richly reflective version of the *arabesque* geometrical style or the *grotesque*, which their French friends Clérisseau and Bélanger, both ardent Anglophiles, also specialised in. The treatment of space, which characterised Robert Adam, resulted in airy virtuoso stairwells in Syon House, Middlesex (1762-1769), the great salon in Saint James's, London (1772), Osterley Park, Middlesex (1775-1779), or Culzean Castle, Ayrshire (1779-1790). The linking together of rooms was set off by the transparency of the intercolumniation and the mobility of the volumes that were varied and contrasted thanks to surprise effects created by chiaroscuro. No less prolific and inventive, James Wyatt (Heaton Hall, Lancashire, 1772), Henry Holland, George Dance the Younger, Thomas Harrison and John Soane created a new insular Classicism, that was also well suited to landscaping large natural spaces inspired by Poussin's paintings and the Italian *vedutistas*.

d'architecture relevés en Chine (1757), un *Treatise on Civil Architecture* (1759) et les plans et dessins de *Kew Gardens* (1763), œuvre capitale de l'histoire du jardin paysager dit également, en France, « anglo-chinois ». Piranésien devenu palladien pour débuter sa carrière, Chambers introduit en Grande-Bretagne le goût « à la grecque » à la française (Casino, Marino, près de Dublin, 1758), non seulement dans l'architecture, mais aussi dans le mobilier et les arts appliqués pour lesquels il dessine des modèles destinés à la Couronne. Son chef-d'œuvre, l'immense palais abritant des services publics, qui domine les berges de la Tamise à Londres, Somerset House (1776-1786), décline des ordonnances puissantes, arcades et parements à bossages, qui rappellent le répertoire de Piranèse et illustrent ici l'architecture d'État. Robert Adam et son frère James, infatigables aménageurs d'espaces au « goût du jour » dans d'anciennes demeures où ils amalgament, à l'extérieur, les valeurs ancestrales (parfois gothiques ou élisabéthaines) avec le renouveau classique, ont publié d'innombrables dessins dans leur *Works in Architecture* (1773-1779). Adaptant le style *pompéien* (on parle aussi d'« étrusque ») aux parois, aux plafonds et dans le mobilier de somptueux salons, galeries et vestibules, les frères Adam ont donné une version allégée, élégante et riche d'intention, du style d'*arabesques* géométriques ou de *grotesques* dont en France leurs amis Clérisseau et Bélanger, anglomanes notoires, se faisaient également une spécialité. Le traitement de l'espace, caractéristique de Robert Adam, culmine dans les cages d'escalier aériennes et techniquement virtuoses : Syon House, Middlesex (1762-1769) ; Saint Jame's Square, grand salon, Londres (1772) ; Osterley Park, Middlesex (1775-1779) ; Culzean Castle, Ayshire (1779-1790). Les enchaînements de pièces y sont favorisés par la transparence des entrecolonnements, la mobilité des volumes variés et contrastés grâce à des effets de surprise que le clair-obscur sollicite. Non moins inventifs et prolifiques, James Wyatt (Heaton Hall, Lancashire, 1772), Henry Holland, George Dance le Jeune, Thomas Harrison et John Soane, illustrent un nouveau classicisme insulaire, au demeurant admirablement adapté au style *paysager* des grands espaces naturels qui s'inspirent des tableaux de Poussin ou des védutistes italiens.

di Blondel e discepolo di Laugier, Chambers pubblica in particolare i suoi disegni d'architettura realizzati in Cina (1757), un *Treatise on Civil Architecture* (1759) e le piante e i disegni di Kew Gardens (1763), opera capitale della storia del giardino paesaggistico detto ugualmente, in Francia, "anglo-cinese". Piranesiano divenuto palladiano per iniziare la sua carriera, Chambers introduce in Gran Bretagna il gusto "alla greca" alla francese (Casino, Marino, vicino a Dublino, 1758), non solo in architettura, ma anche nel mobilio e nelle arti applicate per le quali disegna dei modelli destinati alla Corona. Il suo capolavoro, Somerset House l'immenso palazzo destinato ai servizi pubblici, che domina le sponde del Tamigi a Londra, (1776-1786), declina degli ordini potenti, arcate e rivestimenti a bugne, che ricordano il repertorio di Piranesi ed illustrano così l'architettura di stato. Robert Adam e suo fratello James, infaticabili pianificatori degli spazi secondo il "gusto del giorno" in antiche dimore in cui si mescolano, all'esterno, valori atavici (a volte gotici o elisabettiani) con il rinnovamento classico, hanno pubblicato numerosissimi disegni nel loro *Works in Architecture* (1773-1779). Adattando lo stile pompeiano (si parla anche di "etrusco") alle pareti, ai soffitti e al mobilio dei sontuosi saloni, gallerie e vestiboli, i fratelli Adam hanno donato una versione alleggerita, elegante e ricca di intenzione, dello stile d'*arabeschi* geometrici o di *grottesche* di cui in Francia i loro amici Clérisseau e Bélanger, famosi anglomani, facevano la loro specialità. Il trattamento dello spazio, caratteristico di Robert Adam, culmina nelle sue trombe delle scale aeree e tecnicamente virtuose: Syon House, Middlesex; 1762-1769, Saint James Square, Grand Salon, Londres, 1772; Osterly Park, Middlesex, 1775-1779; Culzen Castle, Ayshire, 1779-1790. La concatenazione dei locali qui è favorita dalla trasparenza degli intercolunni, la mobilità dei volumi variati e in contrasto grazie agli effetti di sorpresa sollecitati dal chiaroscuro. Non meno inventivi e prolifici, James Wyatt (Heaton Hall, Lancashire, 1772), Henry Holland, George Dance junior, Thomas Harrison e John Soane, illustrano un nuovo classicismo insulare, del resto straordinariamente adattato allo stile paesaggistico dei grandi spazi naturali che si ispirano ai quadri di Poussin o dei vedutisti italiani.

France
and the "Greek" taste

In France under Louis XV (1715-1774), the Classical revival began in the middle of his reign with the advent of "Greek" taste. This fact is still not taken properly into account by art historians who classify styles according to reigns, political periods and formal evolutions. For the chronological appearance and the aesthetic affirmation of such styles as Régence, Louis XV, Louis XVI or Directoire are far more complex than their names imply. Rocaille ornamentation appeared during the Régence and flourished until the middle of the eighteenth century, but it has wrongly been equated with the Louis XV style. In fact, alongside the modernising trend which European Baroque expressed in Rococo architecture, there was, as we have seen, a survival of the "grand style" or "grand taste" in French monumental architecture, which derived from the precepts of the *Académie royale d'architecture* and the examples of Perrault and Hardouin-Mansart, followed by Jacques V. Gabriel and J-A Gabriel, Louis XV's Royal Architects. Great artists such as Cotte or Boffrand produced both Rocaille decorations and Classical buildings. Meanwhile, between 1735 and 1745, Servandoni in Paris (the façade of Saint Sulpice) and Soufflot in Lyons (Hôtel Dieu) tried to revive the Graeco-Roman example of expressive order and regular yet powerful decorative effects. The call of Rome seemed irresistible and these two innovators were to be followed by an entire generation of French Piranesians who let their imaginations be guided by a free interpretation of archaeological models. A second Louis XV style, during the last twenty years of his reign, could be termed a "Greek" style. It was stripped down, varied, and was to run through the next reign, before experiencing a second purification at the end of the 1780s and finally disappearing into the more blatant eclecticism of the First Empire.

One journey made by a Frenchman, in imitation of the British Grand Tour, stands out for its symbolic importance and its immediate consequences on France's arts. It was when M. de Vandières, Mme de Pompadour's brother, who was to

La France
et le goût « à la grecque »

En France, sous Louis XV (1715-1774), le renouveau classique commence au milieu du règne par l'épisode du « goût à la grecque », encore trop peu pris en compte par les historiens de l'art qui classent en styles, selon les règnes et les périodes politiques, l'évolution des formes artistiques. Or l'apparition chronologique et l'affirmation esthétique de ces formes sont bien plus complexes que le laisse apparaître la nomenclature des styles : Régence, Louis XV, Louis XVI, Directoire, etc. L'ornement rocaille est formé sous la Régence et il s'épanouit jusqu'au milieu du XVIIIe siècle, mais on l'a abusivement identifié au style Louis XV. En effet, parallèlement à cette tendance moderne, que l'Europe baroque illustre dans l'architecture rococo, nous avons vu qu'en France l'architecture monumentale perpétue le « grand style » ou « grand goût » issu des préceptes de l'Académie royale d'architecture et des exemples de Perrault ou de Hardouin-Mansart dont se réclament les deux premiers (et derniers) architectes de Louis XV, Jacques V et J.-A. Gabriel. De grands artistes comme de Cotte ou Boffrand réalisent simultanément des décors rocaille et des édifices classiques, tandis que, dès les années 1735-1745, un Servandoni à Paris (façade de l'église Saint-Sulpice) ou un Soufflot à Lyon (Hôtel-Dieu), cherchent à revivifier l'exemple gréco-romain de l'ordre expressif et de son appareil décoratif régulier et puissant. L'appel de Rome paraît irrésistible et ces deux novateurs seront suivis par la génération des Piranésiens français qui laissent guider leur imagination suivant la libre interprétation des modèles archéologiques. Un second style Louis XV, durant les vingt dernières années du règne, mérite d'être appelé « à la grecque » : épuré, varié, il accompagnera le règne suivant, avant de connaître une seconde épuration à la fin des années 1780, pour disparaître enfin avec l'Empire dans un éclectisme plus voyant.

À l'imitation du « Grand Tour » des Anglais, un voyage français retient particulièrement l'attention par son rayonnement symbolique et ses conséquences immédiates sur les arts du royaume. C'est celui qu'effectua à Rome, en 1750, le frère de Mme de Pompadour, M. de Vandières, appelé à

La Francia e il gusto
"alla greca"

In Francia, sotto Luigi XV (1715-1774), il rinnovamento classico comincia a metà del regno con l'episodio del "gusto alla greca", ancora troppo poco preso in considerazione dagli storici dell'arte che classificano in stili, secondo i regni e i periodi politici, l'evoluzione delle forme artistiche. Ora, l'apparizione cronologica e l'affermazione estetica di queste forme sono ben più complesse di quanto non lasci trasparire la nomenclatura degli stili: Reggenza, Luigi XV, Luigi XVI, Direttorio, ecc. L'ornamento Rocaille si forma sotto la Reggenza e si espande fino alla metà del XVIII secolo, ma lo si è abusivamente assimilato allo stile Luigi XV. In effetti, parallelamente a questa tendenza moderna, che l'Europa barocca manifesta nell'architettura Rococò, abbiamo visto che in Francia l'architettura monumentale perpetua il "gran stile" o il "gran gusto" nato dai precetti dell'*Académie Royale d'Architecture* e dagli esempi di Perrault o di Hardouin-Mansart e dove Jacques V e J.-A. Gabriel rivendicano di essere i primi (e ultimi) architetti di Luigi XV. Dei grandi artisti come de Cotte o Boffrand realizzano allo stesso tempo delle decorazioni rocaille e degli edifici classici, mentre dagli anni 1735-1745, un Servandoni a Parigi (facciata della chiesa di Saint-Sulpice) o un Soufflot a Lione (Hôtel Dieu), cercano di far rivivere l'esempio greco-romano dell'ordine espressivo e del suo apparato decorativo regolare e potente. Il richiamo di Roma sembra irresistibile e questi due innovatori saranno seguiti dalla generazione dei piranesiani francesi che lasciano guidare la loro immaginazione seguendo la libera interpretazione dei modelli archeologici. Un secondo stile Luigi XV, durante gli ultimi venti anni del regno, merita di essere chiamato "alla greca": depurato, variato, esso accompagnerà il regno seguente, prima di conoscere una seconda purificazione alla fine degli anni 1780, per sparire infine con l'impero in un eclettismo più vistoso.

A imitazione del "Gran Tour" degli Inglesi un viaggio francese attira particolarmente l'attenzione per la sua diffusione simbolica e le sue conseguenze immediate sulle arti del regno. Si tratta di quello che effettuò a Roma, nel 1750, il

succeed his uncle as general director of the King's Buildings, Gardens, Arts and Workshops (a post he was to hold as the Marquis de Marigny, between 1751 and 1774) went to Rome in 1750. The architects Soufflot and Dumont, as well as the illustrator-engraver Cochin (later the perpetual secretary of the *Académie royale de peinture et de sculpture*) were his enlightened mentors. Soufflot even went to Paestum, where he drew the Doric temples that Dumont published in 1764. Its success was due to the great interest in original Greek art which had already been created by the rival publications of his artistic colleagues Le Roy (*Les Ruines des plus beaux monuments de la Grèce*, 1758) and Stuart and Revett in London. The expression "Greek taste", which was used at the time, stood for a new movement of the *Antiquarian* decorative arts then, by extension, of painting and architecture, which aimed to recover authentic classical Greek models and use them to promote modern artistic progress (because of their exemplary efficiency in civil society). Cochin organised a press campaign against ornamental Rocaille productions and mocked architects that subjugated their art to the caprices of an unreasoned undulating form (*Supplication aux orfèvres, and Lettre à l'abbé R*, in *Mercure de France*, December 1754 and February 1755). Around Cochin and other famous scholars, antiquarians, collectors, polygraphs, Caylus, Mariette and the architect-archaeologist Le Roy, Paris became the main centre of a new production of decorative arts inspired from the objects and fragments of recently discovered ancient monuments. Among Europe's most widely distributed publications of engravings can be cited those of F. de Neufforge (*Recueil élémentaire d'architecture*, 8 vols., Paris, 1757-1768) and Delafosse (*Nouvelle iconologie historique*, Paris, 1767-1785). From such works, architects, ornamenters and master masons from Bordeaux to Lille and from Brussels to Stockholm learnt new lessons.

The new structures and decorative patterns varied according to a stately, intentionally heavy style: strict geometric figures, regular scrolls, wave scrolls, symmetrical friezes, flutes, bucranes, vases, tripods, oak garlands, triglyphs, guttae, and

succéder à son oncle à la direction générale des Bâtiments, Jardins, Arts et Manufactures du roi (charge qu'il remplira sous le nom de marquis de Marigny, entre 1751 et 1774). Les architectes Soufflot et Dumont, et le dessinateur-graveur Cochin, futur secrétaire perpétuel de l'Académie royale de peinture et de sculpture, sont ses mentors éclairés. Soufflot se rend même à Paestum où il dessine les temples doriques que Dumont publie en 1764. Son succès bénéficie de l'extrême curiosité pour l'art grec originel qu'ont déjà fait découvrir les publications concurrentes de ses confrères, Le Roy (*Les ruines des plus beaux monuments de la Grèce*, 1758) et Stuart et Revett à Londres. L'expression « goût à la grecque », reprise de l'époque elle-même, désigne dans le cadre de l'*Anticomanie* un nouveau mouvement des arts décoratifs, puis, par extension, de la peinture et de l'architecture, soucieux de retrouver l'authenticité du modèle grec classique et de s'en inspirer pour promouvoir le progrès des arts modernes (c'est-à-dire leur efficacité exemplaire dans la société civique). Le premier, Cochin, organise une campagne de presse contre la production rocaille des ornemanistes et ridiculise les architectes qui assujettissent leur art aux caprices de la forme ondulante irraisonnée (« Supplication aux orfèvres… » et « Lettre à l'abbé R… », *Mercure de France*, déc. 1754, fév. 1755). Autour de Cochin et des célèbres érudits, antiquaires, collectionneurs, polygraphes, Caylus, Mariette et l'architecte-archéologue Le Roy, Paris devient le foyer principal d'une nouvelle production d'arts décoratifs inspirés des objets et des fragments de monuments antiques récemment découverts. Parmi les publications de gravures les plus diffusées en Europe, celles de F. de Neufforge (*Recueil élémentaire d'architecture*, 8 vol., Paris, 1757-1768) et de Delafosse (*Nouvelle iconologie historique*, Paris, 1767-1785) initièrent des architectes, des ornemanistes ou des maîtres maçons, de Bordeaux à Lille ou de Bruxelles à Stockholm…

Les nouvelles structures et motifs décoratifs varièrent sur un mode digne, volontiers lourd : figures strictement géométriques, rinceaux réguliers, frises symétriques, lignes de poste, cannelures, pattes de lion, bucrâne, vases, trépieds, guirlandes de chêne, triglyphes, gouttes, etc., imi-

fratello di Mme de Pompadour, M. de Vandières, chiamato a succedere a suo zio alla Direzione Generale degli Edifici, Giardini, Arti e Manifatture del re (incarico che egli svolgerà sotto il nome del marchese de Marigny, tra il 1751 e il 1774). Gli architetti Soufflot e Dumont, e il disegnatore-incisore Cochin, futuro segretario perpetuo dell'Accademia reale di pittura e scultura, sono i suoi mentori illuminati. Soufflot stesso si reca a Paestum dove disegna i templi dorici che Dumont pubblica nel 1764. Il suo successo gode dell'estrema curiosità per l'arte greca originaria che era già stata fatta conoscere grazie alle pubblicazioni dei suoi colleghi, Le Roy (*Les ruines des plus beaux monuments de la Grèce*, 1758) e Stuart e Revett a Londra. L'espressione "gusto alla greca", ripresa dall'epoca stessa, designa nel quadro dell'Anticomania un nuovo movimento delle arti decorative, poi, per estensione, della pittura e dell'architettura, ansioso di ritrovare l'autenticità del modello greco classico e di prendervi ispirazione per promuovere il progresso delle arti moderne (cioè la loro efficacia esemplare nella società civile). Il primo, Cochin, organizza una campagna stampa contro la produzione rocaille degli ornatisti e ridicolizza gli architetti che asserviscono la loro arte ai capricci della forma ondulante sconsiderata ("Supplica agli orafi..." e "Lettera all'abate R...", *Mercure de France*, dic. 1754, feb. 1755). Attorno a Cochin e ai celebri eruditi, antiquari, collezionisti, poligrafi, Caylus, Mariette, e l'architetto-archeologo Le Roy, Parigi diventa il fulcro principale di una nuova produzione di arti decorative ispirata a degli oggetti e a dei frammenti di monumenti antichi recentemente scoperti. Tra le pubblicazioni di stampe più diffuse in Europa , quelle di F. de Neufforge (*Recuil élémentaire d'architecture*, 8 vol., Parigi, 1757-1768) e di Delafosse (*Nouvelle Iconologie Historique*, Parigi, 1767-1785), iniziarono degli architetti, degli ornatisti o dei direttori dei lavori, da Bordeaux a Lille o da Bruxelles a Stoccolma…

Le nuove strutture e i motivi decorativi si spostarono su un modello degno, decisamente pesante: figure rigorosamente geometriche, viticci regolari, fregi simmetrici, linee di posta, scanalature, zampe di leone, bucranio, vasi treppiedi, ghir-

so on, all imitated from Antiquity. The famous furniture that was produced in about 1757 for Lalive de Jully, a rich collector (and, like Soufflot, a regular at Mme Geoffrin's salon), from designs by the Piranesian painter Le Lorrain, started off a real "Greek" fashion in every sort of artistic expression. Cochin soon became worried about this Parisian antiquarianism, while others found it highly amusing (for example, Petitot, a Piranesian friend of Soufflot and architect for the Bourbon court of Parma, who in 1771 published some humorous costumes for a *Mascarade à la grecque*). In 1763, Grimm was already informing other European courts of this Parisian revolution: "For the last few years, people have been searching for antique forms and ornaments. Taste has consequently improved and this fashion has become so general that everything nowadays is 'Greek'. Everything is 'Greek' in Paris, the interior and exterior decorations of buildings, furniture, fabrics, all sorts of jewellery. This taste has passed from architecture to fashionable shops. Our ladies' hair is now cut in 'Greek' fashion. (…) Such excess is undoubtedly ridiculous, but what does it matter? If abuse cannot be avoided, it is better to abuse something good than something bad." (*Literary Correspondence*, 1 May 1763.) The head of the king's builders thought likewise and encouraged this style.

The fine architecture that Marigny wished to develop in the service of Louis XV was to be produced by Soufflot and his imitators, the young French Piranesians who won prizes at the *Académie royale d'architecture* between 1745 and 1760. This resolutely modern policy was to be carried on under Louis XVI by Marigny's successor, the Comte d'Angivillier, a friend of Turgot. By giving back the original values to ancient orders and structural functions (imitated from peristylar temples), this "Greek" taste became the "grand taste" of the royal ideology. In other words, it was an allusion to the powerful Classicism of the seventeenth century, and an illustration of the domination of the arts under Louis XIV, guaranteed by the *Académie royale* and the king's head architect. After the palace of the Sun King in Versailles, the cities (Paris, or other provincial cities) were to become a new Rome or Athens.

tés de l'Antiquité. Le fameux mobilier, exécuté vers 1757, sur les dessins du peintre piranésien Le Lorrain, pour le riche amateur Lalive de Jully (un familier du salon de Mme Geoffrin, comme Soufflot), déclenche une véritable mode « à la grecque » dans tous les domaines de l'expression. Cochin finit par s'inquiéter de cette *Anticomanie* parisienne, tandis que d'autres s'en amusaient franchement (témoin le piranésien Petitot, ami de Soufflot, architecte de la cour des Bourbons de Parme, qui publie en 1771 les costumes bouffons d'une *Mascarade à la grecque*). En 1763, Grimm informe déjà les cours européennes de cette révolution parisienne : « Depuis quelques années on a recherché les ornements et les formes antiques ; le goût y a gagné considérablement, et la mode est devenue si générale que tout se fait aujourd'hui à la grecque. La décoration extérieure et intérieure des bâtiments, les meubles, les étoffes, les bijoux de toute espèce, tout est à Paris à la grecque. Ce goût a passé de l'architecture dans les boutiques de mode ; nos dames sont coiffées à la grecque (…). Cet excès est ridicule, sans doute ; mais qu'importe ? Si l'abus ne peut s'éviter, il vaut mieux qu'on abuse d'une bonne chose que d'une mauvaise » (*Correspondance littéraire*, 1ᵉʳ mai 1763). La direction des Bâtiments du roi ne pense pas différemment et favorise ce nouveau style.

La bonne architecture que Marigny souhaite voir se créer au service de Louis XV va être illustrée par Soufflot et ses émules, ces jeunes Piranésiens français qui, dans les années 1745-1760, ont été les lauréats de l'Académie royale d'architecture ; cette politique résolument *moderne*, sera poursuivie sous Louis XVI par le successeur de Marigny, le comte d'Angivillier, un ami de Turgot. En redonnant à l'ordre antique et à sa fonction structurelle, plastique et symbolique (imitée des temples péristyles) sa valeur d'origine, le « goût à la grecque » sert l'idéologie royale du « grand goût » ; c'est-à-dire une référence au classicisme puissant du XVIIᵉ siècle, illustration de l'hégémonie des arts à l'époque de Louis XIV dont étaient garants l'Académie royale et le premier architecte du roi. Après l'épisode du palais du Soleil à Versailles, la ville (Paris, comme les capitales provinciales) devient une nouvelle Rome ou une nouvelle Athènes.

lande di quercia, triglifi, gocce, ecc. imitate dall'Antichità. Il famoso mobile, realizzato verso il 1757, sui disegni del pittore piranesiano Le Lorrain, per il ricco amatore Lalive de Jully (un intimo del salone di Mme Geoffrin, come Soufflot), fa scattare una vera moda "alla greca" in tutti i domini dell'espressione. Cochin finisce per preoccuparsi di questa Anticomania parigina, mentre altri se ne divertivano senza problemi (testimone il piranesiano Petitot, amico di Soufflot, architetto della corte dei Borboni di Parma, che pubblica nel 1771 i costumi buffi di una *Mascherata alla greca*). Nel 1763, Grimm informa già le corti europee di questa rivoluzione parigina: "Da qualche anno si ricercano gli ornamenti e le forme antiche; il gusto vi ha guadagnato considerevolmente, e la moda è diventata così generale che tutto oggi si fa alla greca. La decorazione esteriore ed interna degli edifici, i mobili, le stoffe, i gioielli di tutte le specie, tutto a Parigi è alla greca. Questo gusto è passato dall'architettura alle boutiques di moda, le nostre dame sono acconciate alla greca (…). Questo eccesso è ridicolo, senza dubbio; ma che importa? Se l'abuso non può essere evitato, è meglio abusare di una cosa buona che di una cattiva." (*Correspondence littéraire*, 1 maggio 1763). La direzione degli edifici del re non ha un'opinione diversa e favorisce questo nuovo stile.

La buona architettura che Marigny si augura di vedere creata al servizio di Luigi XV, sarà illustrata da Soufflot e dai suoi imitatori, questi giovani piranesiani francesi che, negli anni 1745-1760 sono stati i laureati dell'*Académie Royale d'Architecture*; questa politica, decisamente moderna, sarà portata avanti sotto Luigi XVI dal successore di Marigny, il conte d'Angivillier, un amico di Turgot. Restituendo all'ordine antico e alla sua funzione strutturale, plastica e simbolica (imitata dai templi peristili) il suo valore originario, il "gusto alla greca" è al servizio dell'ideologia reale del "gran gusto"; cioè un riferimento al classicismo potente del XVII secolo, illustrazione dell'egemonia delle arti all'epoca di Luigi XIV di cui erano garanti l'*Académie Royale* e il Primo Architetto del re. Dopo l'episodio del Palazzo del Sole a Versailles, la città (Parigi, come le capitali provinciali) diventa una nuova Roma o una nuova Atene.

Civic responsibility
and the beautification of cities

Gabriel, influenced by recent work by Potain, the head of his studio, also paid a certain measured homage to this new taste – in Versailles with the Petit Trianon (1761-1770) and the Opera (1770), and in Paris with the Place Louis XV (now the Place de la Concorde) and the chapel in the Ecole Militaire. The Classical revival then produced a series of highly original urban productions of grandiose proportions that were finally to transform the capital of the Enlightenment. In the field of religious architecture, the century's most significant project was Soufflot's basilica of Saint Geneviève (now the Panthéon) between 1757 and 1780. After the peace of 1763, money was once again circulating freely and a frenzied construction of private housing led to a flourishing of the new style in aristocrat and bourgeois dwellings. Town houses and, what is new, rented apartments were built in this ancient style. The young French Piranesians back from Rome (Trouard, Chalgrin, Moreau-Desproux, Peyre, De Wailly and Pâris) with other young architects destined for brilliant careers (Ledoux, Boullée, Bélanger, Lenoir Le Romain or Brongniart) created a novel formal repertoire, in which a free arrangement was allied with monumental sculpture, varied bossage or ornamental joint lines, and pure geometric forms. Robert and Clérisseau invented landscape or arabesque decorations that were in no way inferior to the new British style. One Parisian masterpiece illustrates the art of suburban *follies*: the Pavillon de Bagatelle, which Bélanger built for the Comte d'Artois in the Bois de Boulogne (1777).

English or "Anglo-Chinese" gardens and landscapes, punctuated by Greek, Turkish, Chinese or Egyptian follies (the parks of the Désert de Retz, Monceau, Méréville, the Petit Trianon with its hamlet) reflected a yearning for Arcadia and for escape expressed in these ancient or exotic imaginings. Even the city opened up to nature and courtyards planted with elms or lime trees, malls, promenades and landscaped riverbanks replaced the now unnecessary ramparts. Enlightenment Man, the lover of *vedute* and architectu-

Édilité
et embellissement des villes

Gabriel, influencé dans ses dernières œuvres par Potain, son chef d'agence, sacrifie lui-même, avec mesure, au nouveau goût: à Versailles dans la réalisation du Petit Trianon (1761-1770) et de l'opéra (1770), à Paris place Louis XV (actuelle place de la Concorde) et à la chapelle de l'École militaire. Le renouveau classique s'illustre alors dans un ensemble d'œuvres urbaines d'une grande originalité, à une échelle grandiose qui doit, à terme, métamorphoser la capitale des Lumières. Dans le domaine de l'architecture religieuse, le plus important chantier du siècle est celui de Soufflot à la basilique Sainte-Geneviève entre 1757 et 1780 (actuel Panthéon). Tandis qu'à la faveur de la paix de 1763, les capitaux circulent à nouveau dans le royaume, une fièvre de constructions privées favorise l'éclosion du nouveau style dans l'habitat noble et bourgeois: hôtels particuliers et, ce qui est neuf, immeubles de rapport, se parent du décor antiquisant. Les jeunes Piranésiens français à leur retour de Rome (Trouard, Chalgrin, Moreau-Desproux, Peyre, De Wailly, Pâris) avec d'autres jeunes architectes appelés à une brillante carrière (Ledoux, Boullée, Bélanger, Lenoir le Romain ou Brongniart), créent un répertoire formel inédit, où l'ordonnance libre s'allie à la sculpture monumentale, au jeu des bossages variés ou des parements à refend, et aux formes géométriques pures. Robert et Clérisseau inventent des décors de paysages ou d'arabesques qui ne le cèdent en rien au nouveau style anglais; un chef-d'œuvre du genre, à Paris, symbolise l'art des *folies* suburbaines: le pavillon de Bagatelle, construit par Bélanger pour le comte d'Artois au bois de Boulogne (1777).

Jardins à l'anglaise, « anglo-chinois » ou paysagers, ponctués de fabriques grecques, turques, chinoises ou égyptiennes (parc du Désert de Retz, de Monceau, de Méréville, Petit Trianon avec son hameau), traduisent une nostalgie de l'Arcadie et un rêve d'évasion propices au cadre de l'imaginaire à l'antique ou exotique. La ville elle-même s'ouvre sur la nature et les cours plantées d'ormeaux ou de tilleuls, les mails, les promenades et quais monumentaux se substituent aux remparts devenus

Edlizia e abbellimento
delle città

Gabriel, influenzato nelle sue ultime opere da Potain, suo capo di agenzia, si sacrifica, con moderazione, al nuovo gusto: a Versailles nella realizzazione del Petit Trianon (1761-1770) e dell'Opera (1770), a Parigi Piazza Luigi XV (attuale piazza della Concordia) e alla Cappella della Scuola Militare. Il rinnovamento classico si manifesta allora in una serie di opere urbane di una grande originalità, su scala grandiosa che deve, alla fine, far cambiare forma alla città degli Illuministi. Nel campo dell'architettura religiosa, il più importante cantiere del secolo è quello di Soufflot alla basilica Sainte-Geneviève tra il 1757 e il 1780 (attuale Pantheon). Mentre grazie alla Pace del 1763 i capitali circolano di nuovo nel regno, una febbre di costruzioni private favorisce lo sbocciare del nuovo stile nell'ambiente nobile e borghese: edifici privati e, ciò che è nuovo, costruzioni per alloggi borghesi, si rivestono di una decorazione antichizzante. I giovani piranesiani francesi al loro ritorno da Roma (Truard, Chalgrin, Moreau-Desproux, Peyre, De Wailly, Pâris) con altri giovani architetti chiamati a una brillante carriera (Ledoux, Boullée, Bélanger, Lenoir le Romain o Brongniart), danno vita a un repertorio formale inedito, dove l'ornamento libero si allea alla scultura monumentale, al gioco delle bugne variate o dei paramenti divisori e alle forme geometriche pure. Robert e Clérisseau inventano delle decorazioni di paesaggio o d'arabeschi che non cedono per nulla al nuovo stile inglese; un capolavoro del genere, a Parigi, simboleggia l'arte delle ville suburbane: il *pavillon de Bagatelle*, costruito da Bélanger per il conte d'Artois nel Bois de Boulogne (1777).

Giardino all'inglese, "anglo-cinese" o paesaggistico, punteggiato di costruzioni greche, turche, cinesi o egizie (parco del Deserto di Retz, di Monceau, di Méréville, Piccolo Trianon con il suo villaggio) traducono una nostalgia dell'Arcadia e un sogno di evasione propizi al quadro dell'immaginario all'antica o esotico. La città stessa si apre sulla natura e i suoi corsi alberati di olmi e di tigli, i viali e le passeggiate e le banchine monumentali si sostituiscono alle mura diventate inutili. L'Uomo degli Illuministi, amante di vedute e di capricci architettonici, scopre il paesaggio della sua

ral caprices, now discovered the landscape of his own city. This new *art of building* communicated to him the specific places where the public gathered and were served.

The notion of town planning, then expressed as *beautification*, pushed public architecture towards the adoption of evocative characteristics: clarity, simplicity of mass, affirmation of arrangements, measured sculptures and, above all, the opening of entrances and thoroughfares thus setting off the relationships between the interior and exterior, as well as the play of light on strongly contrasted or uniformly linear façades. The art of Piranesian chiaroscuro and the power of strikingly up-dated ancient forms inspired a dramatic dialogue between public buildings and their urban environment. Series of buildings, with programmed façades, led to the emergence of monumental estates. Examples in Paris, designed in the 1760s and completed under Louis XVI, are the Halle aux Blés and its surroundings by Le Camus de Mézières (1762-1766), Gondoin's Ecole de Chirurgie (1769-1775), Antoine's Hôtel de la Monnaie (1767-1775), Heurtier's Comédie Italienne and, above all, the new Comédie Française (now the Théâtre de l'Odéon and its quarter), designed by De Wailly and Peyre (1768-1782).

The town theatres, a symbol of the Enlightenment as though they were temples to society, which raised their porticoes in front of the churches, also became a success in the provinces. They were always built in neighbourhoods of fitting proportions: Victor Louis's Grand Théâtre in Bordeaux (1771-1780), Graslin de Crucy's theatre in Nantes (1784-1787), Ledoux's playhouse in Besançon (1776-1784) or Lequeux's in Lille. Every mercantile town or large port became involved in antique *beautification*, where porticoes with colonnades associated with promenades seemed to extend the spaces inherited from the royal squares. This golden age of town planning, which stretched from Britain and France to the cities of northern Europe, then to Russia and the German states (Berlin, Cassel, Karlsruhe, etc) came about from a consensus between municipal authorities, artists and the public.

inutiles. L'homme des Lumières, amateur de *vedute* et de caprices architecturaux, découvre le paysage de sa propre cité. Il lui faut désormais, à travers l'*art de bâtir*, reconnaître les lieux spécifiques qui rassemblent ou servent le public.

La notion d'urbanisme, alors exprimée sous le terme d'*embellissement*, oriente l'architecture publique vers la recherche de caractères suggestifs : clarté, simplicité des masses, affirmation des ordonnances, mesure du décor sculpté et, surtout, ouverture des espaces d'entrée et de circulation libre, qui valorise le rapport entre l'intérieur et l'extérieur, ainsi que le rôle de la lumière sur les façades fortement contrastées ou uniformément linéaires. L'art du clair-obscur piranésien, la puissance des formes antiques singulières et *actualisées*, inspirent une véritable dramaturgie des rapports entre le monument public et son environnement urbain ; l'immeuble en série, aux façades à programme, aboutit à l'émergence du lotissement monumental. Tels sont à Paris, dessinés dans les années 1760 et achevés sous Louis XVI : la Halle aux blés et son quartier rayonnant (1762-1766) de Le Camus de Mézières, l'École de chirurgie (1769-1775) de Gondoin, l'hôtel de la Monnaie (1767-1775) d'Antoine, la Comédie italienne de Heurtier et, surtout, la nouvelle Comédie-Française (actuel théâtre de l'Odéon et son quartier), mise en œuvre par De Wailly et Peyre (1768-1782).

Symbole des Lumières, le théâtre urbain, tel un nouveau temple de la sociabilité, qui dresse ses portiques face à l'Église, connaît également d'importants chefs-d'œuvre en province, tous implantés dans des quartiers tracés à leur mesure : à Bordeaux, c'est le Grand-Théâtre de Victor Louis (1771-1780), à Nantes le théâtre Graslin de Crucy (1784-1787), à Besançon la salle de Ledoux (1776-1784), à Marseille celle de Bénard, à Lille celle de Lequeux… Toutes les villes de commerce ou grands ports sont gagnés par l'embellissement à l'antique où les portiques à colonnades, associés aux promenades, semblent prolonger l'espace dévolu aux places royales. Cet âge d'or de l'urbanisme qui s'étend, après l'Angleterre et la France, aux villes de l'Europe du Nord, à la Russie et aux Pays germaniques (Berlin, Cassel, Karlsruhe) a pu se concrétiser grâce à une attitude consensuelle des édiles, des artistes et du public.

propria città. Ha ormai bisogno, attraverso l'arte del costruire, di riconoscere i luoghi specifici che raccolgono o servono il pubblico.

La nozione di urbanesimo, allora espressa con il termine di "abbellimento", orienta l'architettura pubblica verso la ricerca di caratteri suggestivi: chiarezza, semplicità delle masse, affermazione degli ordini, misura della decorazione scolpita e, soprattutto, apertura degli spazi di ingresso e di libera circolazione, che valorizza il rapporto tra l'interno e l'esterno, come il ruolo della luce sulle facciate fortemente contrastate o uniformemente lineari. L'arte del chiaroscuro piranesiano, la potenza delle forme antiche singolari e attualizzate, ispirano una vera e propria drammaturgia dei rapporti tra il monumento pubblico e la sua ambientazione urbana; l'immobile in serie, dalle facciate a programma, porta all'emergere della lottizzazione monumentale. Tali sono a Parigi, disegnati negli anni 1760 e compiuti sotto Luigi XVI, il Mercato del Grano e il suo stupendo quartiere (1762-1784) di Le Camus de Mézières, la Scuola di Chirurgia (1769-1775) di Gondoin, la Zecca (1767-1775) di L'Antoine, la Comédie Italienne di Heurtier e, soprattutto, la nuova Comédie Française (attuale teatro dell'Odeon e il suo quartiere), realizzata da De Wailly e Peyre (1768-1782).

Simbolo degli Illuministi, il teatro urbano, questo nuovo tempio della socialità, che eleva i suoi portici davanti alla Chiesa, conosce parimenti degli importanti capolavori in provincia, tutti situati all'interno di quartieri tracciati a loro misura: a Bordeaux, è il grande teatro Victor Louis (1771-1780), a Nantes il teatro Graslin di Crucy (1784-1787), a Besançon la sala di Ledoux (1776-1784), a Marsiglia quella di Benard, a Lille quella di Lequeux… tutte le città di commercio o i grandi porti sono conquistati dall'abbellimento all'antica in cui i portici con colonnati, associati a passeggiate, sembrano prolungare lo spazio destinato alle piazze reali. Questa epoca d'oro dell'urbanesimo che si estende dopo l'Inghilterra e la Francia, alle città dell'Europa del Nord, alla Russia e ai Paesi Germanici (Berlino, Cassel, Karlsruhe) ha potuto concretizzarsi grazie ad un'attitudine consensuale delle autorità municipali, degli artisti e del pubblico.

Architectural theory and the philosophy of art

Thanks to its freedom from traditional graphic constraints and to the use of attractive pictorial effects, architects were taught to try out new plastic and spatial solutions, and thus captivated the public. Drawing, linked to the promotion of vast municipal programmes, dominated the competition of the *Académie Royale*, whose national and international reputation was uncontested. After returning from Rome, leading artists, such as Crucy or Combes (first prize winners in, respectively, 1774 and 1781) made a career for themselves in their home towns – in this case, Nantes and Bordeaux. Many foreigners who went to study in Paris during the last third of the eighteenth century were also to have excellent careers in their various countries (Scandinavia, Holland, Russia, Switzerland, etc). The prestige of the teachers was combined with a sort of militancy for the progress of the arts, the theory of which had become a vital concern thanks to the Enlightenment. It can even be said that without the revival and the phenomenal growth of architectural theory and of the philosophy of art, in the middle of the eighteenth century, the stylistic renewal would have been no more than a short-lived fad. Basing himself on an age-old tradition, Blondel, who held the chair of the Academy and wrote the architectural articles for the *Encyclopédie*, published *L'Architecture française* (1752-1756) which promoted the "grand taste". Publication of his *Cours d'architecture* (1771-1777), later continued by Patte, another influential theorist, confirmed this frenzied desire for knowledge outside strictly professional circles. Laugier, a Jesuit, journalist and brilliant essayist, even published two best-sellers on architectural theory: an *Essai sur l'architecture* (1753, 1755, edition in English, and in German in 1755 and 1756) and his *Observations sur l'architecture* (1765), a sort of pedagogical pamphlet backing Soufflot's work and praising a reasoned "Greek" taste.

Le Camus de Mézières, with *Le Génie de l'architecture, ou l'analogie de cet art avec nos sensations* (1780), commented on the art of distribution according to a sensual, even sentimental approach. As for Ledoux, his artistic testament,

Théorie architecturale et philosophie de l'art

L'enseignement, grâce à la libération des contraintes graphiques usuelles et à l'attrait d'effets picturaux, entraîne les architectes à tester des solutions plastiques ou spatiales inédites et à captiver le public. Le dessin, lié à la traduction de vastes programmes édilitaires, domine dans les concours de l'Académie royale, dont le prestige national et européen est incontestable. Des artistes de premier plan, comme Crucy ou Combes, respectivement Premier Grand Prix en 1774 et 1781, font carrière à leur retour de Rome dans leur ville d'origine : Nantes et Bordeaux. Nombre d'étrangers qui viennent se former à Paris dans le derniers tiers du XVIIIᵉ siècle connaîtront un bel avenir dans leur pays d'origine (Scandinavie, Pays-Bas, Russie, Suisse…). Le prestige des professeurs se double alors d'une sorte de militantisme pour le progrès des arts dont la théorie, sous l'impulsion des Lumières, devient l'un des véhicules majeurs. On peut même affirmer que sans le renouveau et l'expansion phénoménale de la théorie de l'architecture et de la philosophie de l'art, dès le milieu du XVIIIᵉ siècle, la régénération stylistique aurait stagné à l'état de mode éphémère. S'appuyant sur une tradition déjà séculaire, Blondel, titulaire de la chaire de l'Académie et auteur des textes sur l'architecture dans l'*Encyclopédie*, publie entre 1752 et 1756 *L'Architecture française*, qui témoigne pour le « grand goût » ; l'édition de son *Cours d'architecture* (1771-1777), continué par un autre théoricien influent, Patte, confirme cette frénésie de connaissances qui déborde des milieux strictement professionnels. N'est-ce pas un jésuite, journaliste, essayiste brillant, Laugier, qui publie deux best-sellers de la théorie architecturale : l'*Essai sur l'architecture* (1753, 1755, édition en anglais et en allemand 1755 et 1756) et les *Observations sur l'architecture* (1765), sorte de livret pédagogique accompagnant l'action de Soufflot et panégyrique d'un goût à la grecque *raisonné* ?

Le Camus de Mézières, avec *Le génie de l'architecture, ou l'analogie de cet art avec nos sensations* (1780), commente l'art de la distribution selon une optique sensualiste, toute sentimentale. Quant à Ledoux, son testament d'artiste publié deux ans avant sa mort, *L'Architecture considérée sous le*

Teoria architettonica e filosofia dell'arte

L'insegnamento, grazie alla liberazione dai vincoli grafici usuali e all'influenza degli effetti pittorici, spinge gli architetti a provare delle soluzioni plastiche e spaziali inedite e a conquistare il pubblico. Il disegno, legato alla traduzione di ampi programmi di edilizia, domina nei concorsi dell'*Académie Royale*, il cui prestigio nazionale ed europeo è incontestabile. Degli artisti di primo piano, come Crucy o Combes, rispettivamente Primo Gran Premio nel 1774 e nel 1781, fanno carriera al loro ritorno da Roma nella loro terra d'origine (Nantes, Bordeaux). Molti stranieri che vengono a completare la loro formazione a Parigi durante l'ultimo terzo del XVIII secolo, avranno poi una bella carriera nei loro paesi d'origine (Scandinavia, Paesi Bassi, Russia, Svizzera). Il prestigio dei professori allora raddoppia per una sorta di militanza per il progresso delle arti di cui la teoria, sotto l'impulso degli Illuministi, diventa uno dei veicoli principali. Si può anche affermare che senza il rinnovo e l'espansione fenomenale della teoria dell'architettura e della filosofia dell'arte, dalla metà del XVIII secolo la rigenerazione stilistica sarebbe rimasta ferma allo stato di moda effimera. Appoggiandosi su una tradizione secolare, Blondel, titolare di una cattedra dell'Accademia e autore dei testi sull'architettura nell'*Enciclopedia*, pubblica tra il 1752 e il 1756 *L'Architecture Française*, che reca testimonianza del "gran gusto"; l'edizione del suo *Cours d'Architecture* (1771-1777), continuata da un altro teorico influente, Patte, conferma questa frenesia di conoscenza che si espande al di fuori degli ambienti strettamente professionali. Non è forse un gesuita, giornalista, brillante saggista, Laugier, che pubblica due best-sellers della teoria architettonica: l'*Essai sur l'Architecture* (1753, 1755, ed. in inglese e in tedesco 1755 e 1756) e le *Observations sur l'architecture* (1756), sorta di libretto pedagogico che accompagna l'azione di Soufflot e panegirico per un gusto alla greca *ragionato*?

Le Camus de Mézières, con *Le genie de l'architecture, ou l'analogie de cet art avec nos sensations* (1780), commenta l'arte della distribuzione secondo un'ottica sensualista, tutta sentimentale. Quanto a Ledoux, il suo testamento di artista

published two years after his death, *L'Architecture considérée sous le rapport de l'art, des mœurs et de la législation* (1804), is a defence of pure imagination. Encyclopedic, poetic and utopian, he summarised his career and revealed the secrets of his creative passion. Like a swan-song, Ledoux's book closed the Enlightenment tradition in France. Meanwhile, while Britain was still theorising about the *picturesque* in landscape art and vernacular inspiration, northern Italy experienced a further outbreak of Palladianism, which mingled with Laugier's ideas and British empirical philosophy. After Algarotti, Lodoli and Temenza, Francesco Milizia published a series of theoretical works which, in particular, introduced the Classical revival to Venezia (*Principii di Architettura Civile*, 1781, *Maniere di Architetti antichi e moderni*, 1785).

In France, under the Directoire, a new generation of engineer-cum-artists arrived with the founding of the Ecole Polytechnique. They identified themselves with the austere and strictly functionalist publications of Durand and Quatremère de Quincy. There was no longer any question of Piranesian or convivial imaginings, but of engineering and economic rationalism in service of the State. Dry line drawings replaced the architecture of the brush. Under the First Empire, the nineteenth century ignored the virtues of the expressive architecture and moral art that marked the end of the Ancien Régime and the Revolution.

Revolutionary architecture and Europe

Previously, in the Europe of the Enlightenment, there had been a creative dialectic based on relativism (the pairing of Nature with Antiquity), on sentiment and on the idea of philanthropic happiness which led artists to avoid pastiche and the dry uniformity of a passionless imitation of Antiquity. Architects' contradictory declarations incited debate and new projects were examined in the public eye, while images circulated thus making new models familiar. Architectural theory accompanied the antiquarians' and archaeologists' wealth of scholarly works (in London, Rome and Paris, as we have seen). It made the use of new iconographic trends legitimate and inaugurated a hitherto unk-

rapport de l'art, des mœurs et de la législation (1804), revendique le droit à la pure imagination. Encyclopédique, poétique et utopique, il dresse un bilan de carrière et dévoile les arcanes de la création enthousiaste. Véritable chant du cygne, ce livre de Ledoux clôt en France l'héritage des Lumières… Tandis que l'Angleterre poursuit dans la théorie la définition du *pittoresque*, à travers l'art paysager et l'inspiration vernaculaire, l'Italie du Nord connaît une nouvelle veine palladienne qui se mêle aux idées de Laugier et de la philosophie empirique britannique. Après Algarotti, Lodoli et Temenza, Francesco Milizia publie une série d'ouvrages théoriques qui initient la Vénétie, notamment, au renouveau classique (*Principii di Architettura Civile*, 1781, *Maniere di Architetti antichi e moderni*, 1785).

En France, sous le Directoire, avec la création de l'École polytechnique, une nouvelle génération d'ingénieurs-architectes se reconnaîtra dans les publications austères et profondément fonctionnalistes de Durand ou de Quatremère de Quincy. Il n'est plus question alors de piranésisme ou d'imaginaire convivial, mais d'équipement et de rationalisme économique au service de l'État. Le dessin au trait, sec, remplace l'architecture au pinceau. Le XIXᵉ siècle, avec l'Empire, méconnaît les vertus de l'architecture parlante et de l'art moralisant de la fin de l'Ancien Régime et de la Révolution.

L'architecture révolutionnaire et l'Europe

Auparavant, dans l'Europe éclairée, une véritable dialectique de la création, faisant appel au relativisme (couple nature-antique), au sentiment et à l'idée de bonheur philanthropique, conduisait les architectes à éviter le pastiche, à fuir l'uniformité desséchante de l'antique imité sans passion. Les déclarations contradictoires d'architectes suscitent des débats et les nouveaux chantiers sont auscultés devant le public, tandis que les images circulent et font connaître les modèles. La théorie de l'architecture accompagne l'énorme travail d'érudition des antiquaires et des archéologues (à Londres, à Rome ou à Paris, on l'a vu). Elle légitime le recours aux nouvelles tendances iconographiques et inaugure des rapports jusqu'ici inconnus entre les créateurs et leur public. Par exemple : une gouache exposée

pubblicato due anni prima della sua morte, *L'Architecture considérée sous le rapport de l'art, des mœurs et de la législation* (1804), rivendica il diritto alla pura immaginazione. Enciclopedico, poetico ed utopico, egli traccia un bilancio della carriera e svela gli arcani della creazione entusiastica. Vero e proprio canto del cigno, questo libro de Ledoux chiuse in Francia l'eredità degli Illuministi. Mentre l'Inghilterra prosegue nella teoria la definizione del *pittoresco*, attraverso l'arte paesaggistica e l'ispirazione regionale, l'Italia del Nord conosce una nuova vena palladiana che si mescola alle idee di Laugier e della filosofia empirica britannica. Dopo Algarotti, Lodoli e Temenza, Francesco Milizia pubblica una serie di opere teoriche che iniziano il Veneto, in particolare, al rinnovamento classico (*Principii di architettura civile*, 1781, *Maniere di Architetti antichi e moderni*, 1785).

In Francia, sotto il Direttorio, con la creazione dell'*École Polytechnique*, una nuova generazione d'ingegneri–architetti si riconoscerà nelle pubblicazioni austere e profondamente funzionaliste di Durand o di Quatremère de Quincy. Non è più allora questione di piranesismo o di immaginario conviviale, ma di equipaggiamento e di razionalismo economico al servizio dello Stato. Il disegno al tratto, secco, rimpiazza l'architettura al pennello. Il XIX secolo, con l'Impero, disconosce le virtù dell'architettura parlante e dell'arte moralizzante della fine dell'Ancien Régime e della Rivoluzione.

L'architettura rivoluzionaria e l'Europa

Prima, nell'Europa dei Lumi, una vera e propria dialettica della creazione, facente appello al relativismo (coppia Natura/Antico), al sentimento e all'idea filantropica di fortuna conduceva gli architetti ad evitare il pastiche, a fuggire l'uniformità arida dell'Antico imitato senza passione. Le dichiarazioni contraddittorie degli architetti suscitano dei dibattiti e i nuovi cantieri sono presentati davanti al pubblico, mentre le immagini circolano e fanno conoscere i modelli. La teoria dell'architettura accompagna l'enorme lavoro di erudizione degli antiquari e degli archeologi (a Londra, Roma o Parigi, come si è visto). Essa legittima il ricorso alle nuove tendenze iconografiche e inaugura dei

nown relationship between creators and their public. For example, De Wailly's *Vue du vestibule du nouveau Théâtre français*, a gouache exhibited at the Salon du Louvre in 1771, contains characters "in Athenian dress" and is of course a fine instance of antiquarianism; but it is also a poetically fictional reading of a purely concrete project. The publication in the supplement of the *Encyclopédie* (1777) of plans for this theatre before it was built confirms drawing's educative and publicising role during this period.

De Wailly, a professor particularly prized by Russian students, was one of the most influential Academicians, along with Peyre, Chalgrin and Boullée, in the training of young architects and one of the most persuasive public voices. His great pre-Revolutionary projects became authoritative (the Théâtre des Arts, the Assemblée Nationale, the "Artists' plan for the beautification of Paris") and are reminders of how much these troubled times were interested in symbolic architecture. More generally, the anti-Classical nature of the concept of *revolutionary architecture* has been recognised in many constructions in the last third of the century. Boullée and Ledoux are the uncontested masters of this trend that set utopian art at the service of society. In his drawings for his great projects, which are themselves megalomaniacal in the hugeness of their conception, Boullée reaffirmed the prime position of human and physical nature in architectural designs. His pictures, with their suggestive atmospheric effects and chiaroscuro, are visions that show that architecture was still "in its childhood". The geometric purity, the simple strength of his arrangements set up before immense perspectives and the use of the poetry of mythology display the theatrical urban life that antiquarians dreamt of. Was not the Revolution placed under the sign of the democracy of the Roman and Athenian republics?

With Ledoux, who was responsible for several works of a revolutionary formal and functional nature under the Ancien Régime (the Hôtel Thélusson in Paris, 1781, the Saline Royale in Arc-et-Senans, 1775-1779, the toll gates of the Mur des Fermiers Généraux in Paris, 1785-1789), the art of powerful contrasts and the poetry of shadows subjugated to a geometrical or sculptural arrangement of masses became fixed in stone. In his 1804 book,

au Salon du Louvre en 1771, la « Vue du vestibule du nouveau Théâtre français », que De Wailly anime de personnages « vêtus à l'athénienne », est un beau symbole de l'*Anticomanie*, certes, mais encore plus un mode de lecture d'une fiction poétique dans le projet bien concret. La publication des plans de ce théâtre, avant même sa réalisation, dans le supplément de l'*Encyclopédie* (1777), confirme le rôle pédagogique et médiatique du dessin à cette époque.

Professeur, recherché par les élèves russes, notamment, De Wailly est avec Peyre, Chalgrin ou Boullée un des académiciens les plus influents dans la formation des jeunes architectes et des plus persuasifs auprès du public. Ses grands projets, durant la Révolution, font autorité (Théâtre des Arts, palais d'Assemblée nationale, Plan des Artistes pour l'embellissement de Paris) et rappellent que cette période troublée s'est intéressée à l'architecture symbolique. Plus généralement, le concept d'*architecture révolutionnaire* a été reconnu dans le caractère anticlassique de toute une production du dernier tiers du siècle. Boullée et Ledoux sont les maîtres incontestés de cette tendance qui illustre l'utopie de l'art au service de la société. Dans ses grands dessins de projets, eux-mêmes mégalomanes par le programme démesuré qu'ils traitent, Boullée affirme la primauté de la nature, physique et humaine, dans l'art de concevoir l'architecture. Ses *tableaux*, aux effets suggestifs d'atmosphère et de clair-obscur, sont des visions qui font comprendre que l'architecture était encore « dans son enfance ». L'épuration géométrique, la force simple des ordonnances dressées devant d'immenses perspectives et le recours à la poésie des mythes révèlent la théâtralité de la vie urbaine rêvée par les *anticomanes* : la Révolution n'était-elle pas placée sous le signe de la démocratie et des républiques de Rome et d'Athènes ?

Avec Ledoux, responsable de plusieurs chantiers aux caractères fonctionnels et formels révolutionnaires sous l'Ancien Régime (hôtel Thélusson à Paris, 1781, saline royale d'Arc-et-Senans, 1775-1779, pavillons d'octroi du mur des Fermiers généraux à Paris, 1785-1789), l'art des contrastes puissants, la poésie des ombres soumises à l'agencement géométrique ou sculptural des masses, se sont concrétisés dans la pierre. Son livre de 1804,

rapporti fino a qui sconosciuti tra i creatori e il loro pubblico. Per esempio: un gouache esposto al salone del Louvre nel 1771, la "Veduta del vestibolo del nuovo teatro francese", che De Wailly anima di personaggi "vestiti all'ateniese", è un bel simbolo dell'Anticomania, certamente, ma ancora più un modo di lettura di una finzione poetica nel progetto ben concreto. La pubblicazione delle piante di questo teatro, prima ancora della sua realizzazione, nel supplemento dell'*Encyclopédie* (1777), conferma il ruolo pedagogico e mediatico del disegno di questa epoca.

Professore, ricercato dagli allievi russi, in particolare, De Wailly è, insieme a Peyre, Chalgrin o Boullée uno degli accademici più influenti nella formazione dei giovani architetti e dei più persuasivi nei confronti del pubblico. I suoi grandi progetti, durante la Rivoluzione, fanno autorità (Teatro delle Arti, Palazzo dell'Assemblea Nazionale, Piano degli Artisti per l'abbellimento di Parigi) e ricordano che questo periodo tormentato si è interessato all'architettura simbolica. Più in generale, il concetto di architettura rivoluzionaria, è stato riconosciuto nel carattere anti-classico di tutta una produzione dell'ultimo terzo del secolo. Boullée e Ledoux sono i maestri incontrastati di questa tendenza che illustra l'utopia dell'arte al servizio della società. Nei suoi grandi disegni di progetti, essi stessi megalomani per il programma smisurato che trattano, Boullée afferma il primato della natura, fisica ed umana, nell'arte di concepire l'architettura. I suoi quadri, dagli effetti suggestivi d'atmosfera e di chiaro scuro, sono delle visioni che fanno comprendere che l'architettura era ancora "nella sua infanzia". L'epurazione geometrica, la forza semplice degli ordini innalzata davanti alle immense prospettive e il ricorso alla poesia dei miti rivelano la teatralità della vita urbana sognata dagli anticomani: la Rivoluzione, non era forse situata sotto il segno della democrazia e delle repubbliche di Roma e di Atene?

Con Ledoux, responsabile di parecchi cantieri dai caratteri funzionali e formali rivoluzionari sotto l'*ancien régime* (Hôtel Thélusson a Parigi, 1781, Saline Royale d'Arc-et-Senans, 1775-1779, Pavillons d'octroi du mur des Fermiers généraux a Parigi, 1785-1789), l'arte dei contrasti potenti, la poesia delle ombre sottomesse alla disposizione geometrica o scultorea delle masse, si sono concretizzate nella

magnificently illustrated with engravings, he left a message for posterity that was clearly not understood in nineteenth-century France. However, many of the students of the Academy (from the reign of Louis XVI onwards), certain colleagues and above all some great foreign artists (themselves with a Piranesian background) were open to Ledoux's libertarian example. Soane in London, Selva in Venice and Perez in Spain participated in a new international current, whose most spectacular productions are to be found in Scandinavia and Russia. Desprez, a disciple of De Wailly, worked for the Swedish court where he transferred Piranesian and historicist visions of architecture to the theatre. Thomas de Thomon, one of Ledoux's students, built a commodities exchange in Saint Petersburg that is as solid as any temple in Paestum. De Wailly, Ledoux and Clérisseaux sent their own designs to Catherine II or Paul I. Meanwhile, new Russian architects, trained in Paris, developed an original, grandiose, highly coloured art whose lyricism was tempered by an Italo-British Palladianism, directly represented in Saint Petersburg and Moscow by Cameron, a Scot, and Quarenghi, an Italian. Chalgrin's and De Wailly's Russian pupils were to promulgate Enlightenment architecture on the banks of the Neva until the middle of the nineteenth century. Bajenov, Starov and Zakharov were in turn to become masters. Earlier, in about 1790-1800, Italy and Germany also adopted the Classical revival. Gilly, a revolutionary architect deeply marked by France, became the symbol of a brilliant Germanic school where, influenced by Winckelmann and Goethe, a neo-Hellenic nationalism would dominate nineteenth-century Romantic art. From Langhans (the Brandenburg Gate in Berlin, 1789-1791) to masterpieces by Weinbrenner, Schinkel and Klenze, in Munich or Berlin, Germany exported an increasingly *archaeological* imitation of ancient art even to Greece, which had recently been liberated from Turkish rule. Finally Spain, though distinctly Baroque and dominated by Italian and French trends during the entire eighteenth century, at last accepted the Classical revival. The San Fernando academy in Madrid, with a new theoretical approach, encouraged the exceptional career of de Villanueva, the designer of the Prado Museum (1785-1819).

magnifiquement illustré de gravures, offrira à la postérité un message qui, à l'évidence, ne sera pas compris en France au XIXᵉ siècle. Toutefois, bien des élèves de l'Académie (dès le règne de Louis XVI), certains confrères et, notamment, de grands artistes étrangers (eux-mêmes de formation piranésienne), sont sensibles à l'exemple libertaire de Ledoux. Soane à Londres, Selva en Vénétie, Perez en Espagne, participent à un nouveau courant international dont les réalisations les plus spectaculaires se trouvent à l'évidence dans les Pays scandinaves et en Russie. Disciple de De Wailly, Desprez, au service de la cour de Suède, transpose au théâtre ses visions piranésiennes et historicistes d'architecture ; élève de Ledoux, Thomas de Thomon dresse à Saint-Pétersbourg une Bourse de commerce solide comme un temple de Paestum. De Wailly, Ledoux, Clérisseau, envoient leurs propres dessins à Catherine II ou à Paul Iᵉʳ, tandis que les nouveaux architectes russes, formés à Paris et à Rome, développent un art original, grandiose, très coloré, mais dont le lyrisme est tempéré par l'exemple du *Palladianisme* italo-anglais, directement illustré à Saint-Pétersbourg et à Moscou par l'Écossais Cameron et l'Italien Quarenghi. Les élèves russes de Chalgrin et de De Wailly projetteront jusqu'au milieu du XIXᵉ siècle l'image de l'architecture des Lumières sur les bords de la Néva : Bajenov, Starov, Zakharov font à leur tour figure de maîtres… Plus tôt, vers 1790-1800, l'Italie et l'Allemagne s'initient elles aussi au renouveau classique. Architecte révolutionnaire, très marqué par la France, Gilly devient le symbole d'une École germanique très brillante où, sous l'influence de Winckelmann et de Goethe, un nationalisme néo-hellénique dominera l'art romantique du XIXᵉ siècle. De Langhans (porte de Brandebourg, à Berlin, 1789-1791), aux chefs-d'œuvre de Weinbrenner, Schinkel et Klenze, à Munich ou à Berlin, l'Allemagne diffuse alors, jusque vers la Grèce nouvellement libérée des Turcs, l'imitation de plus en plus *archéologique* de l'art des Anciens. Enfin, dominée par les courants italiens et français durant tout le XVIIIᵉ siècle, l'Espagne, farouchement baroque, s'initie tardivement au renouveau classique. L'Académie de San Fernando de Madrid, avec une ouverture théorique nouvelle, favorise la carrière exceptionnelle de J. de Villanueva, le créateur du musée du Prado (1785-1819).

pietra. Il suo libro del 1804, magni-ficamente illustrato con incisioni, offrirà ai posteri un messaggio che evidentemente non sarà compreso in Francia nel XIX secolo. Tuttavia, parecchi allievi dell'Accademia, (fin dal regno di Luigi XVI), alcuni colleghi e, in particolare, dei grandi artisti stranieri (essi stessi di formazione piranesiana) sono sensibili all'esempio libertario di Ledoux. Soane a Londra, Selva in Veneto, Perez in Spagna, partecipano a una nuova corrente internazionale le cui realizzazioni più spettacolari si trovano senza dubbio nei paesi Scandinavi e in Russia. Discepolo di Wailly, Desprez, al servizio della corte di Svezia, traspone al teatro le sue visioni piranesiane e storicistiche dell'architettura; allievo di Ledoux, Thomas de Thomon innalza a San Pietroburgo una Borsa del commercio solida come un tempio di Paestum. De Wailly, Ledoux, Clérisseau, inviano i loro disegni a Caterina II o a Paolo I, mentre i nuovi architetti russi, formati a Parigi e a Roma, sviluppano un'arte originale, grandiosa, molto colorata, ma il cui lirismo è temperato dall'esempio del Palladianesimo italo-inglese, direttamente illustrato a San Pietroburgo e a Mosca dallo scozzese Cameron e dell'italiano Quarenghi. Gli allievi russi di Chalgrin e di De Wailly proietteranno fino al XIX secolo l'immagine dell'architettura dell'Illuminismo sulle sponde della Neva: Bajenov, Starov, Zakharov fanno a loro volta figura di maestri… Più tardi, verso il 1790-1800, l'Italia e la Germania intrapresero anch'esse il rinnovamento classico. Architetto rivoluzionario, molto marcato dalla Francia, Gilly diventa il simbolo di una scuola germanica molto brillante in cui, sotto l'influenza di Winckelmann e di Goethe, un nazionalismo neo-ellenico dominerà l'arte romantica del XIX secolo. Da Langans (Porta di Brandeburgo a Berlino, 1789-1791), ai capolavori di Weibrenner, Schinkel e Klenze, a Monaco o a Berlino, la Germania diffonde allora, fino verso la Grecia nuovamente liberata dai turchi l'imitazione sempre più "archeologica" dell'arte degli Antichi. Infine, dominata dalle correnti italiane e francesi durante tutto il XVIII secolo, la Spagna, prepotentemente barocca, s'inizia in ritardo al rinnovamento classico. L'Accademia di San Fernando di Madrid, con una apertura teorica nuova, favorisce la carriera eccezionale di J. da Villanueva , il creatore del Museo del Prado (1785-1819).

LOUIS-JEAN DESPREZ (1743-1804)

Reconstruction of the temple of Isis in Pompeii.
Pen, brown ink, brown and grey wash, watercolour

Reconstitution du temple d'Isis à Pompéi.
Plume, encre brune, lavis brun et gris, aquarelle.

Ricostruzione del tempio d'Iside a Pompei.
Penna, inchiostro bruno, inchiostro acquarellato
bruno e grigio, acquerello.

Besançon, musée des Beaux-Arts et d'Archéologie.

CHARLES-LOUIS CLÉRISSEAU (1721-1820)

View of the Parrot Chamber in the Minim monastery at the Trinità dei Monti in Rome.
Pen, brown ink, brown and grey wash, watercolour and gouache highlights.

Vue de la chambre du Perroquet au couvent des Minimes à la Trinité-des-Monts à Rome.
Plume, encre brune, lavis brun et gris, aquarelle et rehauts de gouache.

Vista della camera del Pappagallo al convento dei Minimi alla Trinità dei Monti di Roma.
Penna, inchiostro bruno, inchiostro acquarellato bruno e grigio, acquerello e lumeggiature di gouache, 368 x 530 mm.

Cambridge, Fitzwilliam Museum.

JACQUES-FRANÇOIS BLONDEL
(1705-1774)

Projected decoration for the picture gallery at the Academy of Fine Arts of the University of Moscow, transversal section, 1756-1758.
Pen, India ink, wash and watercolour.

Projet de décoration de la galerie des tableaux de l'Académie des beaux-arts de l'université de Moscou, coupe transversale, 1756-1958.
Plume, encre de chine, lavis et aquarelle.

Progetto di decorazione della galleria di quadri dell'Accademia delle Belle Arti de'l'Università di Mosca, spaccato trasversale, 1756-1758.
Penna, inchiostro di china, inchiostro acquarellato ed acquerello, 570 x 498 mm.

Saint Pétersbourg, musée de l'Ermitage.

◀ **Julien-David Le Roy (1724-1803)**

Elevation of a temple of Peace,
2nd prize at the Académie Royale, 1749.
Pen, India ink and wash.

Élévation d'un temple de la Paix,
2ᵉ grand prix de l'Académie royale, 1749.
Plume, encre de chine et lavis.

Elevazione di un tempio della Pace,
2° gran premio Dell'Académie Royale, 1749.
Penna, inchiostro di china e inchiostro acquarellato,
964 x 1080 mm.

Paris, École nationale supérieure des Beaux-Arts.

▲ **Jean-Charles Delafosse (1734-1791)**

Elevation of a projected prison entrance, the "Temple of Immortality".
Pen, brown ink, brown and blue-grey wash.

Élévation d'un projet d'entrée de prison, « Temple de l'Immortalité ».
Plume, encre brune, lavis brun et gris-bleu.

Elevazione di un progetto di entrata di prigione, "Tempio dell'immortalità".
Penna, inchiostro bruno, inchiostro acquarellato bruno e grigio-blu,
153 x 238 mm.

New York, Cooper Hewitt Museum.

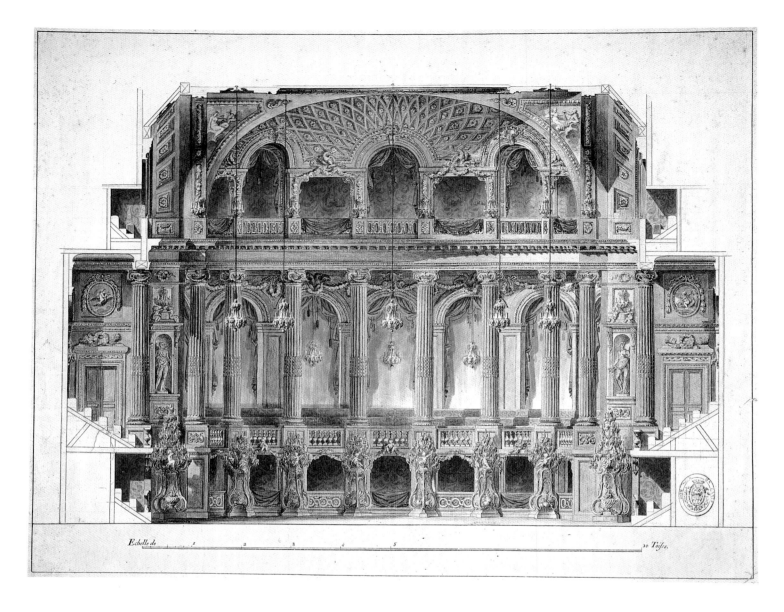

Echelle de   1   2   3   4   5   10 Toises.

▲ CLAUDE-JEAN-BAPTISTE JALLIERS-DE-SAVAULT
(d'après Jacques-Ange Gabriel 1698-1782) **(1738-1807)**

Section of the Opera house of Versailles: elevation of the room
for the costumed ball arranged for the Dauphin's wedding, 1770.
Pen, brown ink, wash and watercolour.

Coupe de l'opéra du Château de Versailles : élévation de la salle
de bal paré montée sur la scène pour le mariage du Dauphin, 1770.
Plume, encre brune, lavis et aquarelle.

Spaccato dell'Opera del Castello di Versailles: elevazione della sala da
ballo addobbata allestita sulla scena per il matrimonio del Delfino, 1770.
Penna, inchiostro bruno, inchiostro acquarellato ed acquerello, 497 x 620 mm.

Besançon, Bibliothèque municipale.

► JEAN-FRANÇOIS-THÉRÈSE CHALGRIN **(1739-1811)**

View of the ballroom built at the Petit Luxembourg
for the costumed ball of 29 May 1770
(marriage of the Dauphin and Marie Antoinette).
Pen, ink, wash and watercolour.

Vue de la salle de bal construite au Petit Luxembourg
pour le bal paré du 29 mai 1770
(fête du mariage du Dauphin et de Marie-Antoinette).
Plume, encre, lavis et aquarelle.

Vista della Sala da Ballo costruita al piccolo Lussemburgo per
il ballo allestito del 29 maggio 1770
(festa di matrimonio del Delfino e di Maria Antonietta).
Penna, inchiostro, inchiostro acquarellato ed acquerello, 582 x 585 mm.

Paris, musée du Louvre, cabinet des Arts graphiques.

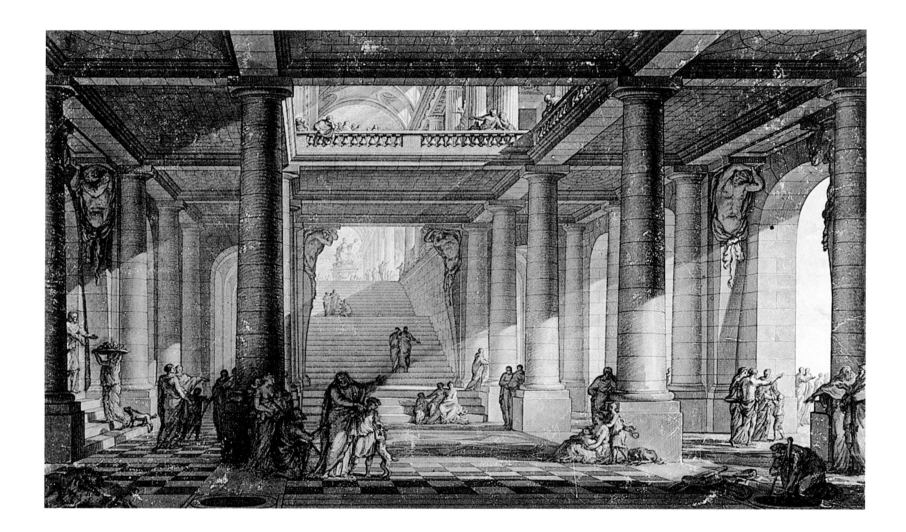

Charles De Wailly (1730-1798)

View of the hall of the new Comédie Française (now Théâtre de l'Odéon) in Paris.
Pen, black and brown inks, wash.

Vue du vestibule de la nouvelle Comédie Française (actuel théâtre de l'Odéon) à Paris.
Plume, encres noire et brune, lavis.

Veduta del Vestibolo della Nouvelle Comédie Française (attuale Teatro dell'Odeon) a Parigi.
Penna, inchiostro nero e bruno, inchiostro acquarellato.

Paris, musée du Louvre, cabinet des Arts graphiques.

INTÉRIEUR DE LA NOUVELLE SALLE DE COMÉDIE FRANÇAISE DE L'ANCIEN PROJET.

CHARLES DE WAILLY (1730-1798)

Longitudinal section of the projected Comédie Française, 1771.
Pen, black ink and wash.

Coupe longitudinale du projet de la nouvelle Comédie Française, 1771.
Plume, encre noire et lavis.

Spaccato longitudinale del progetto della Nouvelle Comédie Française, 1771.
Penna, inchiostro nero e inchiostro acquarellato.

Paris, musée Carnavalet.

These two versions of the same drawing show De Wailly's dramatic skill in depicting two different preaching "atmospheres".
To the left, the eye falls back towards the auditorium, driven by the threatening gesture of the priest demanding repentance.
To the right, in an inverted perspective, the priest's open arms raise the eye towards the calm, divine light (the oculus to the left of the pulpit's cope). The pulpit is no longer a piece of *furniture* but an expressive, symbolic structure.

Ces deux versions du même dessin montrent le talent de dramaturge de Charles De Wailly qui évoque deux « climats » du prêche.
À gauche, le regard qui s'élève redescend vers l'auditoire, porté par le geste menaçant qui invite au repentir.
À droite, devant une perspective inversée, les bras ouverts du prêtre font élever le regard vers la lumière divine, apaisante (l'oculus est à gauche de l'abat-voix). La chaire n'est plus un meuble, mais une *structure* expressive et symbolique, parlante.

Queste due versioni dello stesso disegno mostrano il talento drammaturgico di Charles De Wailly che evoca due "atmosfere" di preghiera.
Nella prima, lo sguardo che si innalza ridiscende verso l'uditorio, condotto dal gesto minaccioso che invita al pentimento.
Nella seconda, davanti a una prospettiva rovesciata, le braccia aperte del prete fanno alzare lo sguardo verso la luce divina, tranquillizzante (l'oculo è a sinistra del pulpito). Il pulpito non è più un mobile, ma una struttura espressiva e simbolica, parlante.

CHARLES DE WAILLY (1730-1798)

"*A sermon in Saint Sulpice*", 1789,
projected pulpit for the church of Saint Sulpice (second version).
Pen, black ink, wash, watercolour
and gouache highlights.

« *Un prêche à Saint-Sulpice* », 1789,
projet de chaire à prêcher pour l'église Saint-Sulpice (2ᵉ version).
Plume, encre noire, lavis, aquarelle
et rehauts de gouache.

"*Una preghiera a Saint-Sulpice, 1789,*
progetto di pulpito per la chiesa di Saint-Sulpice (seconda versione).
Penna, inchiostro nero, inchiostro acquarellato,
acquerello e lumeggiature di gauche,
678 x 473 mm.

Paris, musée Carnavalet.

CHARLES DE WAILLY (1730-1798)

Projected pulpit for the church of Saint Sulpice (first version).
Pen, black ink, wash, watercolour and gouache highlights.

Projet de chaire à prêcher pour l'église Saint-Sulpice (1re version).
Plume, encre noire, lavis, aquarelle et rehauts de gouache.

Progetto di pulpito per la chiesa di Saint-Sulpice (prima versione).
Penna, inchiostro nero, inchiostro acquarellato, acquerello e lumeggiature di gouache,
678 x 473 mm.

New York, Cooper Hewitt Museum.

◄ ▲ **CHARLES DE WAILLY** (1730-1798)

*Elevation of the decoration of the large round
salon in the Château de Montmusart near Dijon.*
Pen, black ink, brown and grey wash, watercolour.

*Élévation du décor du grand salon rond
du château de Montmusart près de Dijon.*
Plume, encre noire, lavis brun et gris, aquarelle.

*Elevazione della decorazione del Gran Salone Rotondo
del castello di Montmusart vicino Dijon.*
Penna, inchiostro nero, inchiostro acquarellato bruno
e grigio, acquerello.

Montréal, Centre Canadien d'Architecture.

► **JACQUES-DENIS ANTOINE** (1733-1801)

Elevation of the gates of the Hôtel des Monnaies in Paris.
Pen, black ink, brown and grey wash.

*Élévation des grilles d'entrée de l'hôtel
des Monnaies à Paris.*
Plume, encre noire, lavis brun et gris.

Elevazione del cancello di entrata della Zecca a Parigi.
Penna, inchiostro nero, inchiostro acquarellato
bruno e grigio, 604 x 426 mm.

New York, Cooper Hewitt Museum.

ROBERT ADAM (1728-1792)

Elevation of the decoration for Kedleston Hall, Derbyshire.
Pen, ink and watercolour.

Élévation du décor pour Kedleston Hall, Derbyshire.
Plume, encre et aquarelle.

Elevazione della decorazione per Kedleston Hall, Derbyshire.
Penna, inchiostro ed acquerello.

London, National Trust.

Section of York House. Chambers A. 1759

SIR WILLIAM CHAMBERS (1723-1796)

Transversal section of York House in London.
Pen, brown ink, wash and watercolour.

Coupe tranversale de York House à Londres.
Plume, encre brune, lavis et aquarelle.

Spaccato trasversale di York House a Londra.
Penna, inchiostro bruno, inchiostro acquarellato ed acquerello.

London, Royal Institute of British Architects.

▲ ROBERT ADAM (1728-1792)

Landscaped project for Kedleston Hall, 1759.
Pen, brown ink and watercolour.

Projet paysager pour le parc de Kedleston, 1759.
Plume, encre brune et aquarelle.

Progetto paesaggistico per il parco di Kedleston, 1759.
Penna, inchiostro bruno ed acquerello.

London, National Trust.

► ROBERT ADAM (1728-1792)

Elevation of Culzean Castle, sea view.
Pen, black and brown inks, wash.

Élévation de Culzean Castle, vue de la mer.
Plume, encres noire et brune, lavis.

Elevazione di Culzean Casle vista dal mare.
Penna, inchiostro nero e bruno, inchiostro acquarellato.

London, Sir John Soane's Museum.

Plans, Elévations, et Coupes, du Sallon et de la Salle a Manger du Hameau

Coupe prise sur la ligne C.D.

Coupe prise sur la ligne C.D.

Coupe prise sur la ligne A.B.

Coupe prise sur la ligne A.B.

Exterieur du Sallon

Exterieur de la Salle a Manger

Plan du Sallon

Plan de la Salle a Manger

ANONYME

Salon and dining room at the Hamlet of Chantilly.
Pen, ink and watercolour.

Salon et salle à manger du Hameau de Chantilly.
Plume, encre et aquarelle.

Salone e sala da pranzo del villaggio di Chantilly.
Penna, inchiostro e acquarello.

Chantilly, musée Condé.

Colonne.   Planche VII.e

Élévation Géométrale.

FRANÇOIS BARBIER

Elevation of the column-house at the Désert de Retz.
Pen, brown ink, wash.

Élévation de la maison-colonne du Désert de Retz.
Plume, encre brune, lavis.

Elevazione della casa-colonna del deserto di Retz.
Penna, inchiostro bruno, inchiostro acquarellato.

Stockholm, Statens Konstmuseer.

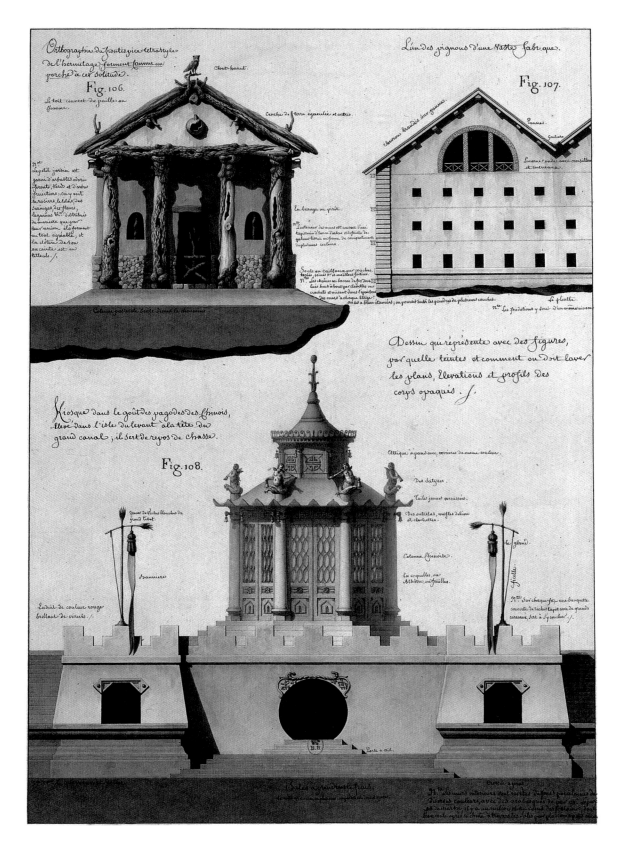

JEAN-JACQUES LEQUEU (1757-1826)

Inscription on the frontispiece of hermitage.
Pen, wash and watercolour.

Orthographie du frontispice de l'ermitage.
Plume, lavis et aquarelle.

Prospetto del frontone dell'Ermitage.
Penna, inchiostro acquarellato e acquerello.

Bibliothèque nationale de France, cabinet des Estampes.

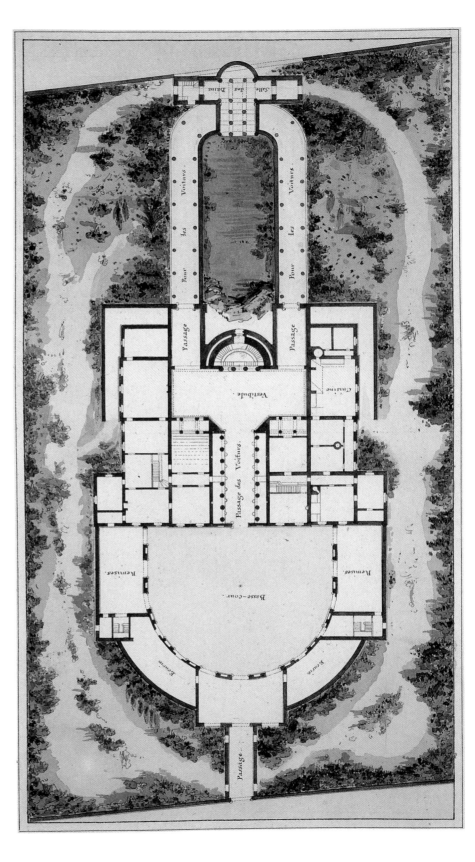

CLAUDE-NICOLAS LEDOUX (1736-1806)

(attributed to) *The Hôtel Thélusson in Paris,* plan of ground floor.
Pen, wash and watercolour.

(attribué à) *L'hôtel Thélusson à Paris,* plan du rez-de-chaussée.
Plume, lavis et aquarelle.

(attribuito) *L'hôtel Thélusson a Parigi,* pianta del pian terreno.
Penna, inchiostro acquarellato, acquerello.

London, British Library..

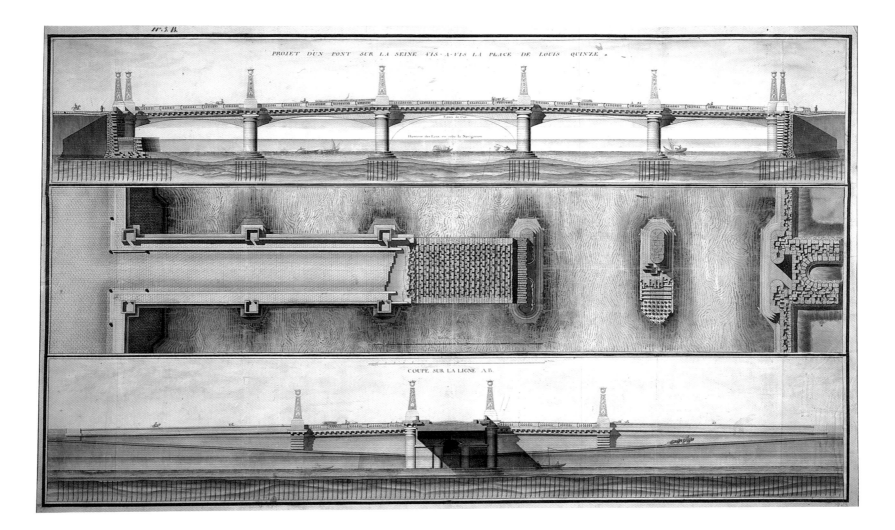

Jean-Rodolphe Perronet (1708-1794)

Section and elevation of the Pont Louis XVI in Paris, 1786.
Pen, black and brown inks, wash and watercolour.

Coupe et élévation du pont Louis XVI à Paris, 1786.
Plume, encres brune et noire, lavis et aquarelle.

Spaccato ed Elevazione del ponte Luigi XVI a Parigi, 1786.
Penna, inchiostro bruno e nero, inchiostro acquarellato ed acquerello.

Paris, École nationale des ponts et chaussées.

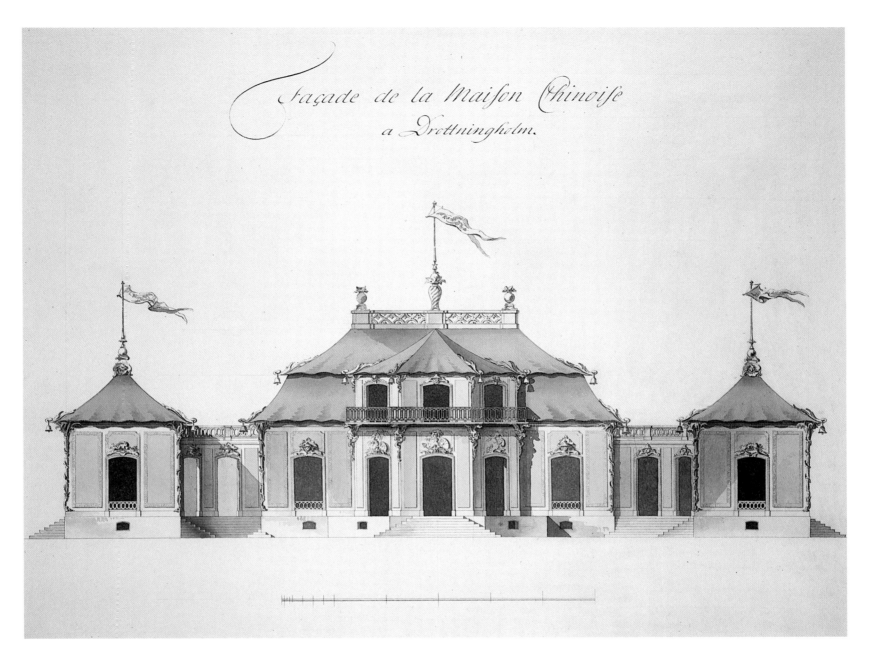

Façade de la Maison Chinoise a Drottningholm.

CARL FREDRIC ADELCRANTZ

Elevation of the main façade of the Chinese house of Drottningholm, circa 1760.
Pen, brown ink, brown and grey wash, watercolour.

Élévation de la façade principale de la maison chinoise de Drottningholm, vers 1760.
Plume, encre brune, lavis brun et gris, aquarelle.

Elevazione della facciata principale della casa cinese de Drottningholm, verso il 1760.
Penna, inchiostro bruno, inchiostro acquarellato bruno e grigio, acquerello, 439 x 644 mm.

Stockholm, Riksarkivet.

▲ **FRANÇOIS-JOSEPH BÉLANGER (1744-1818)**

Longitudinal section of the projected gallery for Lord Shelburne in London.
Pen, brown ink, brown grey and pink wash.

Coupe longitudinale du projet de galerie pour Lord Shelburne à Londres.
Plume, encre brune, lavis brun, gris et rose.

Spaccato longitudinale del progetto di galleria per Lord Shelburne a Londra.
Penna, inchiostro bruno, inchiostro acquarellato bruno, grigio e rosa.

Paris, musée Carnavalet.

► **JEAN-ARNAUD RAYMOND (1742-1811)**

Section of the Hôtel Lebrun in Paris.
Pen, black and brown inks, wash and watercolour.

Coupe de l'hôtel Lebrun à Paris.
Plume, encres noire et brune, lavis et aquarelle.

Spaccato dell'Hôtel Lebrun a Parigi.
Penna, inchiostro nero e bruno, inchiostro
acquarellato e acquerello.

Paris, Archives nationales.

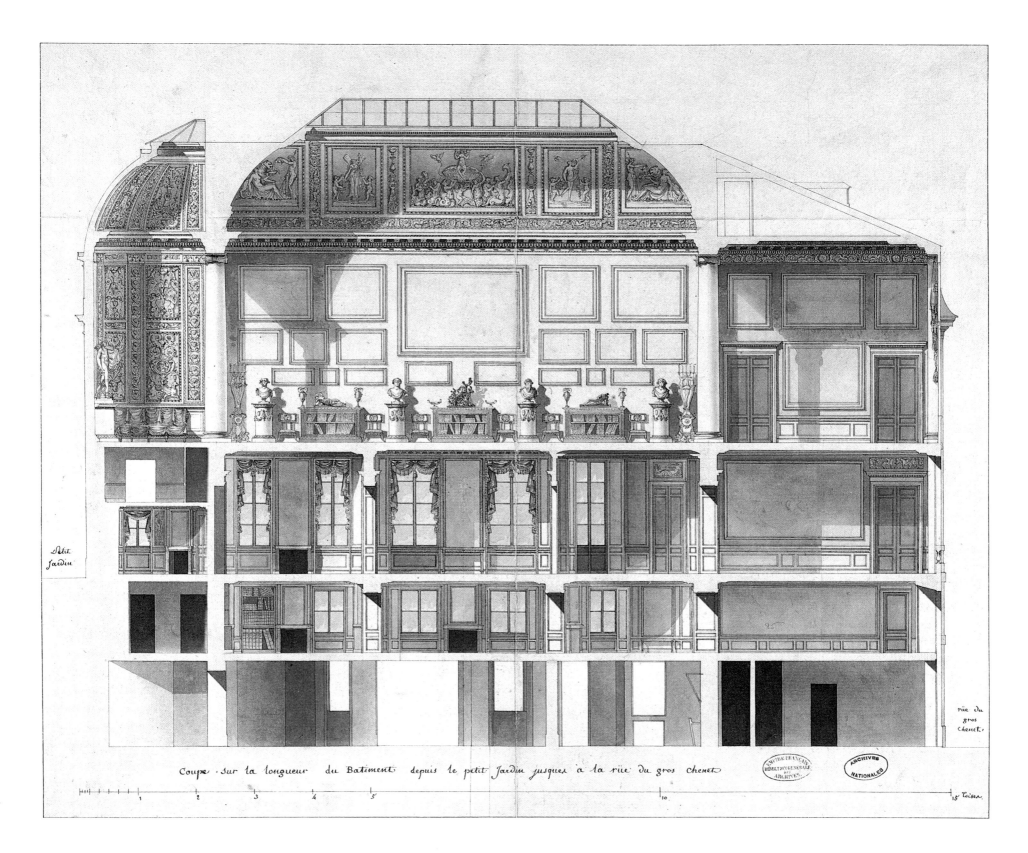

Coupe sur la longueur du Batiment depuis le petit Jardin jusquez à la rüe du gros chenet

Petit Jardin

rüe du gros chenet

1   2   3   4   5   10   15 Toises

JACQUES-GERMAIN SOUFFLOT (1713-1780)

Lateral section of a projected staircase for the king's library in the Louvre.
Pen, black ink and coloured wash.

Coupe latérale du projet de l'escalier pour la biblothèque du Roi au Louvre
Plume, encre noire et lavis de couleur.

Spaccato laterale del progetto della scala per la Biblioteca del Re al Louvre.
Penna, inchiostro nero, inchiostro acquarellato di colore.

Paris, musée du Louvre, cabinet des Arts graphiques.

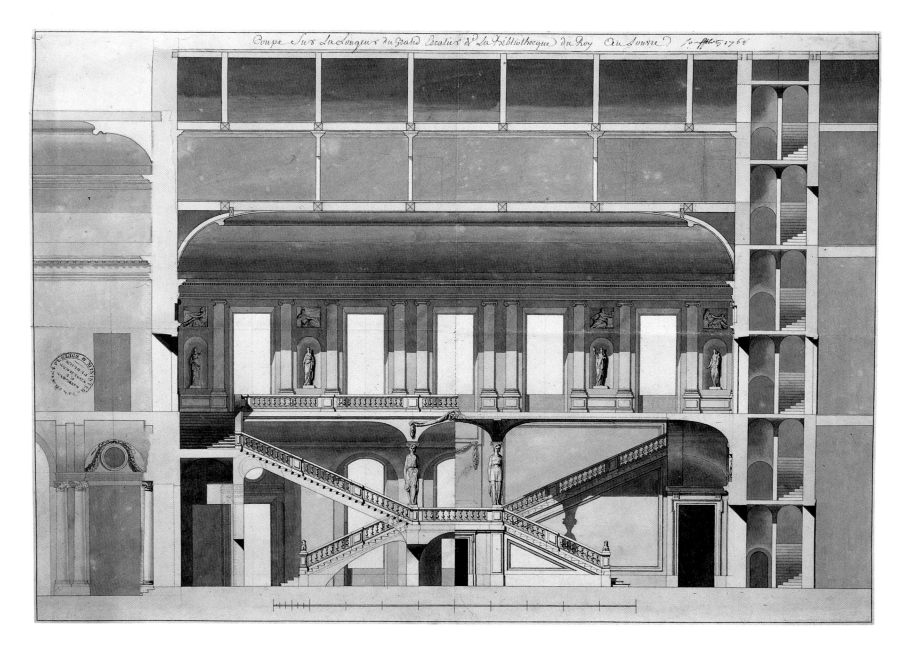

Coupe Sur La Longeur du Grand Escalier de La Bibliothecque du Roy au Louvre. Souflot 1768

JACQUES-GERMAIN SOUFFLOT (1713-1780)

Longitudinal section of a design for the staircase of the King's library at the Louvre.
Pen, black ink and coloured wash.

Coupe longitudinale du projet d'escalier pour la Bibliothèque du Roi au Louvre.
Plume, encre noire et lavis de couleur.

Spaccato longitudinale del progetto di scalinata per la Biblioteca del Re al Louvre.
Penna, inchiostro nero e inchiostro acquarellato di colore.

Paris, musée du Louvre, cabinet des Arts graphiques.

127

ALEXANDRE THÉODORE BRONGNIART (1739-1813)

Design for reinforcing the columns of the Pantheon in Paris.
Pen, wash and watercolour.

Projet de renforcement des piliers du Panthéon de Paris.
Plume, lavis, aquarelle.

Progetto di rinforzo dei pilastri del Panthéon di Parigi.
Penna, inchiostro acquarellato, acquerello.

Montréal, centre Canadien d'Architecture.

128

Coupe sur la Longueur de la Nouvelle Église de S.te Geneviève.

JACQUES-GERMAIN SOUFFLOT (1713-1780)

Longitudinal section of the projected Saint Geneviève church (now the Panthéon) in Paris.
Pen, black ink and wash.

Coupe longitudinale du projet d'église Sainte-Geneviève (actuel Panthéon), à Paris.
Plume, encre noire et lavis.

Spaccato longitudinale del progetto di chiesa Sainte-Geneviève, (attuale Pantheon), a Parigi.
Penna, inchiostro nero e inchiostro acquarellato.

Paris, Archives nationales.

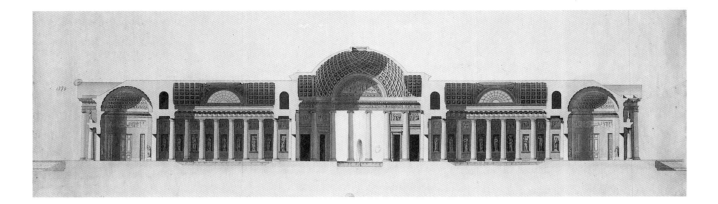

MATHURIN CRUCY (1749-1826)

*Public baths of mineral water,
longitudinal section*, first Grand Prix, 1774.
Pen, ink, wash and watercolour.

*Bains publics d'eau minérale,
coupe longitudinale*, premier Grand Prix, 1774.
Plume, encre, lavis et aquarelle.

*Bagni pubblici d'acqua minerale,
spaccato longitudinale*, primo Gran Premio, 1774.
Penna, inchiostro, inchiostro acquarellato ed acquerello,
910 x 1875 mm.

Paris, École nationale supérieure des Beaux-Arts.

ARNAUD CORCELLE (1765-1843)

Navigation school, emulation prize, 1786.
Pen, ink and wash.

École de navigation, prix d'émulation, 1786.
Plume, encre et lavis.

Scuola di navigazione, premio d'emulazione, 1786.
Penna, inchiostro, inchiostro acquarellato.

Paris, École nationale supérieure des Beaux-Arts.

CHARLES JOACHIM BÉNARD (1750-?)

(attributed to) *Design for a triumphal bridge* (1784).
Pen and wash.

(attribué à) *Projet d'un arc triomphal* (1784).
Plume, lavis.

(attribuito) *Progetto di un arco di trionfo* (1784).
Penna e inchiostro acquarellato.

Royal Institute of British Architects.

MARIE-JOSEPH PEYRE (1730-1785)

Elevation of a public fountain, first Grand Prix, 1751.
Pen, ink, wash and watercolour.

Élévation d'une fontaine publique, premier Grand Prix, 1751.
Plume, encre, lavis et aquarelle.

Elevazione di una fontana pubblica, primo Gran Premio, 1751.
Penna, inchiostro, inchiostro acquarellato ed acquerello, 889 x 1400 mm.

Paris, École nationale supérieure des Beaux-Arts.

PIERRE-LOUIS MOREAU-DESPROUX (1727-1793)

The temple of Hymen. View of the arrangements for the firework display to celebrate the birth of the Dauphin, 1782.
Pen, brown ink, wash, watercolour and gouache highlights.

Le temple de l'Hymen. Vue du corps de feu d'artifice de la fête en l'honneur de la naissance du Dauphin, 1782.
Plume, encre brune, lavis, aquarelle et rehauts de gouache.

Il tempio dell'Hymen. Vista del corpo di fuoco d'artificio della festa in onore della nascita del Delfino, 1782.
Penna, inchiostro bruno, inchiostro acquarellato, acquerello e lumeggiature di gauche.

Paris, musée Carnavalet.

VICTOR LOUIS (Nicolas dit) **(1721-1800)**

Main vertical section of the Chateau de Bouilh.
Pen, brown and black ink, wash and watercolour.

Élévation principale du château de Bouilh.
Plume, encres brune et noire, lavis et aquarelle.

Alzato principale del castello di Bouilh.
Penna, inchiostro bruno e nero, inchiostro acquarellato e acquerello.

Bordeaux, Archives municipales.

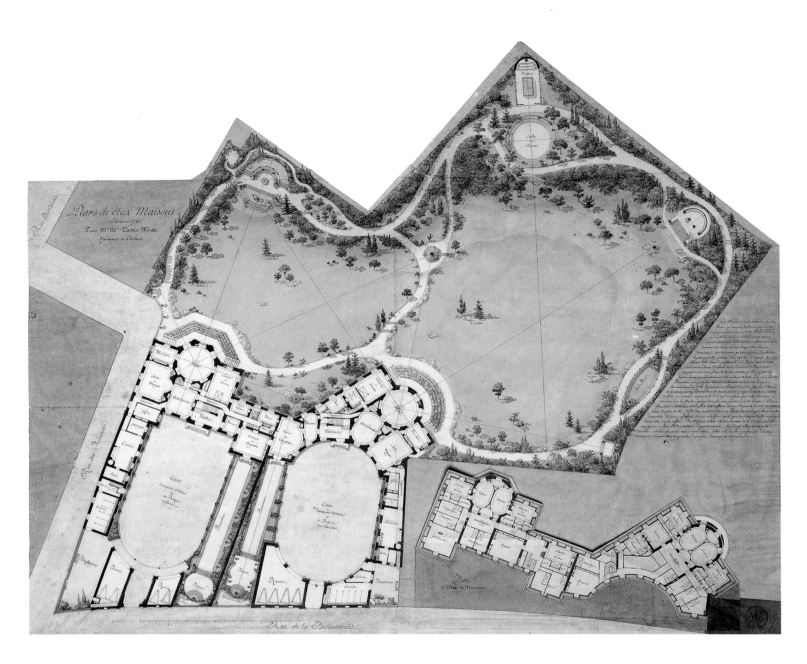

PIERRE-ADRIEN PÂRIS (1745-1819)

Designs for two houses built in Orleans.
Pen, wash and watercolour.

Plans de deux maisons construites à Orléans.
Plume, lavis et aquarelle.

Piante di due case costruite a Orléans.
Penna, inchiostro acquarellato e acquerello.

Besançon, Bibliothèque municipale.

135

ANTOINE-LAURENT-THOMAS VAUDOYER
(1756-1846)

Sketch of a dairy, Prix d'Emulation, 1782.
Pen, ink and watercolour.

Esquisse d'une laiterie, prix d'émulation, 1782.
Plume, encre, aquarelle.

Schizzo di una latteria, premio di emulazione, 1782.
Penna, inchiostro e acquerello.

Paris, École nationale supérieure des Beaux-Arts.

LOUIS PIERRE BALTARD (1764-1846)

(attributed) *Interior of a temple*.
Pen ink and gouache.

(attribué à) *Intérieur d'un temple*.
Plume, encre, gouache.

(attribuito) *Interno di un tempio*.
Penna, inchiostro, gouache.

Paris, musée des Arts décoratifs.

LOUIS-JEAN DESPREZ (1743-1804)

The port of Stockholm. The attack on the castle of Three Crowns, décor for Act III, Scene 8, by Gustaf Wasa.
Graphite, pen, brown and black inks, wash, watercolour and gouache,.

Le port de Stockholm. L'assaut du château des Trois Couronnes, décor pour l'acte III, scène 8, de Gustaf Wasa.
Mine de plomb, plume,encres brune et noire, lavis, aquarelle et gouache.

La porta di Stoccolma. L'assalto del castello delle Tre Corone, decoro per l'atto III, scena 8, di Gustaf Vasa.
Mina di piombo, penna, inchiostro bruno e nero, inchiostro acquarellato, acquerello e gauche, 365 x 568 mm.

Stockholm, Statens Konstmuseer.

PIERRE-ADRIEN PÂRIS (1745-1819)

Stage décor for Numitor, performed at Fontainebleau, 1783.
Pen, sepia and wash.

Décor de scène pour Numitor représenté à Fontainebleau, 1783.
Plume, sépia et lavis.

Decoro per la scena per Numitore rappresentato a Fontainebleau, 1783.
Penna, seppia, inchiostro acquarellato .

Besançon, Bibliothèque municipale.

◀ JEAN-CHARLES DELAFOSSE (1734-1789)

The hall of Pluto's palace.
Red chalk, pen, black ink, brown and grey wash.

Le vestibule du palais de Pluton.
Sanguine, plume, encre noire, lavis brun et gris.

Il vestibolo del Palazzo di Plutone.
Sanguigna, penna, inchiostro nero, inchiostro acquarellato
bruno e grigio, 457 x 559 mm.

London, Royal Institute of British Architects.

▲ CHARLES MICHELANGE CHALLE (1718-1778)

Courtyard of a château with two towers.
Pen, black ink, brown and grey wash.

La cour d'un château avec deux tours.
Plume, encre noire, lavis gris et bruns.

La corte di un castello con due torri.
Penna, inchiostro nero, inchiostro acquarellato
grigio e bruno, 284 x 434 mm.

London, Royal Institute of British Architects.

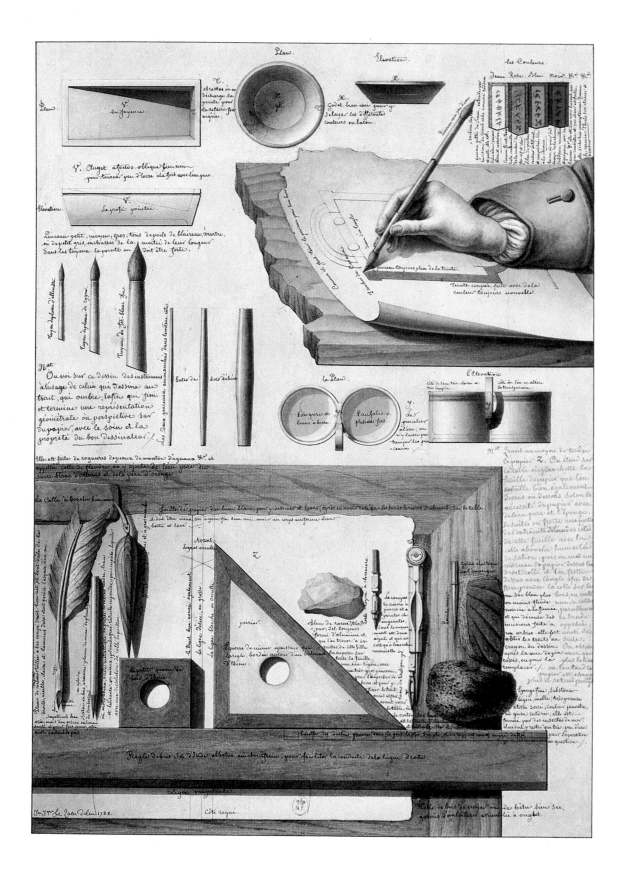

142

◄ **Jean-Jacques Lequeu (1757-1826)**

Instruments to be used by a good draughtsman, 1782.
Pen, ink and wash.

Instruments à l'usage du bon dessinateur, 1782.
Plume, encre et lavis.

Strumenti a disposizione del buon disegnatore, 1782.
Penna, inchiostro e inchiostro acquarellato.

Paris, Bibliothèque nationale de France, cabinet des Estampes.

▲ **Etienne-Louis Boullée (1738-1799)**

Projected façade for the entry to the King's library.
Pen, ink and wash.

Projet de façade pour l'entrée de la bibliothèque du Roi.
Plume, encre et lavis.

Progetto della facciata per l'entrata della Biblioteca del re.
Penna, inchiostro e inchiostro acquarellato.

Paris, Bibliothèque nationale de France, cabinet des Estampes.

◄ ÉTIENNE-LOUIS BOULLÉE (1738-1799)

View of the interior of the King's library, project.
Pen, ink and wash.

Vue de l'intérieur de la bibliothèque du Roi, projet.
Plume, encre et lavis.

Veduta dell'interno della Biblioteca del re, progetto.
Penna, inchiostro, inchiostro acquarellato.

Paris, Bibliothèque nationale de France, cabinet des Estampes.

▲ ÉTIENNE-LOUIS BOULLÉE (1738-1799)

Elevation of a projected cenotaph in Newton.
Pen, black ink and wash.

Élévation du projet de cénotaphe à Newton.
Plume, encre noire et lavis.

Elevazione del progetto di cenotafio a Newton.
Penna, inchiostro nero e inchiostro acquarellato .

Paris, Bibliothèque nationale de France, cabinet des Estampes.

ÉTIENNE-LOUIS BOULLÉE (1738-1799)

Interior view of the Metropole for the harrowing of hell.
Pen, ink and wash.

Vue intérieure de la Métropole au temps des ténèbres.
Plume, encre et lavis.

Veduta interna della Metropoli ai tempi delle tenebre.
Penna, inchiostro e inchiostro acquarellato.

Paris, Bibliothèque nationale de France, cabinet des Estampes.

ÉTIENNE-LOUIS BOULLÉE (1738-1799)

Interior view of the Metropole for Corpus Christi.
Pen, ink and wash.

Vue intérieure de la Métropole au temps de la Fête-Dieu.
Plume, encre et lavis.

Veduta interna della Metropoli ai tempi della Festa di Dio.
Penna, inchiostro e inchiostro acquarellato.

Paris, Bibliothèque nationale de France, cabinet des Estampes.

147

▲ PIERRE-FRANÇOIS-LÉONARD FONTAINE (1762-1853)

A monumental tomb for sovereigns of a great empire, second Grand Prix,
general section with elevation of the main monument, 1785.
Pen, India ink and wash.

*Un monument sépulcral pour les souverains d'un grand empire, deuxième
Grand Prix, coupe générale avec élévation du monument principal, 1785.
Plume, encre de chine, lavis.*

*Un monumento sepolcrale per i sovrani di un grande impero, secondo
Gran Premio, spaccato generale con alzato del monumento principale, 1785.
Penna, inchiostro di china, inchiostro acquarellato, 765 x 1275 mm.*

Paris, École nationale supérieure des Beaux-Arts.

▼ PIERRE-FRANÇOIS-LÉONARD FONTAINE (1762-1853)

Section of a graveyard monument, 1785.
Pen, ink and wash..

*Coupe d'un monument funéraire, 1785.
Plume, encre et lavis.*

*Spaccato di un monumento funebre, 1785.
Penna, inchiostro e inchiostro acquarellato.*

Paris, École nationale supérieure des Beaux-Arts.

FRANÇOIS VERLY (1760-1822)

Projected theatre and baths for Lille.
Pen, ink, wash and watercolour.

Projet de théâtre et de bains publics pour Lille.
Plume, encre, lavis et aquarelle.

Progetto del teatro e dei bagni pubblici per Lille.
Penna, inchiostro,
inchiostro acquarellato ed acquerello.

Lille, musée des Beaux-Arts.

149

FRIEDRICH GILLY (1772-1800)

Projected monument for Frederick the Great, 1797.
Pen, ink, wash and watercolour.

Projet d'un monument à Frédéric le Grand, 1797.
Plume, encre, lavis et aquarelle.

Progetto di un monumento a Federico il Grande, 1797.
Penna, inchiostro, inchiostro acquarellato ed acquerello.

Berlin, Kupferstichkabinett.

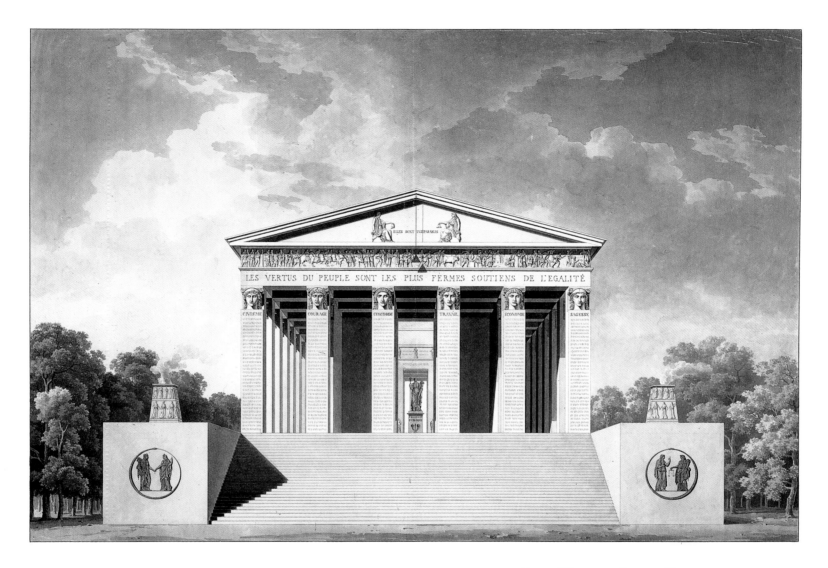

JEAN-NICOLAS-LOUIS DURAND (1760-1834)
and/et/e JEAN-THOMAS THIBAULT (1757-1826)
Copy of/Copie de/Copia di LEO VON KLENZE (1784-1864)

Temple to Equality.
Pen, ink, and wash.

Temple à l'Égalité.
Plume, encre et lavis.

Tempio dell'Uguaglianza.
Penna, inchiostro, inchiostro acquarellato.

München, Staatliche Graphische Sammlung.

CLAUDE-NICOLAS LEDOUX (1736-1806)

Elevation of gatehouse of Gentilly, Glacière or Lourcine.
Pen, ink, wash and watercolour.

Élévation de la barrière de Gentilly, Glacière ou Lourcine.
Plume, encre, lavis et aquarelle.

Elevazione della barriera di Gentilly, Glacière o Lourcine.
Penna, inchiostro, inchiostro acquarellato ed acquerello.

Paris, musée Carnavalet.

CLAUDE-NICOLAS LEDOUX (1736-1806)

Elevation of a projected palace for Aix-en-Provence.
Pen, black ink and wash.

Élévation de projet de palais d'Aix-en-Provence.
Plume, encre noire et lavis.

Elevazione di un progetto di palazzo d'Aix-en- Provence.
Penna, inchiostro nero e inchiostro acquarellato.

Aix-en-Provence, Bibliothèque Mejanes.

154

CHARLES DE WAILLY (1730-1798)

*Details of a central pavilion, of an angle pavilion
and view of the projected Assemblée Nationale
in the Tuileries, from the park.*
Pen, ink, wash and watercolour.

*Détails du pavillon central, détails d'un pavillon
d'angle et vue du projet d'Assemblée nationale
aux Tuileries, du côté du jardin.*
Plume, encre, lavis et aquarelle.

*Dettagli del pavillon centrale, dettagli di un pavillon
d'angolo e veduta del progetto d'Assemblea Nazionale
alle Tuileries, dal lato del giardino.*
Penna, inchiostro, inchiostro acquarellato ed acquerello.

Paris, galerie Talabardon.

Giovanni Campana

Project for a sepulchral chapel, Clementino Competition, 1795.
Pen, ink, wash and watercolour.

Projet de chapelle sépulcrale, concours Clementino, 1795.
Plume, encre, lavis et aquarelle.

Progetto di cappella funebre, Concorso Clementino, 1795.
Penna, inchiostro, inchiostro acquarellato ed acquerello.

Roma, Accademia nazionale di San Luca, Archivio storico.

BENJAMIN HENRY LATROBE (1764-1820)

Perspective view of the porch of the prison house in Richmond, 1797.
Pen, ink, and watercolour.

Vue perspective du porche du pénitencier de Richmond, 1797.
Plume, encre et aquarelle.

Veduta prospettica dell'atrio del penitenziario di Richmond, 1797.
Penna, inchiostro ed acquerello.

Virginia, State Library and Archives.

Jacques Molinos (1743-1831)

Design for a roof for the corn market in Paris.
Pen, wash and watercolour.

Projet de couvrement de la halle aux blés à Paris.
Plume, lavis et aquarelle.

Progetto di copertura del mercato del grano a Parigi.
Penna, inchiostro acquarellato e acquerello.

Paris, musée Carnavalet.

FRIEDRICH GILLY (1772-1800)

Study of perspective in a landscape.
Pen, wash and watercolour.

Étude de perspective dans un paysage.
Plume, encre, lavis et aquarelle.

Studio di prospettiva all' interno di un paesaggio.
Penna, inchiostro, inchiostro acquarellato e acquerello.

Berlin, Kunstbibliothek.

160

► **CHARLES PERCIER (1764-1828)**

View of a Roman house, 1797.
Pen, ink, wash and watercolour.

Vue d'une maison romaine, 1797.
Plume, encre, lavis et aquarelle.

Veduta di una casa romana, 1797.
Penna, inchiostro, inchiostro acquarellato
ed acquerello.

Paris, musée du Louvre.

◄ **JOHANN JACOB FRIEDDRICH
WEINBRENNER (1766-1826)**

*Reconstruction of the Baths of Hippias
in Rome*, 1794.
Pen, ink, wash and watercolour.

*Restitution des bains d'Hippias
à Rome*, 1794.
Encre, plume, lavis et aquarelle.

*Ricostruzione dei bagni d'Hippias
a Roma*, 1794.
Inchiostro, penna, inchiostro
acquarellato ed acquerello.

Karlsruhe, Staatliche Kunsthalle.

GLOSSARY

Antiquarian: in the eighteenth century, a scholar fascinated by ancient history and archaeology, a connoisseur and collector of antiquities.

Antique revival: renaissance of an "antique" taste (a less pejorative expression than Neo-Classicism for the new influence of Antiquity on eighteenth-century artistic creation).

Caprice (Italian *capricio*): in the vocabulary of painting and music, a piece of totally free invention. In architectural drawing, it designates an imaginary view of monuments, ruins or towns.

Chicorée ('chicory' in French): the cut leaf of the herbaceous plant, used in Rocaille ornamentation at the beginning of the eighteenth century. A pejorative symbol of this style as opposed to the classical acanthus.

Connoisseur: a person with a thorough knowledge and critical judgement in the fields of art and culture.

Genre: designates different categories of painting according to the subject; the hierarchy of genres in the language of the eighteenth-century Academy gave them in decreasing order of importance: historical or religious painting (the grand genre), landscapes, portraits, flowers, still lifes. Genre painting: depictions of everyday life.

Grand Tour: in Great Britain, the compulsory tour of Europe made by all young gentlemen. In the eighteenth century, the stay in Rome was one of its high points.

Order: ornate, proportioned structure of ancient architecture reused in western art since the Renaissance. The order is composed of a column whose capital supports an entablature. The five architectural orders are: Tuscan, Roman Doric, Greek Ionic, Greek Corinthian and Composite. The Greek Doric (baseless column) was reused only as of the second half

GLOSSAIRE

Antiquaire: au XVIIIᵉ siècle, désigne un érudit passionné d'histoire antique, d'archéologie, fin connaisseur et collectionneur d'antiquités.

Antique revival (anglais): renouveau antique, renaissance du goût « à l'antique » (expression moins péjorative que néo-classicisme pour désigner au XVIIIᵉ siècle la nouvelle influence de l'Antiquité sur la création artistique).

Caprice (italien: capricio): dans le vocabulaire de la peinture et de la musique, désigne une pièce totalement libre d'invention. Dans le dessin d'architecture, il s'agit d'une vue inventée de monuments, de ruines, de ville imaginaire.

Chicorée: désigne la feuille découpée d'une plante herbacée (salade), utilisée dans l'ornement rocaille au début du XVIIIᵉ siècle. Elle symbolise d'une manière péjorative ce style et s'oppose à l'acanthe classique.

Connoisseur (anglais): amateur, au sens fort de vrai connaisseur, dans le domaine de l'art et de la culture.

Contre-épreuve: double inversé d'un dessin, à la sanguine par exemple, obtenu en pressant l'original à l'envers sur une seconde feuille, la première ayant été mouillée au verso.

Genre: exprime différentes catégories de peintures selon le type de sujet; hiérarchie des genres, dans le langage de l'Académie au XVIIIᵉ siècle, désigne les genres par importance décroissante; peinture d'histoire ou religieuse (grand genre), paysage, portrait, fleurs, nature morte. Peinture de genre: qui traite des sujets de la vie quotidienne.

Grand Tour (anglais): désigne, en Grande-Bretagne, le voyage obligé de tout jeune Lord sur le continent européen. Le séjour à Rome en était un des points culminants au XVIIIᵉ siècle.

Ordre: structure ornée et proportionnée de l'architecture antique réemployée dans l'art occidental

GLOSSARIO

Antiquario: nel XVIII secolo, designa un erudito appassionato di storia antica, d'archeologia, fine conoscitore e collezionista di antichità

Antique revival (inglese): rinnovamento antico, rinascimento del gusto "all'antica" (espressione meno peggiorativa di neoclassicismo per designare nel XVIII secolo la nuova influenza dell'Antichità sulla creazione artistica).

Capriccio: nel vocabolario della pittura e della musica, designa un pezzo d'invenzione totalmente libero. Nel disegno di architettura, si tratta di una veduta fantastica di monumenti, di rovine, di città immaginarie.

Cicoria: designa la foglia tagliata di una pianta erbacea (insalata), utilizzata nell'ambito dell'ornamento rocaille all'inizio del XVIII secolo. Essa rappresenta in modo peggiorativo questo stile e si oppone all'acanto classico.

Connoisseur (inglese): amatore, nel senso forte di vero intenditore, nell'ambito dell'arte e della cultura.

Contro-stampa: doppia versione del disegno, alla sanguigna per esempio, ottenuta pressando l'originale al contrario su un secondo foglio, dopo che il primo è stato inumidito sul retro.

Genere: esprime diverse categorie di pittura secondo il tipo di soggetto; gerarchia di generi, nel linguaggio dell'Accademia del XVIII secolo, designa i generi per importanza decrescente; pittura di storia o pittura religiosa (gran genere), paesaggio, ritratto, fiori, natura morta. Pittura di Genere: tratta dei soggetti della vita quotidiana.

Grand Tour (inglese): designa, in Gran Bretagna, il viaggio obbligato di ogni giovane lord sul continente europeo. Il soggiorno a Roma ne era uno dei punti culminanti nel XVIII secolo.

Ordine: struttura ornata e proporzionata dell'architettura antica riutilizzata nell'arte occidentale a partire dal Rinascimento. L'ordine comprende una colonna

of the eighteenth century. Theory of orders: codification of each order's relative proportions.

Palladianism: from the famous Italian architect Andrea Palladio (1508-1580), whose classic work and theories (*Quattro libri*, Venice, 1570) influenced western architecture from the sixteenth to the twentieth century. Adjective: Palladian.

Piranesian: from the famous architect, designer and engraver G-B Piranesi, born near Venice in 1720 and died in Rome, where he worked, in 1778. His architectural style greatly influenced all of Europe during the second half of the eighteenth century.

Picturesque: relating to painting, the use of a pictorial effect. In the eighteenth century, the art of gardens and architectural drawings drew inspiration from the motifs, themes or techniques (chiaroscuro, perspective, coloured accessories) used in painting so as to animate the subject (landscape environment, attractive views, reflections, shadows, etc).

Quadratura (Italian): in frescoes, canvases and architectural drawings, a use of scholarly perspective which gives the impression of a deep, modelled architectural space. Scenographers, particularly in the eighteenth century with the Galli Bibiena, developed this technique which was to be integrated into drawings of architectural fancy and caprices.

Relevé (fr.): an *in situ* sketch or final drawing of a building, prepared with actual measurements and shown as plan, section and flat elevation.

Reverse-proof: inverse copy of a picture, for example in red chalk, obtained by pressing the original against a second sheet of paper, after wetting its back.

Sensualism: philosophical term designating an important current of eighteenth-century liberal thought, illustrated by the writings of Locke and Condillac. According to this doctrine, all our knowledge and faculties come from our sensations, which education can perfect. Writers and artists were deeply influenced by this current which emphasised sensibility and feeling in creation.

---

depuis la Renaissance. L'ordre comprend une colonne dont le chapiteau supporte un entablement. Les cinq ordres de l'architecture sont : le toscan, le dorique, le ionique, le corinthien, le composite. Le dorique grec (colonne sans base) ne fut réutilisé qu'à partir de la seconde moitié du XVIIIᵉ siècle. Théorie des ordres : codification des proportions relatives à chaque ordre.

Palladianisme : substantif dérivé du nom du célèbre architecte italien Andrea Palladio (1508-1580) dont les œuvres et les théories (*Quattro libri*, éd. à Venise en 1570) classiques ont influencé l'architecture occidentale du XVIᵉ au XXᵉ siècle. Adjectif : palladien.

Piranésien : substantif et adjectif dérivés du nom du célèbre architecte, dessinateur et graveur, G.-B. Piranesi (Piranèse), né près de Venise en 1720 et mort à Rome, en 1778, où il exerça. Son style de dessin d'architecture eut une influence considérable dans l'Europe entière dans la seconde moitié du XVIIIᵉ siècle.

Pittoresque : relatif à l'art de peindre, qui emprunte ses effets à la peinture. Au XVIIIᵉ siècle, l'art des jardins, l'art du dessin d'architecture, s'inspirent de motifs, de thèmes ou de techniques (clair-obscur, perspective, accessoires colorés) propres à la figuration peinte, afin d'animer le sujet (environnement paysager, vue attrayante, reflets, ombres, etc.).

Quadratura (italien) : dans le domaine de la fresque, du tableau et du dessin d'architecture, technique de figuration en perspective savante qui donne l'illusion d'un espace architectural profond et modelé. La scénographie, notamment au XVIIIᵉ siècle avec les Galli-Bibiena, développe ce procédé qui sera intégré au dessin de fiction architecturale ou au caprice.

Relevé : croquis exécuté in situ ou dessin au net d'un bâtiment (préparé par des mesures prises sur le terrain), exprimés en plan, coupe et élévation géométrale.

Sensualisme : terme de philosophie qui désigne un important courant de pensée libérale au XVIIIᵉ siècle, illustré par les écrits de J. Locke et, surtout, Condillac. Selon cette doctrine, toutes nos connaissances et facultés viennent des sensations, perfectibles grâce à l'éducation. Écrivains et artistes ont été profondément touchés par ce courant qui valorise la sensibilité, le sentiment dans la création.

---

il cui capitello supporta una trabeazione. I cinque ordini architettonici sono: il toscano, il dorico, lo ionico, il corinzio, il composito. Il dorico greco (colonna senza base) fu riutilizzato solo a partire dalla seconda metà del XVIII secolo. Teoria degli ordini: codificazione delle proporzioni relative a ciascun ordine.

Palladianesimo: sostantivo derivato dal nome del celebre architetto italiano Andrea Palladio (1508-1580) le cui opere e teorie (Quattro Libri, pubblicato a Venezia nel 1750) classiche hanno influenzato l'architettura occidentale dal XVI al XX secolo. Aggettivo: palladiano.

Piranesiano: sostantivo e aggettivo derivati dal nome del celebre architetto, disegnatore ed incisore G.B. Piranesi, nato vicino a Venezia nel 1720 e morto a Roma, nel 1778, dove operò. Il suo stile di disegno d'architettura ebbe un'influenza considerevole nell'Europa intera nella seconda metà del XVIII secolo.

Pittoresco: relativo all'arte di dipingere, che prende in prestito i suoi effetti dalla pittura. Nel XVIII secolo, l'arte dei giardini, l'arte del disegno di architettura, si ispirano a dei motivi, a dei temi, a delle tecniche (chiaroscuro, prospettiva, accessori colorati), propri della raffigurazione dipinta, al fine di animare i loro soggetti (ambiente paesaggistico, veduta seducente, riflessi, ombre, ecc.).

Quadratura: nel campo degli affreschi, del quadro o del disegno di architettura, tecnica di raffigurazione in prospettiva colta che dona l'illusione di uno spazio architettonico profondo e modellato. La scenografia, in particolare nel XVIII secolo con i Galli-Bibiena, sviluppa questa procedura che sarà integrata al disegno di finzione architettonica o al capriccio.

Rilievo: schizzo eseguito in situ o disegno in bella copia di un edificio (preparato attraverso misure prese sul campo), espresse in pianta, spaccato ed alzato geometrico.

Sensualismo: termine di filosofia che designa una importante corrente di pensiero liberale nel XVIII secolo, illustrata dagli scritti di J. Locke e, soprattutto, Condillac. Secondo questa dottrina, tutte le nostre conoscenze e facoltà provengono dalle sensazioni, perfettibili grazie all'educazione. Scrittori e artisti sono stati profondamente toccati da questa corrente che valorizza la sensibilità e il sentimento nella creazione.

Veduta (Italian): a landscape view of architecture or of a town, drawn *in situ*, and faithful to its model. For example, the painters Canaletto and Guardi are among the most famous eighteenth-century Venetian *vedutistas*. The *veduta* is opposed to the architectural caprice.

Vitruvius: a famous first-century BC Roman architect, author of a famous treatise, the ten books of the *De Architectura*, translated, illustrated, annotated and imitated from the Renaissance onwards. Vitruvius's theories, especially those concerning the orders, have influenced western architecture from the fifteenth to the twentieth century. Adjective: Vitruvian. Noun: Vitruvianism.

Veduta (italien) : vue paysagère d'architecture ou de ville, dessinée in situ, avec le souci d'être fidèle au modèle. Les peintres Canaletto ou Guardi, par exemple, sont parmi les plus célèbres vedutistes vénitiens au XVIIIᵉ siècle. La veduta s'oppose au caprice d'architecture.

Vitruve : nom d'un célèbre architecte romain du Iᵉʳ siècle av. J.-C., auteur du traité théorique, les *Dix livres de l'Architecture,* qui fut traduit, illustré, commenté et imité à partir de la Renaissance. Les théories de Vitruve, sur les ordres notamment, ont influencé l'architecture occidentale du XVᵉ au XXᵉ siècle. Adjectif : vitruvien, substantif : vitruvianisme.

Veduta: vista paesaggistica d'architettura o di città, disegnata sul posto, con lo sforzo di essere fedele al modello. I pittori Canaletto o Guardi, per esempio, sono tra i più celebri vedutisti veneziani nel XVIII secolo. La veduta si oppone al capriccio d'architettura.

Vitruvio: nome di un celebre architetto romano del primo secolo a.C., autore del trattato teorico *Dieci Libri di Architettura*, che fu tradotto, illustrato,commentato e imitato a partire dal Rinascimento. Le teorie di Vitruvio, in particolare sugli ordini, hanno influenzato l'architettura occidentale dal XV al XX secolo. Aggettivo: vitruviano, sostantivo: vitruvianesimo.

INDEX

BIBLIOGRAPHY • **BIBLIOGRAPHIE** • BIBLIOGRAFIA

Berckenhagen E., *Architektenzeichnungen 1479-1979*, Köln, 1980.

Boudon P., Guillerme J., Tabouret R., *Figuration graphique en Architecture*, Paris, 1976.

Braham A., *L'architecture des Lumières de Soufflot à Ledoux*, Paris, 1982.

Harris J., *Catalogue of the R.I.B.A. Drawings Collection*, London, 1968-1976.

Pérouse de Montclos J.-M., *Les prix de Rome. Concours de l'Académie royale d'architecture au XVIIIe siècle*, Paris, 1984.

Middleton R. et Watkin D., *Architecture moderne, du Néo-classicisme au Néo-gothique*, Paris, 1983.

Images et imaginaire d'architecture, exposition du Centre Georges Pompidou, Paris, 1984.

Piranèse et les Français 1740-1790, catalogue de l'exposition de la Villa Médicis, Rome, 1976.

Roland Michel M., *Le dessin français au XVIIIe siècle*, Fribourg-Paris, 1987.

Voronikina A. N., *Dessins d'architectes français aux XVIIIe et XIXe siècles conservés à l'Ermitage (en russe)*, Léningrad, 1971.